Early
Medieval Jewish Policy
in Western Europe

Published with assistance
from the Roger E. Joseph Memorial Fund
for greater understanding of history and public affairs,
a cause in which Roger Joseph believed.

Early Medieval Jewish Policy in Western Europe

by
Bernard S. Bachrach

UNIVERSITY OF MINNESOTA PRESS
Minneapolis

Copyright © 1977 by the University of Minnesota.
All rights reserved.
Printed in the United States of America
at the University of Minnesota Printing Department, Minneapolis.
Published by the University of Minnesota Press,
2037 University Avenue Southeast, Minneapolis, Minnesota 55455,
and published in Canada by Burns & MacEachern Limited,
Don Mills, Ontario

ISBN 0-8166-0814-8

This study is dedicated
with appreciation and affection
to the man from whom I learned
the historian's craft
Bryce D. Lyon

Preface

For almost two millennia persecution and suffering have been the fundamental themes of Jewish history. This is made clear by Yitzhak Baer's rationalization: "It is the privilege of the oppressed people to arouse the conscience of the victors."[1] The theme is treated with far less sympathy by the *doyen* of specialists in Jewish history, Salo Baron, when he writes: "I was the first to coin the term 'lachrymose conception'... when my scholarly conscience... made me impatient with the eternal self-pity characteristic of Jewish historiography."[2]

Traditionally students of Jewish history have found in medieval Western Europe a vast store of disasters to document the suffering of the Exile. Among our contemporaries modern parallels—Nazi Germany, Fascist Italy, Communist Russia—are often evoked to bring to the reader the full impact of the medieval debacle. In discussions of anti-Jewish legislation enacted by either secular or religious powers during the Middle Ages, it is not uncommon to see the Nuremberg Laws introduced as the ineluctable finale to a centuries-long process.[3]

In the prevailing lachrymose conception of Jewish historiography the early Middle Ages—the subject of this study—have been reduced to a formula by which "the Jews became a class of human beings marked out for religious and political persecution throughout the world. The rulers of Christian countries, guided by the Church, subjected the Jews to a fitful system of forced conversion and expulsion, backed up by artificially contrived pogroms."[4] In this context, Visigothic Jewish policy from 589-711 has received the bulk of attention. Solomon Katz observed: "For a century and a quarter kings and bishops united in an effort to convert the Jews of Spain or to drive them from the kingdom."[5] Bernhard Blumenkranz, more recently, has argued: "En 589, se place la point de départ de la plus tragique adventure des Juifs pendant le haut moyen âge."[6] Thus scholars generally agree that the Jews who dwelled in Visigothic Spain were subjected to severe legislation which at various times was intended to limit their freedom, to control their economic capabilities, and ultimately to reduce them to slavery.[7]

Generally Visigothic Jewish policy as interpreted above has served as a model, in the sense of Baer's formula, for dealing with early medieval Jewish policy. When discussing places where the anti-Jewish record is less clear than in Spain, specialists have served the lachrymose tradition by emphasizing anti-Jewish *acta* which though perhaps anomalies in their own time "boded ill" for the future. Thus, the putative persecution ordered by King Chilperic (d. 585) in Merovingian Gaul is detailed in connection with discriminatory conciliar enactments, and these anti-Jewish acts are seen as leading naturally to Dagobert I's alleged order to expel the Jews from Gaul (ca. 632). Similar orders attributed to the Lombard ruler Perctarit and the Carolingian Louis II are prominent in discussions of Italy. Any consideration of Carolingian Jewish policy tends to focus on the anti-Jewish writings and policies of Archbishop Agobard of Lyons and of his like-minded confreres.[8] The thrust of such an approach is to seek out for emphasis the work of persecutors or would-be persecutors and to relegate to relative obscurity those figures who might be seen to have been pro-Jewish.

Such treatments of early medieval Jewish policy have generally been presented in conjunction with a view of barbarian Europe that depicts Christian secular rulers as powerful and religiously oriented, the Church as the dominant institution in society with immense influence over the political process, and the Jews as very few in number, powerless, and easily victimized though innocent. This picture of strong monarchs, a powerful church, and an insignificant Jewry, however, does not fit the evidence for early medieval conditions.[9]

Preface ix

It is indeed curious that specialists in early medieval history, notorious for their contentiousness, have permitted historical thinking about early medieval Jewish policy to be dominated by the lachrymose conception presented within a secular-ecclesiastical framework of dubious accuracy.[10] The usual linguistic reasons for ignoring Jewish history carry little weight for this period since there are few Hebrew sources. Indeed, as Gavin Langmuir recently observed: "In general, majority historiography as it relates to Jews has been marked by lack of interest and by ignorance, when it has not been marked by derogatory attitudes."[11] For the early Middle Ages the first point is well illustrated by the massive four-volume *Festschrift* honoring Charlemagne which appeared in 1965-1967. More than 1,400 quarto pages were devoted to the man and his reign and more than 400 additional pages to the *Nachleben*.[12] Articles were written on Charles's Avar policy, his English policy, his policy toward Islam, the papacy, and Byzantium.[13] But, as one might have predicted on the basis of Langmuir's careful examination of past practices, there was no study of Charlemagne's Jewish policy.

In the present study an effort has been made to examine early medieval Jewish policy in the West from the emergence of the barbarian kingdoms to the dissolution of the Carolingian empire under Louis the Pious's sons. Much of the material used in this work has been employed by one or another specialist in Jewish history from the point of view of those subject to the policies under consideration and almost invariably within the lachrymose framework of cataloguing the suffering and persecution of the Jewish people. There has never been a systematic and comprehensive effort to establish the nature of early medieval Jewish policy from the perspective and aims of its formulators. Nor have the nuances inherent in unique situations been examined to differentiate and elaborate the complex elements of the historical process as it unfolded during a period of four hundred years over the greater part of Western Europe. It is hoped that these lacunae will be filled in the following pages.

Little need be said concerning the starting point of this study since it would be difficult to find a more reasonable beginning for the early Middle Ages than the emergence of the Germanic kingdoms in the West. The other terminus is somewhat less obvious. In deciding upon 877

x *Preface*

I was influenced by the plethora of heirs who succeeded Charles the Bald and Louis the German. With the deaths of these two monarchs in 877 and 876 respectively, the fragmentation of the Carolingian Empire is a fact. Policy making during the last decades of the ninth century, especially in *Francia Occidentalis* and Italy, is much more like that during the subsequent two centuries than that during the preceding hundred years.

This volume has two basic parts. The first three chapters focus upon the barbarian kingdoms in the Christian West. All of these, however, disappeared before the end of the eighth century. The areas in the West that remained Christian and where Jews dwelled either were incorporated directly into the Carolingian Empire or, like the kingdom of Asturias or southern Italy, fell more or less under Carolingian domination. Thus the second part of this work is devoted to the Carolingian Empire and its environs.

It remains only to thank several people who in one way or another have earned my gratitude during my work on this volume. My colleagues James Tracy and Kay Reyerson read the manuscript and saved me from more than one error. My wife Deborah read the work several times in various drafts and also provided much helpful criticism. Mrs. Keefe, my typist, did a fine job of copying my messy drafts, and Mrs. Gertrude Battell and her staff at the Inter-Library Loan Division of the University of Minnesota Library did a heroic job of finding the materials I needed.

It would be unfair if I did not also mention the person who in an indirect way was responsible for my interest in this topic. In the fall of 1966 my former colleague at Queens College the late Cecil Roth invited me to contribute several articles to the new edition of *Encyclopaedia Judaica*. Research for these studies introduced me to the problems of Early Medieval Jewish Policy.[14]

BERNARD S. BACHRACH

Saint Paul
May 14, 1976

Table of Contents

Preface   vii

I Visigothic Jewish Policy   3

II Jewish Policy in Early Medieval Italy (476-774)   27

III Merovingian Jewish Policy   44

IV Jewish Policy in the
Early Carolingian Empire and Its Environs   66

V Jewish Policy under Louis the Pious
(814-840) and in the Environs of the Empire   84

VI Jewish Policy in the Carolingian Empire and Its
Environs during the Period of Dissolution (840-877)   106

VII Conclusions   132

Abbreviations   142

Notes   144

Bibliography   192

Index   207

Early
Medieval Jewish Policy
in Western Europe

CHAPTER I

Visigothic Jewish Policy

For almost a century (418-507) the Visigoths ruled most of Aquitaine in southwestern Gaul, and from the last quarter of the fifth century until 711 they ruled the greater part of the Iberian peninsula. Until 589 the Visigoths were Arian Christians, and scholars generally agree that they pursued a policy of tolerance toward the many Jewish communities that flourished under their rule in both Gaul and Spain.[1]

The letters of Sidonius Apollinaris (d. ca. 489), a Gallo-Roman of the senatorial class who also served as the orthodox Christian bishop of Clermont Ferrand, depict this atmosphere of tolerance and close relations between Jews and Christians in the Visigothic kingdom. For example, Sidonius was in contact with Jewish merchants and thought it not unusual to recommend them to his fellow bishops. Like his friend Felix, a member of the senatorial class from the Narbonnaise, Sidonius also employed Jews in responsible positions.[2] Not all orthodox ecclesiastics living under Visigothic rule were content, however, to permit Christians to maintain close relations with Jews. Thus at the Council of Agde in 506, the prelates objected to popular practices such as the propensity of both Christian laymen and clergy to participate in Jewish festivals and to dine at Jewish homes. Further, the bishops condemned the custom, which they attributed to Jewish influence, whereby Christians violated the rules about fasting during Lent.[3]

These reservations concerning Jews do not seem to have been shared

4   Visigothic Jewish Policy

by the Visigothic rulers or their secular officials who apparently permitted Jews to continue to hold senatorial rank although this was contrary to the law.[4] The Visigoths also recruited and organized Jewish fighting men for garrison service in important strongholds.[5] At the hospital in Mérida, Bishop Masona saw to it that Jews were treated along with Christians. This practice seems not to have raised hostile comment even from clerics.[6] A canon adopted in 506 established a period for the catechumenate of eight months. Thus any overzealous cleric who might be moved to attempt to convert Jews to Christianity by force would violate a conciliar enactment.[7]

Throughout the Visigothic realm during the sixth century, the Roman law code composed at the order of King Alaric II in 506 seems to have been the official embodiment of Jewish policy. According to the *Breviary* of Alaric, Jews were to be considered Roman citizens and were to live under Roman law. In several instances, however, Jews were accorded special treatment. This legislation was intended to insure Jewish *privilegia* in two specific areas: religion and law. In the former, no action was to be permitted that hindered Jewish religious observances, and in the latter, Jewish judicial autonomy was to be respected. The *Breviary* also took into account the vigorous efforts of Jews to convert both pagans and Christians to Judaism and laid down several laws to hinder such activity.[8]

It is difficult to ascertain whether Alaric's code was enforced with regard to the Jews of the Visigothic kingdom during much of the first quarter of the sixth century because Theodoric the Great, the Ostrogothic monarch, ruled there through his agents from ca. 508 until his death in 526. As will be seen in the next chapter, Theodoric pursued a policy intended to insure the Jews their *privilegia* under the law, and he tended to ignore those previous enactments designed to limit Jewish activities. During the period in which Theodoric ruled the Visigothic kingdom, Bishop Caesarius of Arles worked diligently to ransom Christian captives who had fallen into Jewish hands. According to his near contemporary hagiographer, the prelate wanted to stop free men from being enslaved and to keep true believers from being converted to Judaism. The circumstances of Caesarius's private initiative make it clear that government officials did not enforce those laws that prohibited

Jews from converting Christians to Judaism and that barred Jews from owning Christian slaves. At the Council of Orange in 529, the prelates reacted to an apparently related problem. They enacted a canon intended to stop slave owners from seizing runaway slaves who had fled to churches for safety.[9]

For more than half a century after the Ostrogothic dominance of the Visigothic kingdom had been ended, no positive evidence exists concerning Jewish policy there. It is extremely unlikely, however, that an anti-Jewish policy was pursued. The Church councils of the period did not mention Jews. In fact, toward the end of the sixth century, for which information is again available, it is clear that the Jewish communities in the major and minor cities of the Iberian peninsula and Septimania were flourishing despite invasion, civil war, and other similar troubles endemic to early medieval Europe.[10]

In 589 the Visigothic ruler King Reccared I abandoned his Arian Christianity and ordered that all the Goths of his realm were to become orthodox Christians. Scholars generally agree that Reccared also launched an anti-Jewish policy at this time, a claim based on two pieces of evidence.[11] The more important evidence suggests that when Reccared enacted a series of laws for his Gothic subjects that paralleled laws already applied to his Roman subjects he greatly disadvantaged the Jews. He did so, it is charged, by decreeing that the offspring of a sexual union between a Christian and a Jew were to be baptized.[12] At least one noted scholar has characterized this as "the first but not the last instance in Visigothic Spain of forcible conversion to Christianity."[13] The second piece of evidence is found in a letter written by Pope Gregory I who praised the king for refusing bribes from Jews.[14]

In examining the charge that Reccared began a policy of forced conversions of Jews it must be noted that according to ancient and medieval Jewish law and custom a child was Jewish only if born of a Jewish mother or if the child went through the rites of conversion. If a Christian mistress of a Jewish man gave birth to a child, the offspring not only would be illegitimate but would not even be a Jew. Thus neither we nor Jews in Visigothic Spain could consider such a child who was baptized to have been converted to Christianity by force. By contrast it seems reasonable for the Church to have been concerned about the spiritual and material well-being of a non-Jewish bastard born of a Christian woman living in sin; widows, orphans, and other unfortunates were generally taken care of through ecclesiastical institutions.

The illegitimate offspring of the Jewish mistress of a Christian man presents a slightly more ambiguous situation. According to Jewish custom a woman who willingly and openly went to live with a non-Jew was considered dead by her family and by the Jewish community. Legally it was the duty of the community to stone her to death if she could be found. Thus it is likely that such a woman and her offspring had no standing within the Jewish community, and that the community had no interest in them.[15] Whatever the reaction of the Jewish community, it seems reasonable to assume that problems arising from the baptism of the illegitimate offspring of the Jewish concubines of Christian men were not of central importance to Judeo-Christian relations during the reign of King Reccared.[16]

If we consider the law concerning baptism of bastards to have been of little or no moment for the Jewish community, then Reccared seems to have done no more in his legislation than accept the laws of his Arian predecessors who are generally regarded as having been tolerant. The charge that he initiated a policy of persecution and forced conversion cannot be sustained. In fact, Reccared seems to have been pro- rather than anti-Jewish if his reign is examined in perspective. Among the laws promulgated by Alaric II for his subjects was one that decreed the death penalty for Jews convicted of converting or of attempting to convert Christians to Judaism. Reccared eliminated the death penalty for these offenses.[17] When the provincial synod of Narbonne in 589 passed a host of acts severely injurious to Jews, including prohibiting them from performing certain of their religious services, Reccared refused to approve the acts.[18] In 597 Pope Gregory I wrote Reccared to call his attention to the facts that Jews at Narbonne were dealing in Christian slaves contrary to law and that royal officials were doing nothing about it. Reccared ignored the pope's request that he halt the trade.[19] Most important, Reccared refused to enforce the existing laws that in any way disadvantaged the Jews in his kingdom.[20]

Although Reccared seems to have favored the Jews, especially those at Narbonne, some of his subjects in Septimania, particularly the bishops who dominated the provincial council of 589, were intent upon pursuing a vehemently anti-Jewish policy. Narbonne earlier was the focal point of a revolt against Reccared that his army suppressed. Perhaps the Jews there had supported the king against the rebels, and the latter's sympathizers retaliated at the council of 589. But Reccared, knowing who his true friends at Narbonne were, refused to approve the acts of the council. A decade later he again defended the Jews of Narbonne when he refused to succumb to the pressure exerted by the pope to stop the slave trade. Politics not religion seems to have been the key to Reccared's Jewish policy.[21]

Liuva (601-603), Witteric (603-610), and Gundemar (610-612), Reccared's three immediate successors, continued his policy toward the Jews. They made no effort to enforce the existing anti-Jewish laws, and they promulgated no new anti-Jewish laws. At the local level both lay and clerical officials ignored the existing anti-Jewish legislation. In addition Jews continued to own Christian slaves and to hold civil and military positions in which they exercised power over Christians.[22]

When Sisebut succeeded to the Visigothic throne in either February or March of 612, he sharply reversed the Jewish policy of his predecessors and sponsored severe anti-Jewish legislation. Sisebut ordered that all Christian slaves be removed from Jewish ownership and that all Christian freedmen be removed from Jewish patronage. He forbade Jews to hire Christian workers and decreed that all Christian slaves whom the Jews freed and who did not have property of their own were to be given some by their erstwhile owners. These prescriptions were to be carried out by 1 July 612 at the latest. Any Jew who still possessed Christian slaves after that date was to have them taken from him by public officials, the slaves were to be freed, and half the Jew's property was to go to the royal fisc. Sisebut also reversed Reccared's policy on proselytism; he restored the death penalty, and Jews who were convicted were not only to lose their lives but their property as well. The latter went to the royal fisc. Christians who had been converted to Judaism were required to become Christians once again; those who refused were to be whipped in public, to have their heads shaven, and to be made slaves of men chosen by the king. All Jews who were wed to Christians who had converted to Judaism were to convert to Christianity or go into exile outside the kingdom. Slaves who were born from the union of a Jew and a Christian who had converted to Judaism were to be considered Christians. Jews were to be expelled from governmental positions in which they exercised power over Christians.[23]

When Sisebut realized that his anti-Jewish policy was not being enforced, he attempted to bring about the conversion of all Jews in the Visigothic kingdom by coercion. Among those known to have been driven to the baptismal font were important men like Rabbi Isaac of Toledo and Levi Samuel, the head of the synagogue (*archisynagogus*) in the same city. Many other Jews fled into exile to avoid forced conversion.[24]

In attempting to ascertain why Sisebut reversed the Jewish policy of his Catholic predecessors, scholars have advanced three hypotheses: religious piety, greed, and the demands of foreign policy. The last mentioned has met with the least acceptance. This hypothesis suggests that Sisebut attempted to ingratiate himself with the Byzantine Emperor Heraclius who is known to have pursued an anti-Jewish policy. Thus by supporting a Byzantine-inspired anti-Jewish policy in Spain, Sisebut hoped to bring the empire and the Visigothic kingdom into peaceful relations and secure an end to hostilities which had persisted between them for more than half a century. There is, however, no evidence to support this interpretation of Sisebut's motivation. Sisebut began his anti-Jewish policy very soon after assuming power in 612, and he did not come to an agreement with the Byzantines until 616. In the interval of four years the Byzantine and Visigothic armies fought several bloody battles against one another. Finally Heraclius began his policy in 632 well after Sisebut had left the scene.[25]

The contention that Sisebut's strong religious feelings led him to attempt to eliminate Judaism from Spain has received wider support than the foreign policy hypothesis.[26] It is certainly true that Sisebut took a strong proprietary interest in the Church, appointed bishops, admonished the clergy from time to time, and wrote a saint's life.[27] Sisebut's venture into hagiography, however, casts doubt on the pious intent usually associated with such a work. He wrote a *Life of Saint Desiderius of*

Vienne who had been killed ca. 606 or 607 at the order of the Merovingian king Theuderic II and his grandmother Queen Brunhild. Theuderic and Brunhild were enemies of the Visigothic monarch, and Sisebut used the *Life* to attack his foes. Sisebut's praise of Desiderius is juxtaposed with the evil of his tormentors. In short the work is at least as much anti-Merovingian political propaganda as it is religious veneration.[28] The irony, from the religious point of view, is worth noting. Brunhild was originally an Arian Visigothic princess who had converted to the orthodox persuasion some two decades before Reccared's conversion brought orthodoxy to Spain as the official religion.

A letter to the Arian Lombard king Adaloald from Sisebut provides evidence that he viewed religion in political terms. For example, Sisebut pointed out the great material advantages that accrued to the orthodox Christian king. This letter has been called a "trifle cynical" by one modern scholar, especially "the appeal to self-interest when Sisebut goes on to draw the moral from the *locus classicus* for Petrine authority, St. Matthew 16:18-19."[29] Sisebut's use of religion for political purposes, his appointing of bishops, his building of churches, and his admonitions to the clergy seem to have been motivated largely by reasons of state, i.e., the strengthening of his political position. His anti-Jewish policy, moreover, was opposed by the most important cleric in Spain, Isidore of Seville, and it was not approved by a Church council.[30] Sisebut's reputation for piety seems to have been greatly exaggerated by historians.

Scholars who suggest that Sisebut was motivated by greed in pursuing an anti-Jewish policy point to the crown's economic gain from this legislation.[31] Yet if we examine this legislation carefully, the crown seems to have obtained relatively little direct economic advantage from it. Jews who converted to Christianity were not at all disadvantaged economically, and the crown did not gain from them. If the Jews complied with the laws and gave up their Christian slaves, the royal fisc still acquired nothing directly and profited indirectly only if the newly freed slaves became productive, tax-paying subjects. The crown benefited only if the Jews refused to obey the laws and refused to free their Christian slaves. If this were the case, the king could free the slaves and confiscate half of the offenders' remaining property. The fisc would also gain the property of convicted Jews who converted Christians to Judaism. In addition, those who were converts from Christianity to Judaism and refused to return to the Church were to be enslaved, and the king determined their new owners, thus gaining valuable property to give to his loyal followers. It is clear that the monarch benefited economically only if the anti-Jewish laws were not obeyed. Yet if Sisebut was economically motivated, then it seems that his policy was unnecessarily tortuous and less than efficient. First, the violation of law had to be encouraged, hardly a useful precedent even if the violators were a despised cancer in society which incidentally they were not. Second, the royal fisc gained only marginally and indirectly from these laws and then only if they were disobeyed. Third, more efficient means were within the purview of Visigothic monarchs, and later kings did devise more decisive ways to benefit the crown economically through the exploitation of the Jews.

Since we cannot put much faith in piety, greed, and peace as motives for Sisebut's anti-Jewish policy, it seems reasonable to examine the nature of Visigothic politics as a motivating force for his actions. When Sisebut promulgated his anti-Jewish legislation and reversed the policy pursued by his four immediate predecessors, he did so with the advice and support of the palace *officium*. No consultation with the Church or with any individual bishops is mentioned. Sisebut apparently never sought nor did he ever receive the approval of a Church council for this legislation.[32] Not only did Isidore of Seville, whose own anti-Jewish sentiments are well documented, oppose Sisebut's policy, but there was significant opposition from both religious and lay segments of the society. In many areas the anti-Jewish laws simply were ignored. In Toledo, where Bishop Aurasius actually carried out forced baptisms, Froga, the count of the city, opposed him. This opposition led to violence, and the bishop's letter excommunicating the count still survives.[33]

Careful study of Sisebut's anti-Jewish legislation suggests that it was the king's policy to strike a blow at the economic strength of the Jewish community and thus perhaps to weaken its political influence. Jews were to be deprived of their Christian slaves, and thus those Jews engaged in the slave trade would be severely handicapped if not put out of business entirely. Jews who owned large estates that were worked primarily by Christian slave labor would be greatly disadvantaged and would have found difficulty in maintaining their holdings. Sisebut's attempt to prohibit Jews from hiring Christian laborers was probably aimed at keeping Jewish landowners from employing the newly freed slaves and thus maintaining business almost as usual. By legislating the freedom of all Christian slaves owned by Jews, Sisebut probably hoped to create a class of people whose interest lay in supporting the king against their former owners. Sisebut promulgated his anti-Jewish laws very soon after coming to power, and his policy was concocted solely with the support and advice of his palace staff. Many churchmen and noteworthy lay officials like Count Froga of Toledo and Isidore of Seville actively or passively opposed Sisebut's radical attack on the Jews. Sisebut's later policy of conversion or exile was one of desperation and an admission that his earlier legislation had failed. It seems reasonable to suggest that Sisebut reversed the pro-Jewish policy of his predecessors because, in the traditional struggle for power which accompanied the succession to the Visigothic throne, the Jews opposed him. Thus just as the Jews in Spain benefited at the hands of Reccared, the winner in 589, they suffered when they apparently opposed Sisebut, the winner in 612.

In medieval Jewish tradition Suinthila, who succeeded Sisebut in 621, is regarded as a good and tolerant monarch. Suinthila did not enforce Sisebut's anti-Jewish laws, and he encouraged Jews who had gone into exile to return. Jews who had been converted by force and who wanted to return to their former religious practices were not harassed for their apostasy; some Jews were even employed in governmental posts.[34] We do not know why Suinthila reversed Sisebut's policy and returned to the traditional policy of the Visigothic kings. But it may be conjectured that because Suinthila deposed Sisebut's son Reccared II, who survived his father by only a few days, he found support among the Jews who had been the enemies of his predecessor.[35] In addition, Suinthila presumably did not want to follow a policy that had been a manifest failure.

After ruling for a decade, however, Suinthila was overthrown by a noble named Sisenand; the latter's success was due essentially to Frankish aid and to the defection of Suinthila's brother Geila. Opposition to Sisenand, however, was fierce. Geila later conspired against him,

12   Visigothic Jewish Policy

and in the south a certain Iudila ruled for some time, even issuing coins in his own name. In his short reign (631-636) Sisenand returned to the anti-Jewish policy of Sisebut. Unlike Sisebut, however, Sisenand obtained the support of the Church for his program. Jews were once again prohibited from holding public offices in which they exercised power over Christians. In addition persons who were born of Jewish parents were also prohibited from holding such offices. Suinthila, in reversing Sisebut's policy, had once again begun to use Jewish officials; Sisenand in returning to Sisebut's policy sought to eliminate all Jewish officials in government. Officials who did not dismiss the Jews who had gained such public offices and officials who appointed Jews to positions of governmental power were liable to excommunication. Sisenand also struck at Jewish slave traders who dealt in Christian slaves and reaffirmed Sisebut's legislation in these matters.[36]

Sisenand tried to bring about the dejudification of the government, and he sought to weaken the fiscal strength of the Jewish community. Sisenand's approach to purely religious matters was not innovative. He did, however, oppose forced conversions. Nevertheless, those who had converted were not permitted to apostatize, and Jewish proselytizing was handled in the traditional manner.[37]

It is important to note that both the king and the Fourth Council of Toledo were aware that the revival of Sisebut's anti-Jewish policy would meet with strong opposition. It was expected that simple clerics and even bishops, as well as laymen both in and outside the government, would continue to pursue pro-Jewish policies. Therefore, it was decreed that those who refused to enforce Sisenand's anti-Jewish policy would be anathematized and excommunicated.[38] Sisenand came to power through a revolt, and his short reign was wracked by civil wars. At least two of the uprisings against him were carried out by men who were supporters of his predecessor's general policies including favorable treatment of the Jews. It would have been strange indeed if Sisenand had not pursued an anti-Jewish policy after overthrowing the pro-Jewish Suinthila.

When Chintila succeeded Sisenand in 636, he immediately summoned the Fifth Council of Toledo. *Gallia Narbonensis* seems to have been in revolt at the time, and the council was called by a king who "at the earliest possible moment tried to protect himself, his family, and his *fideles* to the best of his feeble ability" by having the Church call down upon the heads of would-be usurpers and rebels the curses of divine vengeance.[39] The Fifth Council, however, did not accomplish Chintila's aims, and eighteen months later he summoned the Sixth Council of Toledo. In the period between these meetings violence continued to disturb the realm. *Refugae*, men who sought foreign aid against the king, were active in Chintila's reign. Important men were imprisoned for opposing Chintila, and other opponents fled into exile.[40]

Throughout Chintila's short reign Spain was wracked by civil wars, and he used both the Fifth and Sixth Councils of Toledo to promulgate legislation intended to deter and punish rebels.[41] Chintila's anti-Jewish acts, supported by the Sixth Council, can be seen, therefore, as part of his general policy of repressing those who opposed him. As Sisenand's legitimate successor and the heir to his palace *officium*, Chintila was very probably opposed by the Jews who had suffered under his predecessor's anti-Jewish policy. Thus Chintila saw to the reaffirmation of the anti-Jewish *acta* of the Fourth Council of Toledo. Jewish officials were to be expelled from governmental service, and Jewish slave owners were to be expropriated, a continuation of Sisenand's policies that had not been successful. In fact Pope Honorius I wrote to the Sixth Council in 638 accusing the bishops and the clergy of Spain of not enforcing the anti-Jewish laws which had already been enacted.[42]

Thus at the Sixth Council, Chintila saw to it that it was decreed that henceforth only Catholics were to remain in Visigothic Spain. Jews were either to convert or to emigrate. Chintila further required those Jews who accepted baptism to sign a document (*placitum*) in which they renounced their beliefs and promised to abstain from Jewish rites and practices such as worship on Saturday and circumcision. They were to give up all of their holy writings and to stone to death any convert who failed to be a true Catholic.[43] Chintila ruled only three years, and little can be ascertained from contemporary sources about the success of his anti-Jewish policy. In 640 he was succeeded by his young son Tulga. Nothing is known of his reign since he was deposed shortly after his succession by the pro-Jewish king Chindasuinth. During the decade or so which ended with Tulga's overthrow, several major and many minor revolts against the several kings occurred. Foreign aid was sought to support some of these rebellions. In brief recapitulation, Suinthila, after succeeding the anti-Jewish Sisebut—perhaps by murdering his son—pursued a pro-Jewish policy, and Sisenand, after overthrowing Suinthila, pursued an anti-Jewish policy. At least some of the revolts against Sisenand were led by supporters of Suinthila's policies. Chintila was a supporter of Sisenand, and he pursued his predecessor's anti-Jewish policies. There were revolts against him as well. Tulga, Chintila's son, was overthrown by Chindasuinth who pursued a pro-Jewish policy.[44]

E. A. Thompson is probably correct, however, when he concludes "It will hardly be thought that the storms of these years centered on the position and liberties of the Jews in Spain. It is safest to think that the conspiracies were the outcome of the rival ambitions of different Gothic noblemen."[45] Yet it seems reasonable to hypothesize that the Jews, as a formidable faction on the Visigothic scene, were supporters of Suinthila and Chindasuinth and were opposed to Sisebut, Sisenand, Chintila, and Tulga. The violent nature of the Visigothic royal succession strongly suggests, for example, that a noble like Chindasuinth who sought to overthrow the dynasty of Chintila would first try to obtain the support of the Jewish party which suffered from the policies of that dynasty. Thus although the issue of Jewish "liberties" was very probably not a *casus belli* for the various Gothic noblemen who sought to seize the throne, the position of the Jewish faction may well have been an important factor in determining the nature of the Jewish policy pursued by the king, whether he was a successful rebel or a legitimate monarch.

When the aged Chindasuinth seized power in 642, he put to death several hundred influential Goths who had taken part in revolts. Many other rebels were forced into exile, and their property was confiscated. Chindasuinth decreed the death penalty for future traitors. He, however, "showed no enthusiasm for persecuting the Jews." He reversed the anti-Jewish policy that Chintila had pursued and returned to the policies followed by Suinthila. Chindasuinth did not enforce the decree that Jews in Spain were either to convert to Christianity or to emigrate. In fact he used Jews in governmental positions. Chindasuinth did, however, take one apparently anti-Jewish measure by decreeing the death penalty for Christians who practiced Jewish rites. Chindasuinth seems to have been taking defensive action to halt conversions. What is truly amazing, however, is that Judaism still held such a powerful attraction for Christians despite the anti-Jewish policies of kings like Sisebut, Sisenand, and Chintila.[46]

It should be noted that Tulga, Chintila's son and successor, was overthrown by Chindasuinth. Thus if it can be assumed that supporters of the young King Tulga preferred the policies of his father, Chintila, then Chindasuinth would have been a natural rallying point for Jews as well as for others who opposed the faction in power. That Chindasuinth found it necessary to legislate against the Christians who were being converted to Judaism might well suggest that Jewish missionary work was successful. In this regard, it is important to note that Chindasuinth was taking action against Christians who were being converted to Judaism and not against the Jews who were converting Christians.[47]

Reccesuinth who was associated as king with his father, Chindasuinth, in 649 ruled alone after the old monarch died in 653. Little information survives concerning Reccesuinth's long reign which ended in 672. It is known, however, that revolts followed upon his succession and that he crushed them. His reorganization of the administrative machinery of the Visigothic kingdom strongly suggests that he had strained relations with some Roman elements of the population; the remarks of ecclesiastics suggest that he was not popular with some of the clergy; and his anti-Jewish legislation would suggest that his relations with the Jews were far from cordial. Thus it is hardly surprising that the meagre extant sources indicate that his reign was not blessed with peace and prosperity.[48]

Reccesuinth's great accomplishment was completing the revision of the laws of the Visigothic kingdom that his father had begun. Though he seems to have been dedicated to his father's policy of revising the laws, he reversed Chindasuinth's policies in many other areas. At the Eighth Council of Toledo in 653, for example, he denounced Jews as polluting the soil of Spain, and at his urging the *acta* concerning Jews passed at the Fourth Council were reaffirmed. Reccesuinth, however, went further in pursuing an anti-Jewish policy. First, he enacted ten laws concerning Jews, and these appeared in the new code. The thrust of these laws was to make it impossible for a Jew to remain in Spain. Anyone who practiced Jewish rites or celebrated Jewish rituals was to be executed.[49] Some scholars have suggested that a distinction can be made between practicing and nonpracticing Jews, and thus they conclude that it was a capital crime only to be a practicing Jew. Other scholars have noted, however, that Reccesuinth's laws explicitly point out that anyone who "in his heart" had even the slightest doubt about the Catholic faith must go into exile. Second, Reccesuinth decreed that all preexisting anti-Jewish laws not explicitly repealed were to be enforced. Thus Chintila's law that all Jews either must convert or go into exile was still in force. It seems reasonable to agree with Parkes who concludes: "Without saying so in so many words, Reccesuinth forced all Jews who remained in Spain to accept conversion."[50]

Reccesuinth's anti-Jewish policy, however, met with strong opposition. In 655 very shortly after his anti-Jewish policy became law, the Ninth Council of Toledo took up the problem of Christians who connived with Jews to resist the new laws.[51] The reaffirmation of the penalties and admonitions of the Ninth Council did not have the desired effect. In 656 Reccesuinth called the Tenth Council of Toledo and produced evidence that large numbers of clerics were still selling Christian slaves to Jews. The religious penalties of excommunication and anathema and the economic penalties of confiscation of up to one-quarter of the lands of anyone who violated the laws seem to have been ineffective. Not only did Reccesuinth's laws fail to destroy the Jewish community, but the Jews apparently were carrying on business as usual in the many areas where the king's power did not reach.[52] For example, from all of Gallia—where, it should be emphasized, Jews were an important element on the political scene—and Tarraconensis only Bishop Quiricius of Barcelona attended the Tenth Council.[53]

In trying to ascertain why Reccesuinth reversed his father's policies concerning the Jews, scholars like Katz have labeled him "fanatical in the extreme."[54] Yet the continuator of Isidore's chronical writing not long after the king's death characterized him as "easy-going" and "debauched." These are hardly the virtues commonly associated with a religious fanatic.[55] If, however, we view Reccesuinth's change of his father's Jewish policy in its political context, there is little need to resort to such characterizations. For example, Reccesuinth reversed his father's policy concerning the supporters of Chintila and Tulga. Whereas Chindasuinth ruthlessly crushed this group, Reccesuinth granted pardons.[56] He favored men whom his father had driven out, men who had helped to formulate and enforce Chintila's anti-Jewish policy.

Another probable factor in the formulation of Reccesuinth's anti-Jewish policy was his close association with Bishop Braulio of Saragossa and his followers. Braulio, as the leader of a powerful faction in the Visigothic Church, had taken the initiative in trying to persuade King Chindasuinth that he should violate canon 75 of the Fourth Council of Toledo and associate Reccesuinth with him in the kingship.[57] Thus Reccesuinth perhaps owed a debt to the faction of the clergy led by Braulio (d. 651), a bishop who had pursued a consistently anti-Jewish policy.[58] It is instructive in this context to note that Braulio had edited Reccesuinth's revision of the Visigothic Code (649-651). Although we have no way of ascertaining the bishop's specific suggestions, it is not unreasonable to assume that he took a hard line against the Jews.[59]

Bishop Eugenius II of Toledo who had been a student and close friend of Braulio was an important advisor to Reccesuinth, and some scholars suggest that he had the task of putting the revision of the Visigothic laws into final form. This same Eugenius wrote an epitaph for Chindasuinth describing him as "impious, obscene, and guilty of every manner of crime." This might suggest that Reccesuinth who was close to Eugenius was not overly partial to his father, King Chindasuinth.[60]

Reccesuinth also maintained a close connection with Bishop Taio, Braulio's supporter and successor as bishop of Saragossa. Curiously, and perhaps by coincidence, no sooner did Chindasuinth die than a revolt broke out in the region of Saragossa. Taio, who was loyal to Reccesuinth, was besieged in the city until the king appeared with an army and crushed the rebels.[61] The connection of Braulio, Eugenius, Taio, and King Reccesuinth with the pardoning of those who had been supporters of Chintila, the denigration of Chindasuinth's memory, the drawing up of the Visigothic Code, and the reversal of Chindasuinth's policies toward the Jews would seem to suggest that political factionalism and not religious fanaticism motivated Reccesuinth's anti-Jewish policies. Addi-

18 Visigothic Jewish Policy

tional evidence for this hypothesis is the failure of the legislation he promulgated and the support the Jews received from both clerics and laymen. Not only did clerics connive to thwart Reccesuinth's laws, but relatively few bishops attended the councils. The Ninth Council of Toledo was in fact no more than a regional synod, and the Tenth Council was attended by only seventeen bishops[62] (compared, for example, with the Third Council in 589 attended by seventy-two bishops or their deputies).

Wamba succeeded to the Visigothic throne at Reccesuinth's death, and like most of his predecessors he found it necessary to fight to keep his newly acquired crown. In the spring of 673 while he was campaigning against the Basques, a serious revolt (led by Count Childeric of Nîmes) broke out in Septimania. Wamba sent Duke Paul to put down the revolt, but the latter developed a plan to usurp the throne. To this end he won over Ranosind, the governor of Tarraconensis. The Jews of Narbonne sided with the rebels and seized control of the city by driving out Bishop Argebad, who had been a loyal supporter of Reccesuinth and remained a supporter of his successor. When Wamba's forces retook Narbonne, however, the Jews were expelled from the city at royal command.[63]

The importance of the Jews of Narbonne in the struggle for power in the Visigothic kingdom was clear to King Reccared as early as 589. Julian, the archbishop of Toledo (680-690), maintained that the Jews in Gaul were not persecuted and lamented that Gaul was "a brothel of blaspheming Jews."[64] In the revolt against Wamba, the only such campaign concerning which we are relatively well-informed, the Jews played an important political and military role; Count Paul chose the city for his coronation and capital.[65] Wamba was the legitimate successor of Reccesuinth, and the Jews probably expected him to carry on his predecessor's anti-Jewish policy: thus they followed their apparent self-interest and opposed him. The military action taken by the Jews of Narbonne reinforces the impression that "la force de l'argent" was not the only power wielded by the Jewish faction in Visigothic politics.

Wamba, however, was not a religious fanatic, and his appreciation of the power of the Jewish community apparently led him to a rapprochement with them. The Jews of Narbonne were allowed to return to their city where for a long time they continued to be a dominant force. Wamba, in addition, did not enforce the existing anti-Jewish laws, and at the councils which met during his reign the Jewish question was not discussed.[66]

Count Erwig succeeded Wamba as king and promptly initiated an anti-Jewish policy. In the very short period from his accession on 21 October 680 to the opening of the Twelfth Council of Toledo on 9 January 681, Erwig drew up twenty-eight anti-Jewish laws. The laws of Reccesuinth were reaffirmed, and in addition baptism was required; the alternative was severe physical punishment, loss of property, and exile. Many other detailed penalties were instituted including beatings and castration. These punishments replaced the death penalty which had been decreed by Reccesuinth for minor infractions like performing a circumcision or refusing to eat pork.[67]

Of equal importance were Erwig's efforts to deter his enemies from providing protection and support for the Jews. For example, individual bishops and abbots had employed and were continuing to employ Jews as agents to administer ecclesiastical estates. These abbots and bishops were warned to stop the practice. Bishops convicted of having sexual relations with Jewish women were to be defrocked and sent into exile. Ecclesiastical and secular officials who failed to enforce Erwig's anti-Jewish laws were liable for a fine of seventy-two *solidi* for each offense they ignored. Anyone who accepted a bribe for not reporting a Jew who broke these laws was also liable for a fine.[68] As part of the dejudification process every Jew was required to sign a statement abjuring Judaism and adhering to Christianity. These statements were to be placed in the archives of the churches in the areas where the new converts dwelled.[69] It should be noted that none of these sworn statements have survived which may suggest a lack of widespread enforcement of Erwig's anti-Jewish policy. In addition we know that as late as 694 Jews still owned Christian slaves and carried on business as usual.[70]

A clue to why Erwig chose to pursue a vigorous anti-Jewish policy may be found in the unorthodox manner in which he succeeded to the throne. On 14 October 680 Wamba was taken ill and "while unconcious was, according to the current custom, made a penitent—tonsured and clothed in penitential garb."[71] When Wamba recovered, he learned that since he had been tonsured he could no longer reign and that Erwig had succeeded him. Erwig then called the Twelfth Council of Toledo where his succession was confirmed despite Wamba's protests that he was still able to reign.[72]

The only contemporary evidence we have for these events comes from the proceedings of the council at which the dominant figure was Bishop Julian, who many scholars maintain was dedicated to the extirpation of Judaism from the Visigothic kingdom.[73] The circumstantial evidence has led many scholars to suggest that Erwig's succession was the result of a conspiracy. Wamba was opposed by some elements in the Church, and his failure to pursue a vigorous anti-Jewish policy could not have pleased Julian, the most important ecclesiastical magnate in the kingdom.[74] Rumors which only found written form several generations after Wamba's illness claimed that he had been drugged so that he could be tonsured and deposed. Of this Thompson writes, "It was inevitable that such a tale should have been told; and it may have been the truth. Indeed the mere fact that the Twelfth Council tried at such length to excuse Erwig suggests that there was something which called for an excuse."[75]

What the council did do to support Erwig's claim does indeed suggest its *parti pris*. Erwig submitted to the council two documents which he said had been signed by Wamba. These appointed Erwig as Wamba's successor. Scholars generally agree that the documents were forgeries, but the council, acting under the influence of Julian, accepted them as genuine and proclaimed Erwig's legitimate right to be king. Even if these documents were not forgeries, they were not valid since they violated canon 75 of the Fourth Council.[76] The Twelfth Council also strengthened the rules concerning the inability of a tonsured king to regain the throne and absolved Wamba's subjects from their oath of fidelity to him.[77] Thus it has been hypothesized often that a conspiracy between Julian of Toledo and Erwig resulted in the recognition of the latter as king. In return for Julian's support, Erwig seems to have promised among other things to pursue a vigorous anti-Jewish policy.[78]

Egica succeeded Erwig and was faced not long afterward with a serious revolt. Bishop Sisebert of Toledo led the attempt to overthrow the king and place a certain Suniefred on the throne in his place. Opposition to Egica was widespread, but he managed to survive and maintain his throne. After putting down Sisebert's revolt, he called the Sixteenth Council of Toledo which opened on 2 May 693. Egica had all those who conspired against him condemned, and it was ruled that their property was to be confiscated and their descendants were to be barred from public office. Bishop Sisebert was deposed and defrocked.[79] Egica also promulgated a new anti-Jewish policy that increased the penalties imposed upon those who dealt with Jews illegally. Important people (*maiores*) were liable for a fine of 216 *solidi*, and unimportant people (*inferiores*) were liable to receive up to a hundred lashes with the whip and be fined at the king's will. All property held by Jews that had been obtained from Christians was to be confiscated by the crown, but compensation was to be paid. Jews were not permitted to carry on trade with Christians within the Visigothic kingdom, nor were they allowed to engage in long-distance commerce beyond its borders. In addition Jews were subjected to very burdensome taxes which they presumably could not pay, having lost their wealth. The bishops at the Sixteenth Council confirmed this law but specifically noted that they did so only at the king's behest.[80]

The mode of attack Egica developed makes it abundantly clear that Erwig's efforts to force all Jews either to convert or to emigrate had failed. There were still many Jews in the Visigothic kingdom in 693, and Egica thought it necessary to issue a series of laws aimed at crippling the economy of the Jewish community. The increase in the penalties decreed for those who violated the laws indicates that Erwig's milder punishments had not deterred offenders.[81]

Although some scholars have maintained that Egica was a religious fanatic, his anti-Jewish policy seems to have been politically motivated. His relations with some Church factions were poor indeed, as indicated by the revolt led by Bishop Sisebert. Further he violated many canons and moved Bishop Felix from Seville to Toledo. Felix was Julian's biographer and apparently shared his anti-Jewish sentiments.[82] While Egica violated Church law, his anti-Jewish legislation was intended to destroy the economic base of the Jewish community. Thus he tried to eliminate a potential source of financial and other support previously available to his many non-Jewish enemies.

22   Visigothic Jewish Policy

During the year after Egica's anti-Jewish policy became law at the Sixteenth Council of Toledo, some elements of the Jewish community attempted to raise support from outside the kingdom to help sustain a revolt against the king. Egica learned of these efforts and called the Seventeenth Council of Toledo which met on 9 November 694. There he spoke of confessions he had obtained from some of the Jews who had schemed to overthrow him. At Egica's order the bishops assembled at Toledo thus decreed that henceforward all Jews should be stripped of their property and be made slaves.[83]

Some scholars have defended the Jews' loyalty to the monarchy and have argued that Egica's claim that the Jews sought foreign support to overthrow him was a "figment or an invention";[84] the "doctors plot" is a ready parallel for the historian of the recent past. Yet Egica's policy was pursued in seventh-century Spain, not in Hitler's Germany or Stalin's Russia; and we must evaluate the evidence in its own context, not in light of more modern events. Is there any reason to disbelieve Egica's charges? Had not *refugae* sought foreign aid to help rebel causes throughout much of the seventh century? Had not Jews actively participated in military operations against Wamba? Were not Jews sufficiently disadvantaged as a result of Egica's policies that they would benefit by opposing him actively? Egica was an extremely unpopular monarch who not long after his death was condemned by a Christian writer as a king who "persecuted the Goths with bitter death."[85]

Against positive evidence asserting that the Jews sought foreign aid to overthrow the king and circumstantial evidence providing additional support for the charges, we have only the timeworn prejudice that Jews are an unwarlike people; Jews do not fight but weep, discuss, and at most try to bribe their enemies.[86] The uselessness of such stereotypes for the historian who is attempting to evaluate the evidence for a particular event at a particular time is manifest. Thus I can find no reason to conclude that Jews did not scheme to overthrow Egica. It would have been strange indeed if they had not opposed him at least as vigorously as they had opposed Wamba when he came to power as the legitimate successor of a king who had pursued an anti-Jewish policy.

In 700 Egica raised his son Witiza to the throne and gave him the northwestern part of Spain to rule with his capital at Tuy. When Egica died in 702, Witiza ruled alone. The latter, like most of his predecessors, was faced with revolts, but he survived and managed to have his young son Achila accepted as co-monarch. Contemporary sources are largely lacking for Witiza's reign, but some nearly contemporary materials portray him as a much more congenial ruler than his father. Nevertheless Witiza did not have good relations with at least a faction of the clergy,[87] nor did he pursue his father's anti-Jewish policies. A medieval tradition that survives in the *Chronicle* of Lucas of Tuy is that Witiza was eager to have the support of the Jews and that he eliminated the disabilities his father had placed upon them.[88]

There is, however, no scholarly consensus concerning the reliability of the tradition found in Lucas's *Chronicle*. Graetz, for example, first accepted it but later changed his mind.[89] Dahn rejected it. He argued that the Church's dislike for Witiza led an ecclesiastic like Lucas to characterize the king as a Jew-lover; in the thirteenth century this was a form of condemnation.[90] Katz follows Dahn, but Ziegler suggests that Witiza may have relaxed the anti-Jewish laws since "he ruled more mildly than his father." Scherer strongly supports the accuracy of Lucas's testimony.[91]

The two most damaging attacks on the evidence Lucas provides are based on his long separation in time from the events themselves and on the alleged enmity of the Church toward Witiza. It is true that Lucas portrays Witiza as a bad king. In doing so, however, he was merely following a well established historiographical tradition. He passed on the picture that he found in his sources and added the "fact" that Witiza pursued a pro-Jewish policy. In defense of Lucas it should be noted that his *Chronicle* is an uncritical grab bag of facts, stories, and legends gleaned from numerous written and oral sources. That Lucas personally shared in the "kirchliche Feindschaft" which is alleged to have motivated Witiza's "bad press" has not been proven. Yet even if it were demonstrated that Lucas shared this bias, it would not in itself constitute proof that he or his source fabricated the story of Witiza's pro-Jewish policy.[92]

What is most important is that Lucas introduced a new "fact" concerning Witiza. In this context it is important to note that Lucas was from Tuy, where Witiza located his first capital. The people of no other region in Spain would have had a better opportunity to retain in their oral traditions information about Witiza. In short Lucas may well have had access to information about Witiza's pro-Jewish policy because of the unique position the king's reign played in the history of Tuy.[93] If Witiza in fact reversed his father's anti-Jewish policy, the clearest evidence would probably have been found in the proceedings of the Eighteenth Council of Toledo which was called ca. 703, shortly after Egica's death. One copy of the minutes (now lost) of this council survived in the Middle Ages; could Lucas have gotten his information from these documents?[94]

The history of the last few years of the Visigothic kingdom is very poorly documented. When Witiza died ca. 710, his young son Achila, who earlier was associated in the kingship, succeeded to the throne. As usual there was opposition to the succession, and a noble named Roderic was able to establish himself as king in the southern part of Spain while Achila retained control in the northeastern region.[95]

The struggle for power within Spain was complicated by the efforts of the Byzantines to reestablish their influence and perhaps their colonies in the south of the peninsula. During the latter part of Witiza's reign a Byzantine invasion fleet was repulsed by the Visigothic general Theudimer. Urban, the Byzantine governor of the fortress at Ceuta, leagued with the Muslims in 710 to raid the coastal towns in the south of Spain. Legend has it that Urban was pursuing a vendetta against Roderic because the king had dishonored his daughter. It is more probable, however, that the Byzantines were pursuing a policy against the Visigoths and saw the Arabs as a useful tool in this endeavor.[96]

The Byzantines, the Muslims, and the armies of Achila were not Roderic's only enemies. The king was campaigning against the Basques in 711 when an army led by Tarik ibn Ziyad landed in the south of Spain. Roderic gathered a large force including contingents led by Achila's supporters, Archbishop Oppas of Seville, and a noble named Sisebert. When Tarik's forces met Roderic's army near the lake of La Janda in southern Spain on either the 25th or 26th of July, those fighting men and magnates loyal to Achila deserted, and the Muslims won a decisive victory. During the next three years the Muslims subdued Roderic's kingdom. The Jews opposed Roderic's supporters and allied with the Muslims. A large number of cities were seized by the Jews, and some cities including Seville, Cordova, and Toledo—the most important in Spain—received Jewish garrisons. The numismatic evidence indicates that Achila's kingdom survived the Muslim conquest for several years.[97]

It is tempting to conclude that the Muslims, King Achila, and the Jews all joined together, at least temporarily, to overthrow Roderic.[98] As the turn of events shows, the Muslims gained the most from this fluid situation; the Jews, however, did not suffer. The importance of the Hispano-Jewish community in the post-Visigothic era is well documented. The Jews were an important faction in the struggles for power that characterized the political life of the Visigothic kingdom during the century and a quarter before its fall, and they continued to be important in Spain for the remainder of the Middle Ages.[99]

If we view the Jews in this light and the anti-Jewish policies pursued by at least some of the Visigothic kings are seen as politically motivated attacks, it may be suggested that these attacks were formulated within a religious framework because the Jewish community was a clearly identifiable entity. The Jews practiced religious rites and ceremonies markedly different from those of the Christian majority including dietary customs, worship on Saturday, and congregation in synagogues. In addition there was in Spain and throughout the lands once constituting the western half of the Roman Empire no dearth of anti-Jewish polemical literature which condemned Jews as perfidious and enemies of Christianity. Some clerics and laymen in Visigothic Spain did not find the persecution of Jews abhorrent, and some saw it as desirable.[100] Thus in pursuing anti-Jewish policies for political purposes, Visigothic kings could expect support from those who preferred persecution of Jews on religious grounds.

It should be emphasized, however, that only six of the Catholic Visigothic kings pursued anti-Jewish policies. The Church as an ongoing institution in Visigothic Spain was a tool of the monarchy and confirmed the anti-Jewish legislation promulgated by the monarchs; at the councils it was usually made clear that the king had commanded their approval. While the Church as an institution tended to support the anti-Jewish policies of the kings, many bishops and abbots in their capacity as powerful magnates opposed or ignored them. The population throughout Visigothic Spain tended not to support the anti-Jewish policies pursued by the kings. The noteworthy role that the allegedly enslaved Jewish population played in the success of the Arab conquest strongly suggests that the Hispano-Jewish community remained a formidable political faction in Visigothic Spain and that in sum the anti-Jewish policies were abject failures. We may conclude with Thompson that "Whatever the reason for the persecution, it may have contributed to the utter destruction of those who initiated and enforced it."[101] In chapters IV, V, and VI, our examination of the Jewish policies pursued by the tiny Christian polities built upon the ruins of the Visigothic kingdom will reveal whether these remnants learned the folly of persecuting the Jews.

CHAPTER II

Jewish Policy in Early Medieval Italy (476-774)

During the some two centuries in which Spain was ruled by the Visigoths, Italy was subjected to a series of conquerors. Odoacer, the leader of a war band comprised of several barbarian peoples, ruled much of Italy for thirteen years (476-489). From 489 until 493 Odoacer and the Ostrogothic king Theoderic fought for control of the peninsula. The latter won, and his dynasty ruled until 554. The last two decades of this period, however, were disturbed by an ongoing war with the Byzantine armies of Justinian I. The Byzantines were victorious but enjoyed the fruits of their conquest for only fourteen years. In 569 the Lombards invaded Italy and played a politically dominant role on the peninsula until they were overcome by Charlemagne in 774. During the period of these major transfers of power, it should be noted that the Merovingians ruled substantial areas in northern Italy (during the late sixth and early seventh centuries); the pope gained control of the city of the Caesars and its environs; and from time to time various *civitates* functioned as autonomous polities.[1]

Each of the powers that ruled in Italy found it necessary to develop policies to deal with the many Jewish communities that flourished in the numerous *civitates* dotting the peninsula. We obtain our first glimpse of these policies from two letters of Pope Gelasius I (492-496). The pope was asked by one of his close associates, a certain Telesinus, to write a letter recommending his relative, Antonius, to Bishop Quinigesius. Gelasius responded to the request affirmatively, and the pope's strong letter of support makes clear that Telesinus who is styled a *vir clarissimus* —a member of the senatorial class—and his relative, Antonius, were both Jews.[2]

At about the same time Pope Gelasius also wrote to three bishops, Siracusius, Constantius, and Laurentius, to investigate a charge that a Jewish slave owner had circumcised and converted to Judaism one of his Christian slaves contrary to the latter's will. In this letter the pope took great care to warn the bishops to act judiciously so that neither the cause of religion nor the exercise of proper authority be damaged.[3]

These two pieces of evidence from the chancery of the most important ecclesiastical authority in Italy not only help to ascertain the nature of papal Jewish policy at this time but are probably of some value in developing an overall understanding of the position assumed by Theodoric the Great shortly after he came to power in 493. It must be emphasized in this context that the Jews in Italy at this time were formally subject to more than fifty special enactments of the *Theodosian Code* that distinguished them from other Roman citizens. For example, Jews were barred from holding high rank, from owning Christian slaves, and from converting Christians or anyone else to Judaism.[4]

Pope Gelasius's letters provide evidence, as in the case of Telesinus, that Jews held positions of high rank. A *vir clarissimus* was of the senatorial rank, the highest class in the empire. Pope Gelasius's close relations with Telesinus and the expected cooperation in support of the Jew Antonius by Bishop Quinigesius speak for themselves.[5] In the case of the Jewish owner of Christian slaves it is clear that the local secular authorities had not enforced the laws against Jews owning Christian slaves or against Jews converting Christians to Judaism. The pope's instructions to the bishops assigned to investigate the matter are circumspect and illustrate the delicate nature of the situation. Parenthetically, it should be noted that Pope Gelasius did not instruct the bishops to investigate or deal with the problem of Jews who owned Christian slaves contrary to both Roman law and the Church canons but only directed the bishops to concern themselves with the case of a Christian slave alleged to have been converted to Judaism. It must also be emphasized that the case involved a Christian who was supposedly converted against his will and not one who had chosen Judaism freely.

From the political point of view it is highly unlikely that Pope Gelasius was in a position to pursue a Jewish policy or for that matter any other that was radically different from Theodoric's policy in the same area. During the earlier part of his reign Theodoric issued a compilation of 154 edicts summarizing the law to be followed by both Romans and barbarians in matters of public order or of potential confrontation between the two peoples. Many of these edicts are restatements in simple form of existing legislation, but although Theodoric indicated in the introduction to his compilation that the old laws still applied, he did make substantive changes.[6] Edict 143 concerns Jews and reads "Circa Iudaeos privilegia legibus delata serventur: quos inter se iurgantes et suis viventes legibus eos iudices habere necesse est, quos habent observatiae praeceptores."[7] The guaranty to Jews of their previously existing privileges including that of using their own law is significant in itself. More important is the omission of any mention of the *Theodosian Code*'s enactments that curtailed Jewish activities, such as laws that barred them from high rank and prohibited them from owning Christian slaves.[8] In any discussion of Theodoric's legal enactments it must be pointed out that at least one Jew is known to have held an important position on his legal staff. Although this particular jurisconsult, Symmachus by name, cannot be shown to have influenced Theodoric's Jewish policy, that he or one of his coreligionists, e.g., a senator like Telesinus, might have been influential cannot be dismissed out of hand.[9]

We can obtain some idea of the relation between Theodoric's edict concerning Jews and the legislation of the *Theodosian Code* from various of the king's letters to Jewish communities or affecting these communities. Thus, for example, in the period 507-511, the Jews of Genoa requested permission to put a new roof on their synagogue. Theodoric granted them permission but warned them not to enlarge the synagogue or to add any kind of adornment. The penalty for violation of these strictures was to be "the king's displeasure."[10]

The *Theodosian Code* seems to have been followed in that it was necessary for the Jews to obtain permission to refurbish their synagogue and in that they were prohibited both from enlarging it and from decorating it conspicuously.[11] When the nature of the punishment delineated in the letter is examined, however, it is clear that the earlier legislation of the *Code* was no longer in force. The penalties stipulated in the *Theodosian Code* for the enlargement or the conspicuous decoration of a synagogue were the confiscation of the building by the government and the transfer of it to the Church.[12] This stringent punishment was replaced by the relatively innocuous rhetoric of Theodoric's secretary Cassiodorus who observed that the violation of these laws would incur the king's displeasure.

A substantial body of evidence from the Ostrogothic period confirms the suspicion that Theodoric and his successors did not enforce the legislation of the *Theodosian Code* that prohibited Jews from bearing arms and serving in a military capacity. For example, accounts of urban strife suggest the participation of armed Jews. More important, however, is the evidence of the use of Jewish fighting men to help garrison fortified places in the name of the king.[13]

In short it seems to have been Theodoric's policy to enforce the *privilegia* of the Jews without making a serious effort to implement the legislation intended to curtail their activities. Jews like Telesinus and Symmachus were permitted to hold high rank and high governmental office, Jews were permitted to carry arms and to serve the government in a military capacity, and Jews were allowed to own Christian slaves and even converted them to Judaism without governmental interference. Theodoric confirmed Jewish *privilegia* not only in edict 143 but also in letters such as one to the community at Genoa in which he wrote: "Privilegia debere servari quae Judaicis institus legum provida decrevit antiquitas."[14] In no text is it indicated, however, that the restrictive legislation of the *Theodosian Code* was enforced rigorously.

On several occasions we catch a glimpse of Ostrogothic Jewish policy in relation to specific incidents of violence that scholars have generally seen as anti-Jewish in character.[15] We learn, for example, of an incident that took place at Rome sometime between 509-511 in which a group of important Jews inflicted very serious punishments on some Christian slaves who had attacked and murdered their Jewish owners. A group of Romans retaliated by burning the synagogues. In ordering an investigation of the matter, Theodoric indicated that those who burned the synagogues were to be severely punished and that the complaints against the Jews were to be examined. Theodoric, moreover, evinced a perplexed attitude at the activities of the supposedly anti-Jewish faction who "foolishly attacked innocent buildings because they were angry at the men who used them."[16]

In 525 other incidents of rioting and burning of synagogues were reported. The Jews of Ravenna were charged with having ridiculed Christians and with having thrown either baptized Christians or their holy water into the river. Concerning the incident at Ravenna it is said that a mob of Christians took offense at the actions of the Jewish troublemakers and retaliated by burning their synagogues. Theodoric then ordered that the entire Roman population of the city be taxed for the purpose of rebuilding the synagogues that had been burned. Those Christian Romans (in contrast to Goths and other folk) who could not pay the tax were to be whipped through the streets of the city as a punishment.[17] At about the same time as the trouble in Ravenna, the Jews of Milan complained to Theodoric that they had been the victims of unwarranted violence and that their *privilegia* were not being respected. The king ordered that no ecclesiastic might infringe upon the privileges of the Jews nor concern himself with the internal affairs of the Jewish community. Theodoric did, however, warn the Jews not to act violently against the Church.[18]

Are we to conclude that this urban violence in Ostrogothic Italy was religiously inspired and pitted Orthodox Christians against Jews, or is the situation more complex? An argument based solely upon the notion of religious hostility appears tenuous, particularly in the face of Pope Gelasius's pursuit of a pro-Jewish policy and Archbishop Peter of Ravenna's support of the tax and the whippings ordered by Theodoric for the Christians of his city who had burned the Jewish synagogues.[19]

When Theodoric observed, perhaps somewhat tendentiously, that he could not understand why people attack innocent buildings because they supposedly have a score to settle with the people who use them, he provided an aid to our understanding of the urban violence discussed above.[20] Synagogues, like churches, were repositories of many valuable objects of gold, silver, and gems. Attacking innocent buildings whether synagogues or churches or shops was a characteristic of the violence endemic to the cities of the late antique Mediterranean world. For example, an illuminating episode at Constantinople is discussed by Professor Sharf: "Demonstrations by Christian extremists protesting that the Judges had been bribed to favor the accused in a trial for 'hellenism' led in the words of John of Ephesus, to violence by which 'the whole city was troubled. The shops were shut and Jews, Samaritans and heretics of all kinds rushed from every quarter, ready to steal whatever came to hand.... They had joined for the loot and were meaning to burn churches, supposing that the Christians would be blamed for it.' "[21]

The role of Jews in the endemic urban violence of the eastern part of the empire is well documented.[22] The material available for Ostrogothic Italy would seem to illustrate similar complex social, economic, political, and religious motives involved in such outbreaks in Theodoric's kingdom. Noteworthy there, however, is Theodoric's consistent support of the Jewish faction and his vigorous use of royal power to sustain his pro-Jewish policy. Scholars have usually underestimated the *parti pris* of Theodoric's policy, and in trying to account for the Ostrogothic position toward the Jews it is usually concluded somewhat lamely that Arians tended to treat Jews better than orthodox Christians treated them.[23]

It seems, however, that Theodoric pursued a clearly defined pro-Jewish policy that called for the recognition and enforcement of their *privilegia*. At the same time he managed to ignore old imperial legislation that restricted the activities of Jews. Those who harmed Jews were effectively and severely punished; alleged or potential Jewish wrongdoing was investigated, admonished, and even threatened with "royal displeasure"; but at no time is there evidence of punishments having been meted out or of anti-Jewish laws having been enforced. Whether the Ostrogoths' Arianism made them more favorable to Jews than they would have been if they were Orthodox Christians is a question that historians cannot hope to answer. In trying to ascertain the Ostrogothic motives in pursuing a pro-Jewish policy, however, it should not be forgotten that the Jews provided educated men for government service, loyal fighting men to defend the new order, and a vigorous faction of armed citizens in the important cities of the realm. The many Jewish communities throughout Italy were rich, powerful, and well organized. It may be asked, what advantage could the Ostrogoths have gained by pursuing a policy that was not pro-Jewish?

Barbarian domination of Italy was shattered in a bloody war with the Byzantines in which the armies of Justinian I devastated the peninsula and rejoined its ruin to the empire.[24] During this conflict Theodoric's successors used Jewish advisors to the extent that their presence attracted public attention. In the popular view these advisors were considered soothsayers.[25] The Ostrogoths also organized Jewish fighting men as garrison troops. At Naples, for example, the Jewish units in the city's garrison fought heroically in defense of the Gothic cause, as noted by the contemporary Byzantine historian Procopius. Procopius, who was knowledgeable in military matters, praised the Jewish fighting men for their ability and remarked on the martial spirit of the Jewish community at Naples. At no time did he register surprise either at the idea or the fact of Jews participating in military operations although such activity was illegal according to the *Theodosian Code*.[26]

In light of the Ostrogoths' pro-Jewish policy which won strong Jewish support, it would be reasonable to expect the Byzantine conquerors to have pursued a vigorous anti-Jewish policy. Such an expectation is strengthened by Justinian's order to confiscate the synagogues of North Africa in 535. This act was intended to punish the Jews who had supported the Vandals and who continued to pursue active military operations against the Byzantines even after the imperial conquest of the Vandal kingdom had been completed.[27]

In addition to the not unreasonable anti-Jewish policy that Justinian instituted in North Africa, his revision of the Roman law severely curtailed the privileges enjoyed by Jews of the empire under the *Theodosian Code*.[28] Jewish legal autonomy was limited,[29] many Jewish protections and immunities were eliminated,[30] and the death penalty was mandated for Jewish ownership of Christian slaves[31] and for trying to or succeeding in converting a Christian to Judaism.[32] Jewish rights in Roman law courts were diminished by Justinian,[33] and heavy fines were ordered imposed upon Jews who contrary to the law exercised either civil or military power over Christians.[34] These portions of the revision include only some of the more important legislative changes which worsened the Jews' legal status in secular matters. In religious affairs Justinian acted to control Jewish ritual; he mandated the use of vernacular translations of Jewish holy writings,[35] banned the use of postbiblical Jewish commentaries,[36] and prohibited the Jewish Passover from being celebrated before the Christian Easter.[37]

During the two generations following the institution of Justinian's legislation and reconquest of Italy, imperial officials on the peninsula seem to have refrained from pursuing an anti-Jewish policy. It is especially noteworthy that at Naples where the activity of Jewish armed forces in support of the Ostrogoths attracted the attention of a contemporary historian of the conquest, the synagogues were not destroyed nor confiscated as they had been in North Africa under not dissimilar circumstances.[38] The Jewish community at Naples was permitted to flourish as it had under the Ostrogoths.[39] Jewish slave owners were allowed to own pagan, Christian, and Jewish slaves as they had before the conquest. Pagan slaves and Jewish slaves who according to Justinian's laws were to be freed if they wanted to become Christians continued to be kept in bondage by their Jewish owners. Naples during this period was an entrepôt for the slave trade, and both Christian and pagan slaves from Gaul were transported by Jewish slave traders to Naples to be transshipped to the Near East. Imperial officials (*judices reipublicae*) helped and encouraged the Jewish slave merchants to break the laws that prohibited Jews from dealing in Christian slaves.[40]

Imperial policy at Naples does not seem to have been very different from that in the many other places where Jewish communities were long established. In general, the synagogues were not confiscated[41] as they had been in North Africa nor was Justinian's legislation concerning the mandated changes in Jewish religious observance systematically enforced.[42] Jews were permitted to continue to own Jewish, pagan, and Christian slaves, the last contrary to law,[43] and officials of both the government and the Church allowed Christian *coloni* to be bound like serfs to the *latifundia* of Jewish landed magnates.[44] Not only did imperial officials cooperate with Jews to break the law with regard to Jewish ownership of and trade in Christian slaves, but prelates such as the bish-

Jewish Policy in Early Medieval Italy 35

ops of Cagliari and Luna did so as well.⁴⁵ Jews were permitted to play a role in merchant shipping and as moneylenders,⁴⁶ and ecclesiastics even sold valuable liturgical objects to Jewish traders contrary to conciliar enactments.⁴⁷

During the two generations following the Byzantine conquest it is clear that Justinian's anti-Jewish policy was not enforced in Italy.⁴⁸ Insofar as can be ascertained, Byzantine officials connived to thwart anti-Jewish measures or failed to take positive action to enforce the law. In trying to account for the Byzantine failure to pursue Justinian's anti-Jewish policy it should be remembered that in 569, only thirteen years after the conquest had been completed, a successful Lombard invasion of the peninsula placed imperial forces on the defensive. Any kind of concerted effort to enforce the imperial will against the Jews or for that matter against anyone was a very difficult proposition indeed.⁴⁹

In the late sixth and early seventh centuries, when the Lombards and the Byzantines had accomplished an uneasy and by no means peaceful division of Italy, an exceptionally able and important pope, Gregory I (590-604), emerged as a major figure on the chaotic political scene. Gregory recognized imperial authority and exercised during his tenure as pope considerable political, economic, and ecclesiastical power throughout the Byzantine-held regions of Italy.⁵⁰ Scholars generally agree that Gregory pursued a benign policy toward Jews, one that protected their legal rights and insured religious toleration to them.⁵¹ Gregory's observation: "Just as no freedom may be granted to the Jews in their communities to exceed the limits legally established for them, so too in no way should they suffer a violation of their rights" is often quoted as the key to understanding his Jewish policy.⁵² While no one is likely to disturb the traditional view that Gregory pursued a benign Jewish policy, certain aspects of his policy are in need of more nuance in understanding.

In 1933 S. Katz accurately observed that scholars had not "recognized Gregory's dependence upon Roman law" in making his decisions concerning Jews.⁵³ Parkes, a year later, emphasized that "Gregory was firm in allowing them [the Jews] exactly the privileges which they enjoyed under Theodosian Law."[54] The researches of Katz and Parkes in this area are of signal importance, not primarily because they discussed in detail Gregory's legal orientation, but because they showed the pope to have relied primarily upon the *Theodosian Code* and not on Justinian's *Code* which was more harsh with regard to Jews. That Gregory, who recognized the authority of the emperor at Constantinople, generally chose in pursuing his Jewish policy to use a law code more favorable to the Jews than the official compilation is a point worth emphasizing. Thus, Gregory was not simply a legalist giving the Jews their due as might any unimaginative bureaucrat. Rather, he was an important political and ecclesiastical policy maker who chose a course of action that would seem to demonstrate a pro-Jewish stance regardless of the latest imperial legislation.

Gregory firmly pursued a policy of protecting Jewish synagogues from those who tried to implement certain of Justinian's anti-Jewish laws. Under these laws bishops were given great flexibility in finding pretexts to confiscate Hebrew houses of worship and their appurtenances.[55] In addition Gregory explicitly prohibited officials from interfering with the internal affairs of Jewish communities. Thus the pope not only implicitly reaffirmed the *privilegia* of self-government that had existed under Theodoric the Great and had been curtailed by Justinian's legislation but also expressly forbade the bishops under his jurisdiction to tamper with Jewish ritual as permitted by the new imperial law.[56]

From time to time, Gregory seems to have employed the harsher laws of Justinian in dealing with the problem of Jewish owners of Christian slaves or of non-Christian slaves when the latter declared their desire to convert to Christianity.[57] More often than not, however, Gregory found that the ambiguities of the *Theodosian Code* suited his aims better than the rigors of Justinian's *Code*. Thus Gregory permitted the flourishing Jewish slave trade to continue by making allowances for Jewish merchants who "accidentally" acquired Christian slaves. The pope made it clear that he did not want Jewish slave dealers to be disadvantaged because of "ignorance" or "accident." Gregory knew that imperial officials were involved with Jews in encouraging the slave trade, and thus Jews who were found to have Christian slaves among their stock were permitted forty days to sell their contraband. Obviously this restriction, even if it were enforced, would do little to hinder business.[58] Gregory also pursued a policy consistent with the *Theodosian Code*, but prohibited by Justinian's legislation, to the effect that Jewish ownership of Christian agricultural slaves was tolerated as long as the latter were permitted to practice their religion without molestation.[59] Finally Gregory allowed landed Jewish magnates to retain Christian *coloni* on their *latifundia* in violation of the laws that prohibited Christians from being under the power of Jews.[60]

Although Gregory admonished ecclesiastical officials who permitted Jews to perpetrate flagrant violations of the Roman law to the gross disadvantage of Christians,[61] he took special care to act on behalf of Jews who gave even the appearance of being wronged. For example, he looked after the interests of a Jewish shipowner who claimed that officials had wrongly confiscated his vessel[62] and saw to it that a Jewish moneylender was not deprived of what was due him.[63] In yet another case Gregory declared that since it was illegal for Christian slaves to work and live in the home of a Jew, it was permissible for the Jews to use Christian domestic slaves who "lived out."[64]

The one vaguely anti-Jewish aspect of Gregory's policy concerned his desire to convert Jews to Christianity. Although a great many poor and heavily burdened Jewish serfs were bound to Church lands, Gregory eschewed the use of force as a means of bringing these dependents to the baptismal font. Rather, he pursued a policy of bribing these poor economic dependents of the Church by promising them less burdensome *onera* and even by offering them gifts of money if they became Christians.[65] When ecclesiastical officials found that preaching and bribery were ineffective, on occasion they used force. When such a violation of his policy occurred, Gregory never hesitated to condemn the use of force.[66]

It is more than a little curious that Gregory's Jewish policy was at odds with the legislation of Justinian's *Code*, but it is startling when one realizes that the pope acted in a manner diametrically opposed to what seems to have been his personal view of Jews. Gregory apparently regarded Jews with "the deepest horror and loathing." In his theological tracts he had "no word of either sympathy or understanding" for them.[67] Scholars who have tried to understand the basic contradiction between Gregory's attitude toward Jews and his policy toward them have generally advanced theological arguments which, in their sum, are not implausible provided certain premises are accepted. They argue that Gregory would have reasoned thus: Basically, the loathsome Jews will "remain unfaithful until the Gentiles are gathered in. Then all Israel was to be saved." The perfidy of the Jews "only added to the miracle of their ultimate salvation." The Jews must continue to be tolerated until God is ready to save them. They should not, however, be favored in any way.[68]

The theology is consistent, but this interpretation of the motivation behind Gregory's Jewish policy hinges upon the accuracy of seeing the pope as a strict legalist who said: "no freedom may be granted to the Jews . . . to exceed the limits legally established for them." As we have seen, Gregory in fact permitted the Jews far more than the law permitted. Therefore it is not unreasonable to ask why Gregory, despite his "personal" attitude toward Jews, pursued a manifestly pro-Jewish policy contrary to the laws of the Byzantine empire and to the will of the emperor whose authority he fully acknowledged?

Any attempt to approach the problem must rely heavily upon an understanding of the circumstances in which the pro-Jewish policy was forged. Even the casual reader of Gregory's letters will not be unaware that the pope was an acute observer of the political scene and knowledgeable about affairs in both the West and the East. Gregory's years of service in Constantinople had likely acquainted him with the powerful influence wielded by Jews in the factionalized cities of the Mediterranean. Widely publicized episodes in which armed bands of Jewish fighting men made serious inroads even against imperial troops could not be ignored by a man of Gregory's power and responsibilities.[69] In the barbarian kingdoms to the north of Italy, the Frankish queen Brunhild and her grandsons King Theuderic II and King Theudebert II pursued pro-Jewish policies.[70] In addition these Franks held important territories in northern Italy and had often defeated the Lombards, who were a significant papal enemy.[71] In Spain the newly Orthodox Visigothic monarch, Reccared I, pursued a pro-Jewish policy,[72] and in North Africa Jewish Berber tribesmen were a power of consequence.[73] In Italy, as we have

Jewish Policy in Early Medieval Italy 39

seen, Byzantine officials pursued pro-Jewish policies and in particular encouraged Jewish slave traders who dealt in Christian slaves.[74] Even at Rome the Christian population evidenced distinct Judaizing tendencies which greatly worried Gregory.[75] In these circumstances could any pope, especially one with the political acumen of Gregory, have pursued any policy but a pro-Jewish one?

In 632 the Byzantine emperor Heraclius ordered that all Jews in the empire were to be converted to Christianity. Curiously this decree was not enforced; there were no serious efforts to baptize whole communities of Jews forcibly, and so far as can be ascertained Jewish life was not greatly disturbed. Heraclius apparently moved against the Jews in an attempt to coerce them to support the empire against the Persians and the Muslims. The danger posed by powerful and potentially hostile Jewish forces within the empire seems to have compelled Heraclius to issue the decree. If the Jews remained loyal, he could rescind the order or simply ignore it, but if the Jews supported the enemies of the empire, then the decree would have been enforced.[76] Ironically the Jews seem to have been so strong that even though they did not give their full support to the empire, the decree was not enforced. In fact the Jews in Constantinople rioted in 641 against the succession of Heraclius's son and again in 661 when they attacked Hagia Sophia.[77]

In the West the Jews living in Byzantine Italy were no more bothered by Heraclius's anti-Jewish order than were their coreligionists in the heart of the empire. In Sicily, for example, the governor (ca. 655) seems to have been on the payroll of the Jewish community, and he was willing to do their bidding contrary to the law.[78] This situation was not dissimilar from that on the island a half-century earlier when Pope Gregory I complained of the unwillingness of the governor of Sicily to enforce the laws designed to limit the "anti-Christian" activities of Jews.[79]

To speak of an imperial Jewish policy in Italy during the later seventh and eighth centuries in any but the most theoretical terms would clearly do violence to the reality of the situation.[80] It should be remembered that the astounding success of Islam which brought the Muslims to the gates of Constantinople in 732 seriously curtailed the empire in all its aspects; therefore, in Italy the growth in power of local factions and of the Lombards was possible.[81]

The evidence for a Lombard Jewish policy is jejune and scattered. Legally Jews in the Lombard kingdom lived under the Roman law. In the northern parts of the Lombard kingdom, the vulgar Roman law contained only three provisions that differentiated Jews from other "Romans" also subject to the code. Under this Roman law Jews were permitted to maintain their traditional judicial autonomy, but in cases that involved Christians the latter could not be compelled to submit to a Jewish court. The Jews were also prohibited from engaging in trade of Christian slaves, and Jews were not permitted to "intermarry" with Christians.[82]

The legislation concerning "intermarriage" is important because, as noted above, Jewish law dictated that a non-Jew who married a Jew must undergo conversion to Judaism. In 731 Pope Gregory III addressed himself to the problem of intermarriage and condemned it according to the relevant canons.[83] In 743 a papal council again took up the question with a similar result.[84] It should be noted, parenthetically, that the Lombards had begun accepting Orthodox Christianity during the latter part of the seventh century. Thus the Lombards were subject to papal policy and canon law insofar as any Christians were.

Intermarriage seems to have been more than a nominal occurrence among the inhabitants of the Italian peninsula. Not only was it the subject of one of the three special Jewry laws chosen from among more than fifty in the *Theodosian Code* to be incorporated into the *Lex Romana Curiensis*, but during a period of thirteen years, two popes found it necessary to address themselves to this practice as a very serious problem. In addition the Lombards may have been particularly susceptible to intermarriage. This is suggested by the fundamental influence exercised by Jewish law on the Lombard marriage laws and upon the Lombard marriage contract itself.[85] It is not impossible that the sharp increase in polygamy among the Lombards mentioned by Paul the Deacon was also due to Jewish influence. That Duke Grimoald of Benevento obtained a divorce from his sterile wife "more hebraico" may be worthy of note in this context also.[86] The practice of intermarriage and the influence of Jewish law upon Lombard law in this area can be seen as important aspects of close relations between Christians and Jews, which though contrary to both Roman law and Church canons, could not have flourished without governmental connivance.

In 692 the "Quinisext" Council had taken cognizance of such close relations between Christians and Jews. In the introduction to the canons it enacted, the council condemned the prevalence of Jewish customs in the Church.[87] In canon eleven of the proceedings specific attention was given to close social relations between Jews and Christians. The latter were prohibited from eating unleavened bread, from using Jewish doctors, and from mixing with Jews in the public baths.[88] In 731 Pope Gregory III echoed this same theme when he railed against Christians who celebrated Easter with Jews.[89] In 743 Pope Zacharias warned that those who continued to sell Christian slaves to Jews would be anathematized.[90]

During the later seventh and well into the eighth century the thrust of the Jewish policy formulated in Italy by those with secular political power seems to have been to ignore close relations between Christians and Jews. When the *Lex Romana Curiensis* was compiled, only three "Jewish laws" were included of more than fifty that were available. Occasionally a pope or council reiterated the laws intended to limit relations between Jews and Christians, but these enactments seem to have had no noteworthy effect. Even more significant is the failure of the periodic attempts by Byzantine emperors to carry out anti-Jewish policies. So far as can be ascertained Justinian's anti-Jewish laws, Heraclius's decree ordering the conversion of all Jews in the empire to Christianity, and Leo the Isaurian's order either in 722 or 723 that Jews thereafter were *de facto* "new Christians" had no impact on the Italian peninsula.[91]

The single overt pursuit of an anti-Jewish policy by any figure in Italy of political consequence may have occurred in 672 when King Perctarit reclaimed possession of the Lombard throne after a decade of exile. According to a poem written in 698 with the intent of praising Perctarit, he is said to have ordered all Jews of his kingdom either to accept baptism or to suffer execution.[92] Scholars have doubted the accuracy of this source because it is not corroborated, and one would expect that an order of such importance if pursued seriously would have left substantial evidence. The silence is particularly noteworthy because Paul the Deacon devoted considerable attention to Perctarit's reign in the *Historia Langobardorum* but failed to mention the anti-Jewish edict.[93] From other sources it is clear that the Jewish community at Pavia was well established. In fact there is a record of a religious disputation between a Jew named Julius and Peter of Pisa in the city during the eighth century.[94] It seems that Perctarit issued his anti-Jewish edict soon after returning to power, but like similar efforts by the Byzantines it had no noteworthy effect.

The circumstances surrounding Perctarit's edict are obscure. In 661 Perctarit and his brother Godepert succeeded their father Aripert I as joint kings of the Lombard realm. Aripert (653-661) was the first Orthodox Christian king of the Lombards, and his sons followed him in rejecting Arianism. In 662, however, a certain powerful magnate named Grimoald went to war against Aripert's sons; Godepert was killed, and Perctarit fled into exile. His wife and son were held as hostages by the new king Grimoald. Grimoald ruled the Lombard kingdom until his death in 672 when Perctarit returned from exile and apparently embarked upon an anti-Jewish policy.[95] It is not unreasonable to suggest that Perctarit's anti-Jewish policy was related to his religious orthodoxy and perhaps to the fact that he had been exiled for a decade. If we hypothesize that the Jews feared Aripert's conversion to Orthodox Christianity, then it is possible that they supported Grimoald against Aripert's son and successor, Perctarit. It will be remembered that during Grimoald's reign the Jewish custom of polygamy gained ground among the Lombards. Finally when Perctarit returned to power, he sought to punish the Jews who had supported his enemy. The pattern of action hypothesized here follows the pattern in the Visigothic kingdom of the same period. Like his Visigothic contemporaries, Perctarit might have issued a vigorous anti-Jewish edict, but he was clearly unable to enforce it.[96]

Insofar as it is possible to ascertain the nature of the Jewish policies pursued by the various powers in Italy during the period under consideration, it would seem that those officials who attempted to curtail Jewish activities failed in these efforts and those who tended to be pro-

Jewish Policy in Early Medieval Italy 43

Jewish gained valuable supporters of substantial economic and military importance. The Ostrogoths enforced Jewish legal *privilegia* and ignored the laws that were aimed at curtailing Jewish activities. The Byzantine conquest and Justinian's anti-Jewish laws seem to have had little impact on the many Jewish communities in Italy. Pope Gregory the Great permitted Jews to stretch the laws beyond reasonable limits, and imperial officials collaborated eagerly in this. The pope's casuistry in defense of Jewish interests—especially the slave trade—and in contravention of imperial law deserves close attention. Heraclius's, Leo's, and Perctarit's attempts to pursue anti-Jewish policies were of no contemporary consequence. In Italy the political situation was simply too fragmented, and the Jews apparently were too numerous, influential, and important to be attacked effectively and systematically even by emperors and kings.

During the three centuries following the collapse of imperial power in Italy, the several polities established on the peninsula pursued a variety of Jewish policies. This diversity makes it impossible to characterize "Italian" Jewish policy in this era. During the later eighth century and throughout most of the ninth century Italy experienced relatively greater unity under Carolingian domination and influence. In chapters IV, V, and VI it will be seen whether political unity as opposed to fragmentation had a significant effect upon the formulation and pursuit of a Jewish policy.

CHAPTER III

Merovingian Jewish Policy

Shortly after Clovis succeeded his father Childeric as the ruler of Tournai in 481, he expanded Frankish control to the region between the Somme and the Seine. In 503-504, about seven years after his acceptance of Orthodox Christianity, Clovis extended his kingdom south of the Seine and then conquered most of Aquitaine. During the next three years Clovis conquered the northeastern quarter of Gaul.[1]

Clovis's rapid rise to dominance in Gaul can be attributed, in part, to his acceptance of Orthodox Christianity which brought him the support of both ecclesiastical and lay magnates of Roman origin.[2] Baptism, however, does not seem to have caused Clovis to change the basically pro-Jewish policy that his father Childeric pursued. At Tournai, Childeric's capital, Jews were welcomed during this period, not only by the secular authorities but also by Bishop Eleutherius who seems to have been favorable to Jews also. Even in the south of Gaul, which at that time was ruled by the Visigoths, it was known that Jewish merchants thrived at Tournai.[3]

As Clovis expanded his power in Gaul, important Jewish communities in cities like Nantes, Poitiers, Tours, and Toulouse came under his control. In 508 when the Merovingians laid siege to Arles, the Jews who garrisoned a part of the city planned to hand over the defenses to Clovis's forces. That the Jews of Arles should prefer the dominance of the Orthodox Clovis to the dominance of the Arian Visigoths suggests that the Frankish ruler had not gained an anti-Jewish reputation during the preceding decade of conquest. In fact the preference of the Jews of Arles for Clovis may suggest that he had been overtly pro-Jewish.[4]

In 511 during what was to be the last year of his reign, Clovis regularized his relations with the Church at the first Council of Orleans and had the laws of the Salian Franks written down.[5] These two accomplishments were of signal importance, both explicit and implicit, to the Jewish communities of Merovingian Gaul. The writing down of *Lex Salica* made clear that the principle of personality of the law would obtain in Clovis's lands as it had under previous rulers. The Franks were to have their own law and the Romans their own law. Within this framework Jews were considered to be Romans.[6] Basically Jews enjoyed the same rights and owed the same obligations as did non-Jews who were subject to the Roman law.[7]

Clovis, however, retained several laws that treated Jews differently than Christians. These laws can be divided into two basic categories. In one group of laws, Jews were given special *privilegia* because of their religion. On their sabbath and on their holy days, Jews are forbidden by their religion to work. To non-Jewish officials who arranged schedules for public work, collection of taxes, court sittings, and other governmental business, these Jewish holy days had no significance. Thus laws were enacted so that Jews would not be scheduled to do public business on their sabbath or on other holy days.[8]

Another *privilegium* based upon their religion was the Jews' special judicial status. In all cases involving only Jews and in cases not covered explicitly by the Roman law, Jewish courts presided over by Jewish judges were to have jurisdiction. Further, in cases that were covered by the Roman law but in which both parties to the suit wished the matter to be adjudicated in a Jewish court under Jewish law, the venue could be changed at the request of the litigants. Finally, all judgments made in the Jewish courts were legally binding and were enforceable by the appropriate governmental officials.[9]

The second category of legislation under which Jews received special treatment included laws dealing with proselytism and appears at first glance to be severely discriminatory. After careful examination, however, it seems more in the nature of defensive action taken by Christians to protect themselves against the proselytizing zeal of the Jews.[10] Those most vulnerable were slaves belonging to Jews. Thus it was decreed that Jews who bought Christian slaves were to give them up and have the purchase price returned. A Jew who was caught trying to convert a Christian or an ex-Christian slave to Judaism was to lose the slave and to be punished capitally. Further, Jews were not to obtain Christian slaves as gifts. Jews could, however inherit Christian slaves or receive them through a trust. Jews who possessed Christian slaves and who made no effort to convert them either by force or by argument were not to be disturbed.[11]

Jewish proselytizing efforts extended to free men and women as well as slaves, and laws were enacted to thwart this activity. Thus it was decreed that a Christian and a Jew who married were considered to be adulterers and were subject to the punishment stipulated for that crime.[12] In any such marriage one party had to convert. If the Jewish partner became a Christian, then the authorities would scarcely have been concerned; therefore it is clear that this law was intended to stop Christian men and women from converting to Judaism for the purpose of marriage. In cases concerning Jews who became Christians, the law makes it clear that no harm was to come to the convert at the hands of the Jewish community.[13] Free Christians who became Jews, however, were to suffer intestacy.[14]

Just as legislation was enacted to keep Jews from converting slaves by force or persuasion and free Christians through social intercourse, so too, laws were passed to prevent free Christians from being placed in positions in which they could be forced to convert. Jews were therefore prohibited from holding the posts of prison guard and *defensor civitatis*. In general it was decreed that Jews were to be barred from positions in the government that gave them power over Christians and especially over the clergy. Since Jews were rigorously restricted from proselytizing in any way, it was ruled that they should build no new synagogues but should be content to repair and restore their old ones.[15]

The first Council of Orleans was called by Clovis, and it was attended by thirty-two bishops most of whom were from Aquitaine. It is clear that Clovis was in control of the council, and among the canons that he had enacted was one stipulating that no one could be ordained a priest without his consent or that of his count.[16] Thus it is particularly noteworthy in any discussion of Clovis's Jewish policy that this council made no pronouncement concerning Jews.[17] Apparently Clovis was satisfied that the Roman law was adequate. The behavior of the Jewish community at Arles may suggest that Clovis was looked upon as pursuing a reasonably pro-Jewish policy.

Under the Merovingians as under the Romans whom they succeeded, the *civitas*, the walled urban nucleus and the surrounding territory that it administered, was the fundamental unit of both local governmental organization and ecclesiastical jurisdiction. Many of the *civitates* in Gaul had long and celebrated histories which sometimes predated the Roman conquest. It was not unusual for the inhabitants of the *civitates* to owe their primary political loyalty to these miniature city states. When Clovis died in 511, his lands were divided among his surviving sons, Theuderic, Chlodomir, Chlotar, and Childebert, each of whom received various *civitates* which were then organized into four distinct kingdoms.[18] In these Merovingian realms one can therefore discern two distinct though not unrelated foci of political power: the *civitates* and the royal courts. The former, though a part of one kingdom or another, are often seen to have been unresponsive to the king's will. Thus in attempting to ascertain the nature of Merovingian Jewish policy during the reigns of Clovis's sons it is necessary to examine not only royal aims but local ones as well.

During the first two decades after Clovis's death, we have no direct information concerning the policies of the monarchs, or of the local powers, or of the Church toward the many Jewish communities throughout Gaul. The silence is noteworthy because no less than six Church synods met in Merovingian territory during this period, and traditionally, it is from the proceedings of such meetings that we are informed about Judeo-Christian relations.[19]

This silence was broken in June of 533 when twenty-six prelates and the representatives of five other ecclesiastical magnates met at the order of Clovis's three surviving sons, Theuderic, Chlotar, and Childebert, in the city of Orleans to deal with the health of the Church. Of the twenty-one canons promulgated by these ecclesiastics only one dealt with the Jews. In canon nineteen the bishops addressed themselves to the question of Christians who married Jews.[20] As noted above, if such a marriage was to have standing within the Jewish community, the Christian had to accept Judaism. The bishops, of course, did not recognize the validity of such an act and declared that unless the marriage were annulled, the "Christian" partner (who in his or her own eyes and that of his or her spouse was a Jew) would be excommunicated. Obviously the excommunication would have had no religious significance for the person in question. The social consequences, however, would have been great. An excommunicated person is by and large supposed to be cut off from contact with all other Christians, and if the rules were obeyed, the "Christian" spouse of a Jew would have forfeited relations with his or her Christian relatives. Thus the convert would have been placed in a dangerous position because of the fundamental role played by the family in providing protection.[21]

That the bishops at the second council of Orleans, the first "national council" of Clovis's successors, addressed themselves to the problem of Christians who marry Jews raises more questions than it answers.[22] It is clear that canon nineteen would have been promulgated only if the bishops had perceived the problem to be serious, and therefore it is not unreasonable to surmise that too many Christians to be ignored were marrying Jews and thereby accepting Judaism as a necessary step to matrimony. But if Jews were proselytizing zealously as rabbinic pronouncements made during the first five centuries after the fall of the Temple seem to suggest they should,[23] why did the bishops at Orleans II not promulgate more stringent and far-reaching measures to deal with the problem? It may be asked, for example, were these bishops who met at royal command less than eager to advocate detailed and decisive action against the Jews because the latter enjoyed royal favor?

Some insight into royal policy toward Jews under Clovis's sons may be gleaned from the actions of the eldest Theuderic and of his son Theudebert. Theuderic and his successors gained control of the largest part of Gaul and ruled many more *civitates* than did their relatives.[24] With regard to Jewish policy, it should be noted that Theuderic, who inherited Tournai, continued Clovis's support of Bishop Eleutherius who dealt favorably with the Jews in his see and took the theological position that Jews were superior to heretical Christians, i.e., the denial of Christ was less worthy of condemnation than the misrepresentation of Him.[25] At Clermont, where a well-established Jewish community dated back to the later Roman empire,[26] Theuderic installed a certain Gallus as bishop. The latter was highly regarded by the Jewish community and may be presumed to have pursued a pro-Jewish policy.[27]

Very soon after Theuderic was succeeded by his son Theudebert in 534, a number of bishops from the realm approached the new king and asked his permission to hold a council at Clermont. This council met with fifteen prelates under the leadership of Honoratus, archbishop of Bourges, and promulgated sixteen canons.[28] Two of these, the sixth and the ninth, dealt directly with Jews. In canon six, the bishops reaffirmed canon nineteen of Orleans II, raising some important questions. For example, did Theuderic fail to support the earlier injunction concerning marriages of "Christians" with Jews, and thus were the bishops requesting that the new king reverse his father's policy?[29] In this context, it should be emphasized that the Council of Clermont was a local gathering and included only prelates from Theudebert's kingdom.

The ninth canon promulgated at Clermont, however, is far more important than the sixth. In the ninth canon the bishops ventured openly and forcefully, though not without both theological and legal justification, into political matters. They proclaimed that Jews must not be permitted to hold the position of *judex*: i.e., "any *state official* from the highest down to the 'comes civitatis'."[30] Theologically the bishops were concerned that Jews should not hold important governmental posts that gave them power over Christians. The bishops seem to have been particularly worried about Jewish governmental officers who used their positions to humiliate bishops and lesser clerics.[31] Jews were also prohibited from holding such positions by the Roman law in Gaul.[32]

Apparently Theuderic ignored both ecclesiastical and secular law in this matter and employed or permitted his officials to employ Jews in these high governmental positions. If this were the situation, the prelates had good cause to be worried; and if the king permitted Jews to be *judices*, it is hardly likely that he did much to enforce other laws intended to limit the activities of the Jews in his kingdom. Within this framework, it is not unreasonable to assume that the bishops who met at Clermont with Theudebert's permission hoped to have the new monarch reverse his father's pro-Jewish policy. During the Merovingian era the period following the death of a monarch when royal power was transferred from father to son was critical, and it was not unusual during this period for various elements on the political scene to attempt to gain concessions or advantages at the expense of the new ruler.[33]

In trying to understand Theuderic's Jewish policy and the policies of his successors, it must be noted that this branch of Clovis's family came to dominate the greater part of the Burgundian kingdom,[34] and thereby ruled over important Jewish communities.[35] Thus Burgundian Jewish policy must be examined to place the Merovingian Jewish policy in its historical perspective. The Jews of the Burgundian kingdom like their coreligionists throughout Gaul were subject to Roman law. But whereas Alaric's *Breviary* contained eleven titles that distinguished Jews from non-Jews and was in use throughout the greater part of Gaul, the Roman law of the Burgundian kingdom had only one such provision. This law prohibited the much-discussed institution of intermarriage.[36]

In addition to this single title in the Roman law, the Burgundian ruler, Gundobad (474-516) or his successor, found it necessary to distinguish between attacks upon Christians by Jews and by non-Jews. Any non-Jew who struck a free Burgundian was to pay a composition of one *solidus* per blow to the victim, and a fine of six *solidi* was to be paid to the royal treasury. If the victim were a freedman, then the composition was one *semissis* and the fine four *solidi*. If the victim were a slave, then the composition was a *tremissis*, and the fine paid to the treasury was three *solidi*. Further it was decreed that the composition for pulling the hair of a free Burgundian was two *solidi* if done with one hand and four *solidi* if done with two hands. The treasury received a fine of six *solidi* in either case. Such an attack on either a freedman or a slave was dealt with as in the case of a blow. If a slave struck a free Burgundian, the offender was to receive 100 blows.[37]

By contrast with these detailed enactments, the Jew who attacked a Christian in any of the above ways, regardless of the victim's status or class, was condemned to lose his hand. The hand might be saved for the sum of seventy-five *solidi* regardless of the number of blows struck.

The royal treasury was to receive a fine of twelve *solidi* if the Jew chose to pay the compensation. It was also decreed that a Jew who attacked a priest was to be executed and that his property was to be given to the treasury.[38]

It would be unwise to conclude from this legislation that the Jews of the Burgundian kingdom were a particularly violent lot who had to be deterred from this predilection by more severe punishments than those decreed to restrain Christians and pagans. The existence of a special enactment stipulating the death penalty for Jews who attacked Christian priests might suggest, however, that the clergy had been victims of Jewish violence or that perhaps they feared such action. Such a conclusion would be tenuous, however, in light of the silence of the many Burgundian Church councils concerning such possible conflict.[39] Only one enactment concerning Jews was passed by these councils. The fifteenth canon of the Council of Epaone in 517 indicates that Christians were to avoid dining with Jews.[40] This pronouncement and the prohibition of intermarriage found in the Burgundian Roman law seem to suggest that Christians and Jews had close relations.[41] It should be reiterated here that when the prelates who gathered at Orleans in 533 promulgated their prohibition against intermarriage, this legislation had jurisdiction in the erstwhile Burgundian realm.[42] When the bishops assembled at Clermont in 535 attacked intermarriage, their legislation included that part of the former Burgundian kingdom that had become a part of Theudebert's kingdom.[43]

In 538 King Childebert I called a council to meet at Orleans. As in all previous Merovingian and Burgundian councils that addressed themselves to Jewish policy, the bishops assembled at Orleans condemned intermarriage. They also forbade Christians to eat with Jews. Further, Christians were to cease celebrating the Jewish sabbath and to cease working on Sunday. Jews and Christians were forbidden each other's company during Holy Week from Maundy Thursday until Easter Monday. Finally, a Christian slave who fled from his or her Jewish owner to a church or to a Christian in order to avoid punishment was to be protected. Christians were encouraged to buy such slaves from the Jewish owners in order to protect them.[44]

These canons not only focus our attention upon ecclesiastical *desid-*

erata with regard to the formulation of Jewish policy, but they highlight what probably had been the general trend of Merovingian Jewish policy during the reign of Clovis's sons. It is clear that the Jewish community was not isolated from the Christian community but that the two groups had close and friendly relations: from the ecclesiastical point of view, this was to the detriment of Christians.[45] For example, intermarriage and conversion to Judaism appear to have been a continuing problem and thus called forth repeated condemnation from the Church. Christians and Jews socialized, and the former were entertained at the homes of the latter with sufficient frequency to disturb the Church fathers. Even more dangerous to the faith of Christians was the common practice of abstaining from labor on Saturday, the Jewish sabbath, and working on Sunday, the Christian sabbath. Incidentally, this practice was not confined to Jewish-owned Christian slaves who could exercise little choice in the matter, but extended to free Christians as well.[46] Finally, Jews seem to have been accustomed to violating the sanctuary of churches by seizing runaway slaves who sought refuge in holy places.[47] In short, as of 538 Jews do not seem to have been subjected to an anti-Jewish policy by any of Clovis's sons nor is there evidence for the enforcement of the existing laws aimed at protecting Christians from Jewish influence and power.

In 541 yet another council met at Orleans. In canon thirty, the ecclesiastics at the council recognized that Jews were permitted to own Christian slaves provided that no effort was made to convert them to Judaism.[48] Nevertheless the bishops continued to demonstrate their anxiety at the apparent continued success of Jewish proselytism, and they also stated that a Jew who converted a Christian slave to Judaism or who converted someone of Christian parents, or who reconverted a convert was to be punished by the loss of his slaves.[49] The recognition of the Jews' right to own Christian slaves by the bishops would hardly have been promulgated in council had not some pressure been exerted on them. It would seem that although Clovis's successors were willing to have the bishops enact canons to protect Christians from the zeal of Jewish missionary activity, they were not prepared to see their Jewish subjects deprived of the labor to work their estates.

Of all Clovis's heirs, Theuderic and his successors as rulers of Austrasia seem to have been most obvious in pursuing a pro-Jewish policy. King Theuderic appointed Bishop Gallus to the see of Clermont. The bishop was permitted to retain his position under Theudebert and Theudebald, Theuderic's son and grandson, respectively. Gallus was highly regarded by the large Jewish community at Clermont, and when he died in 551, they attended his funeral and lamented his passing.[50] Two factions within the city strove to have their respective candidates succeed Gallus. One candidate, Cato, seems to have had the support of the clergy, and the other, Cautinus, was supported by the Jews of Clermont as well as by others. Cautinus took his case to King Theudebald who appointed him as Gallus's successor.[51] Thus Theuderic's branch of Clovis's family appointed two consecutive pro-Jewish bishops to the see of Clermont. Only two years after the appointment of Cautinus, Theudebald chose as bishop of Uzés a certain Ferreolus who is also said to have been pro-Jewish.[52]

When Theudebald died in 555 without a direct heir, his two granduncles Chlotar and Childebert divided his kingdom between themselves. Childebert obtained the city of Uzés and almost immediately exiled Ferreolus. According to a hagiographical account of the bishop's life, Childebert was very perturbed by the prelate's close relations with Jews and is said to have assumed that Ferreolus was plotting with the Jews to hand Uzés over to the enemy. Ferreolus remained in exile at Paris, Childebert's capital, until the ruler's death in 558. In that year Chlotar I assumed control of the entire *regnum Francorum* and permitted Ferreolus to return as bishop to Uzés.[53]

It will be remembered in 538 that Childebert summoned the Council of Orleans where several anti-Jewish canons were promulgated. Similarly, in 541 he sponsored the Council of Orleans where additional anti-Jewish *acta* were promulgated. Childebert's treatment of Ferreolus, then, might be seen as part of an anti-Jewish policy that has been obscured by the limited sources. It also might be mentioned that Childebert's ally, Chramn, attacked Bishop Cautinus of Clermont who had been the candidate of the Jewish party in the city.[54]

Before concluding, however, that Childebert pursued an anti-Jewish policy or assuming that he harbored strong anti-Jewish religious feelings, it should be noted that from 555 until 558 he was at war with his brother Chlotar. Chlotar's eldest son Chramn had revolted against his father and joined forces with Childebert. One of Chramn's first acts was to seize control of Clermont where he was opposed by Cautinus. Both Cautinus and Ferreolus had been appointed by Theudebald, both were pro-Jewish, and both were either opposed to or disturbed by Childebert and his supporters. It is unlikely that Bishop Cautinus and Bishop Ferreolus were subject to attack because of their Jewish policies. The Jews naturally supported Ferreolus and Cautinus and Theudebald who had appointed them because they were pro-Jewish. Chlotar who inherited the major share of Theudebald's kingdom apparently was heir to his Jewish support; therefore Childebert and Chramn not unnaturally took action against two pro-Jewish bishops. An analogy with the somewhat later events in Visigothic Spain discussed in chapter I would seem appropriate.

When King Childebert died in 558, the entire *regnum Francorum* was united under the control of Chlotar I, Clovis's last surviving son. Chlotar died in 561, and his lands were divided among his four surviving sons: Sigibert, Charibert, Guntram, and Chilperic. Throughout this era of rule by Clovis's grandsons, Merovingian Gaul was scourged by civil wars. The greatly unsettling effects of these continuing conflicts during the two decades after Chlotar's death may well have been partially responsible for the convocation of frequent church councils. From 561 to 583 no less than ten councils were called, an average of almost one every two years. It is important to note that only at the Council of Mâcon convoked in 583 by King Guntram were Jews the subject of ecclesiastical legislation. In fact Jews had not been a topic of conciliar action for more than forty years preceding the Council of Mâcon.[55]

The canons promulgated at Mâcon in 583 indicate that during the more than four decades since the Council of Orleans in 541 the Jews in Merovingian Gaul had grown in power and prestige and that neither secular nor ecclesiastical laws restricting their activities had been enforced. Apparently Jews not only continued to hold the high governmental office of *judex* but had become important agents of the royal fisc as *tellonarii*. The latter collected tolls and also served as judges in cases

Merovingian Jewish Policy   55

concerning foreign merchants.⁵⁶ In religious matters Jews seem to have become even bolder in their proselytizing and not only made efforts to convert their slaves to Judaism but even entered convents and had secret dealings with the nuns. The council vigorously concemned such practices and stipulated that any Jew who converted one of his slaves to Judaism was to lose the slave and to suffer intestacy.⁵⁷ It should be pointed out that this punishment was far less severe than that demanded by the Roman law stipulating that a Jew who converted one of his slaves was to be executed and was to have his property confiscated.⁵⁸ In addition the Jewish community was reminded by the council that it should be respectful of priests and not attack them.⁵⁹ Christians were encouraged to buy Christian slaves owned by Jews for twelve *solidi* each.⁶⁰ The council also reiterated the often-violated canon that Christians should not eat with Jews or celebrate festivals with them under the pain of excommunication, and it was reaffirmed that Christians and Jews should not fraternize during Holy Week from Maundy Thursday to Easter Sunday.⁶¹

The canons of the Council of Mâcon make it clear that during the four decades preceding its gathering the Merovingian kings had pursued policies of, at worst, benign neglect toward the Jews. They had done nothing to enforce laws that were intended to limit the activities of the Jewish community. The basic question raised by the promulgations of the council, however, is why after more than forty years of silence were the bishops who gathered at Mâcon permitted to enact a list of anti-Jewish items. It may be suggested that the civil wars that raged throughout Gaul continued to weaken royal power; several anti-Jewish acts had been perpetrated in the course of factional strife during the few years preceding the council, and in 583 King Guntram who called the council was under serious challenge from the pretender Gundovald.

There is a good example of the success of an anti-Jewish policy at the local level at Clermont. When Bishop Cautinus died in 572, a struggle for the bishopric ensued; the two leading candidates were Avitus and Euphrasius. The Jewish community supported the latter, but King Sigibert chose Avitus.⁶² For the next few years no conflict of significance seems to have occurred between the Jewish community at Clermont and the bishop whom they had opposed. In 576, however, shortly after King Sigibert's murder led to the virtual dissolution of his kingdom into its constituent *civitates*, Avitus pressed his case against the Jewish faction at Clermont. During Easter of 576, a band of Jews attacked one of their erstwhile coreligionists while he was going to church. With this act as a *casus belli*, Avitus preached the baptism of the Jews. His followers burned a synagogue, and the bishop ordered that the Jews of Clermont either accept Christianity or leave. According to Gregory of Tours, a contemporary, 500 Jews were baptized, and the remainder emigrated to Marseilles.[63]

Avitus's apparently successful attack on the Jews of Clermont may have encouraged an anti-Jewish faction at Orleans.[64] At about the same time King Chilperic, a man who fancied himself a theologian and evidenced erratic behavior from time to time, ordered some Jews in his kingdom to be baptized. He proclaimed that he would serve as their godfather.[65] The Jews of Merovingian Gaul, however, were not passive victims of these occasional outbursts. For example, Priscus, a wealthy Jewish merchant and governmental official who dealt with kings and controlled the mint at Châlons-sur-Saône, was killed with members of his entourage by the armed followers of a certain Phatir over the issue of conversion to Christianity. Priscus's kinsmen later killed Phatir.[66]

Of more direct bearing on King Guntram's convocation of the Council of Mâcon, however, may well have been the challenge to his position by the pretender Gundovald who claimed to be a son of King Chlotar I (d. 561). Gundovald was a pawn in a Byzantine foreign policy aimed at increasing imperial influence in Gaul, and he was supported by many important magnates in Gaul including Mummolus, the most prominent government official and most successful general in Guntram's kingdom. Gundovald landed with a large treasure at Marseilles and was well received there.[67] At that time the Jewish community at Marseilles was important, and it had recently been enlarged by émigrés from Clermont.[68] We do not know from direct evidence whether the Jewish community supported Guntram or Gundovald in this struggle. We do know that Bishop Theodore who managed to gain the favor of Guntram pursued an anti-Jewish policy after the king was victorious.[69]

Ironically, Theodore had been a member of the conspiracy to support Gundovald, but when the first attempt to establish the pretender failed in the winter of 582, the bishop was made the scapegoat and accused by one of the other conspirators, Duke Guntram Boso, as the leader of the plot.[70] Theodore, however, managed to convince King Guntram that he was loyal, and I suggest that he accomplished this by making the Jews of Marseilles the scapegoat. This conclusion is based upon two hypotheses which when taken together seem to explain several pieces of evidence concerning the Jews at this time. First, there were Jewish communities in some of the coastal cities of Gaul like Marseilles and Bordeaux, where Gundovald was also well-received,[71] and these Jews may have given the usurper their support. Second, King Guntram had the bishops who gathered at his command at Mâcon promulgate, after four decades of silence, a list of anti-Jewish acts for the purpose of threatening or warning would-be defectors from the royal cause. When the council met, Gundovald was still at large. He was ensconced on an island in the Mediterranean from which he could be landed in Gaul by Jewish-owned ships.[72] In seeking a motive for putative Jewish support for Gundovald at the two major port cities of southern Gaul, Marseilles and Bordeaux, and perhaps otherwhere as well, certain facts must be remembered: the usurper was a creature of Byzantine foreign policy,[73] the Jews were much involved in long-distance trade with the East,[74] and the Emperor Tiberius II (578-582) who sent the usurper to Gaul had pursued a pro-Jewish policy as illustrated by his position during the riots of 578.[75]

It seems unlikely that the occasional anti-Jewish effort such as that of Bishop Avitus of Clermont or that of Bishop Theodore of Marseilles, even when considered with Chilperic's capricious desire to godfather a bevy of converts or Guntram's convocation of the Council of Mâcon, could sustain the notion that the Merovingian monarchs of this era engaged in a vigorous anti-Jewish policy. First, it must be reiterated that the canons of Mâcon evidence the high positions held by Jews throughout the government as well as the success that they had in proselytizing. This situation could not have been maintained without the tacit support of the monarchs or, at least, of their officials. A glimpse of Chilperic's behavior as provided by a contemporary indicates that this erratic ruler tolerated and even indulged in friendly theological debate with Jews who frequented his court and with whom he dealt.[76] In 585 after the Gundovald affair had been decided, King Guntram was welcomed by the Jews of Orleans who considered it a realistic possibility that he would rebuild their synagogue at public expense.[77] At Tours, where Gregory was not an unzealous bishop, two Jewish moneylenders flourished and were involved in the collection of taxes. In 585 these Jews and two of their Christian partners were murdered. The alleged criminals, Christians of local importance, were brought to trial at Tours but found innocent. The relatives of the Jewish moneylenders, however, were dissatisfied and appealed to the Austrasian ruler, King Childebert II, who indicated that he would hear the case in his own royal court.[78] On the whole, the thrust of the very limited evidence seems to make clear that Jews were not subject to a royal anti-Jewish policy. In short it seems that the Jews of this era in Gaul were no worse off than any other group trying to survive in the midst of civil war, blood feuds, and rampant local factionalism.

The last ruling Merovingians witnessed civil wars no less violent or widespread than those which had characterized the reigns of Clovis's grandsons. For more than three decades after the promulgation of the above-mentioned canons at Mâcon, no Church council in Gaul acted on the Jewish question despite the meeting of no less than twelve councils during the period.[79] The absence of either secular or ecclesiastical legislation during this period, however, should not be construed to mean that the last of the ruling Merovingians enforced the existing laws. For example, two letters of Pope Gregory I that have survived were written to Queen Brunhild and her grandsons King Theuderic II and King Theudebert II urging them to suppress Jewish slave owners and slave traders. The pope was particularly interested in stopping the trade that brought newly converted barbarians from east of the Rhine to the slave markets of Italy. These letters make it clear that Brunhild and her grandsons had not enforced the laws aimed at keeping Jews from owning and selling Christian slaves and the laws that prohibited the conversion of slaves to Judaism. Parenthetically it may be noted that Byzantine officials in Italy cooperated with and encouraged this trade. The pope's letters seem to have had no effect on Brunhild's policy.[80]

Brunhild and her grandsons seem to have let the Jews of their kingdom do much as they pleased; she was, however, very tough with churchmen and especially with bishops who might be seen to challenge royal power.[81] It is important to note that Brunhild and her grandsons ruled all of the *regnum Francorum* except for twelve *pagi* located between the Oise and Seine rivers and the sea. These lands were held by Brunhild's enemy Chlotar II whose position was very weak.[82] Nevertheless in a rapid turn of events, Chlotar formed a coalition of secular and ecclesiastical magnates which during the period 613-614 won for him the entire *regnum Francorum* and brought about the death of Brunhild and of all her heirs. In October of 614, Chlotar called together his lay and ecclesiastical supporters at Paris. There he promulgated an edict of twenty-four provisions recognizing both abstractly and concretely the rights and privileges of the magnates and particularly of those who had supported him in overthrowing Brunhild. Eight days after Chlotar presented the Edict of Paris, the seventy-nine bishops who had also gathered at the royal court promulgated seventeen canons for the regulation of religious matters. Thus the Paris conclave that met in October of 614 arranged the transfer of power from Brunhild's party to Chlotar's party.[83]

In recompensing his supporters, Chlotar articulated a Jewish policy apparently contrary to that of the recently murdered Brunhild. The king and the council established that no Jew might hold an office in which he could command either the military or the public (fiscal) service of Christians. A Jew who held such an office had to accept baptism.[84]

The focus of both king and council on the question of Jewish officeholders not only illustrates the failure of previous ecclesiastical and Roman legislation to keep Jews from exercising governmental power over Christians but seems to have stemmed from the *parti pris* of the victors. During the two years before Chlotar called together his victorious followers at Paris, a substantial number of Jewish émigrés from Spain established themselves in the *regnum Francorum*. These émigrés had fled from the Visigothic ruler Sisebut who had initiated a vigorous anti-Jewish policy in 612.[85] The Jews were welcomed by Queen Brunhild, Sisebut's enemy, and the newcomers may be assumed to have supported the Merovingian queen whom not even Pope Gregory the Great could sway from a pro-Jewish policy.[86]

In these circumstances it was not unreasonable for Chlotar to take a hard line against the Jews in Gaul and especially against those who had been officials in Brunhild's government. Thus, Chlotar eliminated from royal service men who had supported his enemies. In addition Chlotar repaid the bishops who had supported him by moving against Jews who exercised power over Christians contrary to the canons and who were supporters of Brunhild, a ruler known for very brutal anti-ecclesiastical acts. One may perhaps regard Chlotar's order — Jews who wished to retain their offices were required to accept baptism — as demanding a demonstration of loyalty or an act of submission to the new ruler.

During the last three years of his reign, Chlotar called two councils — one met at Clichy and the other at Rheims — at which the Jewish question was the subject of ecclesiastical legislation. Canon thirteen promulgated at Clichy and the identical canon eleven promulgated at Rheims indicate that Chlotar and his son Dagobert I who ruled with him at that time were intent upon pursuing an anti-Jewish policy. Both councils reaffirmed the previous secular and ecclesiastical enactments that Jews should not hold public office and that Christians should not feast with Jews. Further it was established for the first time that Jews who attempted to convert Christian slaves to Judaism or who punished Christian slaves severely were to lose the slaves to the royal fisc. Finally, both Jews and pagans were prohibited from buying and selling Christian slaves. Any such sale was to be considered void.[87]

These canons may be seen as the backdrop for the vigorous anti-Jewish efforts of Archbishop Sulpicius of Bourges who is credited by hagiographers with having converted the Jews of his city to Christianity.[88] Of even greater importance than Sulpicius's alleged triumph, however, is Dagobert's putative success reported in the *Chronicle* of Fredegar: "The Emperor Heraclius . . . sent a legation to Dagobert, King of the Franks, asking that he order all of the Jews of his kingdom to be baptized into the Catholic faith. Dagobert complied immediately."[89] It does not seem unreasonable to hypothesize that Dagobert pursued an anti-Jewish policy. Scholars, however, have been unable to agree on either the vigor of his efforts or their effects; indeed, despite Fredegar's unambiguous remarks quoted above, the role played by the Byzantines in this aspect of Merovingian policy is generally thought to be insignificant.[90]

In trying to understand Dagobert's Jewish policy it seems worthwhile to view it, basically, more as a continuation of his father's policy than as sharply distinct from it. Indeed Dagobert was Chlotar's co-ruler for a decade, his legitimate successor, and his son. The anti-Jewish legislation of 614 and the *acta* promulgated during their co-rule at Clichy and Rheims can be seen as the starting point for Dagobert's position. It is clear that although both King Chlotar II and the Church endeavored to eliminate Jews from high governmental offices in 614, enough remained influential to incite the action of the bishops and to stimulate the endorsement of the monarchs more than a decade later at two separate councils. Also Christians continued to feast with Jews, and the latter continued to convert their slaves to Judaism presumably severely punishing those who rejected conversion. If the kings were pursuing an anti-Jewish policy, clearly many important people in the *regnum Francorum* were not following royal dictates as they pursued pro-Jewish policies. The plausibility of this interpretation is buttressed by analogy with events during the seventh century in Spain.

Two enactments at Clichy and Rheims were basically innovative in their thrust and may well provide some insight into the kings' aims. The canons stipulating that Jews who attempted to convert Christian slaves to Judaism or who punished recalcitrant Christian slaves severely were to lose those slaves to the royal fisc was one such innovation. While this punishment was far more lenient than that prescribed by the Roman law to which Jews were formally subject, it did bring to the kings a source of wealth and directly involved the monarchs' interest in the enforcement of the canon. The second innovation concerned the emphasis upon the buying and selling of Christian slaves by Jews and pagans. It is noteworthy in this context that during the reigns of Chlotar II and Dagobert I, the Merovingians advanced their influence east of the Rhine and entered into substantial contacts with the Slavs and other pagans. These contacts opened trading opportunities east of the

Rhine and thus enabled Jewish slave traders to deal with the pagans. The new canons prohibiting pagans and Jews from buying and selling Christian slaves may perhaps be seen as a response to this trade.[91]

The apparent connivance of important people in Merovingian society to thwart royal anti-Jewish policy may suggest that the Jews were part of a faction opposed to Dagobert and his father as previously they had been associated with and had been protected by Brunhild and her supporters. Within this framework royal support for ecclesiastical enactments aimed at confiscating Christian slaves belonging to Jews and efforts to limit the activities of Jewish slave traders may be seen as a policy intended to coerce the Jewish communities of the *regnum Francorum* through economic pressure.

Although it is doubtful that Heraclius ever asked Dagobert to baptize all the Jews of his kingdom, it is certainly not impossible that the Merovingian ruler issued such an order on his own.[92] In recreating the circumstance under which Dagobert may have done so it should be noted that ca. 629 he allied himself with a certain Sisenand who finally succeeded in usurping the Visigothic throne in 631. Sisenand, with Dagobert's military aid, overthrew Suinthila. The latter had pursued a pro-Jewish policy after deposing in 621 the son of Sisebut who was known for having pursued a vigorous anti-Jewish policy. Sisebut had been an enemy of Brunhild who was pro-Jewish, and she was the cousin of Reccared who was also pro-Jewish. Brunhild had been the enemy of Dagobert's father, Chlotar II, who was the son of Chilperic. Dagobert, Chlotar, and perhaps Chilperic pursued anti-Jewish policies. Chilperic, incidentally, had murdered Galasuintha, Brunhild's sister.[93]

In trying to draw some conclusions from these "coincidences" it is useful to remember E. A. Thompson's observation concerning a similar situation in the Visigothic realm: "It will hardly be thought that the storms of these years centered on the position and liberties of the Jews."[94] It is indeed unlikely that the Merovingian rulers fought each other because of their respective Jewish policies. Yet it is not unreasonable to suggest that the Jews as a formidable element in Merovingian society supported those rulers who were pro-Jewish and opposed those who were enemies of their benefactors. For example, Brunhild's enemies might well have become the enemies of her Jewish supporters.

Merovingian Jewish Policy 63

Jewish support for Brunhild therefore might have stimulated rulers like Chlotar II and his son Dagobert I to pursue anti-Jewish policies.

Historians have labeled as *rois fainéants*—do-nothing kings—those monarchs who succeeded Dagobert I. For more than a century preceding the fall of the Merovingian dynasty in 751 the real power in Gaul was in the hands of the magnates. Some, like the Carolingians, were far more important than others. Thus even if we assume that Dagobert did order the baptism of all the Jews of his kingdom, it is unlikely that such an order was vigorously enforced by his successors. It is also unlikely that his anti-Jewish policy intended to curtail the activity of the Jews in political, economic, and religious areas was sustained by the "do-nothing" monarchs who followed him.[95]

It is clear from canon nine of the Council of Châlons-sur-Sâone that by the mid-seventh century Jews were still in possession of Christian slaves and that Christians were still being converted to Judaism. In addition the slave trade with pagan Slavs also continued much to the consternation of the assembled bishops.[96] At about this time, the chronicler Fredegar observed that the Roman Emperor Domitian had annihilated the descendants of David and therefore the Jews who were waiting for their messiah were doing so in vain.[97] Fredegar's observation on this point was a typical argument in the ongoing polemic between Christians and Jews throughout the late antique and early medieval era. It is unlikely that Fredegar would have found it important to make such an argument were there not Jews in Gaul at the time who claimed that descendants of David were still living.

In 672 Jews and Franks collaborated in a military action against the Visigothic monarch Wamba.[98] Not long after, Archbishop Julian of Toledo remarked upon how well the Jews of Gaul were treated. He went on to characterize the kingdom of the Franks as a "brothel of blaspheming Jews."[99] At the unlikely city of Auch a Jewish inscription has been found which was originally part of a funeral dedication from the local synagogue. The inscription dates from the late seventh or early eighth centuries and testifies to a flourishing Jewish community at Auch.[100] The marks of several mintmasters from this period indicate that Jews continued to serve in important governmental posts during the later seventh and early eighth centuries.[101]

Throughout the early Middle Ages the decline in legal education and knowledge made necessary the compilation of epitomes of the Roman law for use in local courts. The text of one of these, the *Epitome* of Aegidius which was compiled early in the eighth century, has survived. This text is based upon Alaric's *Breviary* and follows its model closely in legislation concerning Jews. Like Alaric's code, the *Epitome* of Aegidius includes legislation that protected traditional Jewish privileges. Jews were recognized as Roman citizens and enjoyed the privilege of using the Jewish law in cases among themselves. In addition Jewish religious rights were guaranteed; specifically, Jews were free to celebrate their sabbath undisturbed. Aegidius's *Epitome* also includes several enactments intended to protect Christians from the proselytizing efforts of their Jewish neighbors or owners. Thus Jews were forbidden to own non-Jewish slaves because of the not unwarranted fear that the slaves would be converted to Judaism as mandated by Jewish law. The *Epitome* also prohibited intermarriage because of the necessity of one partner's conversion to Judaism. Free Christians who did convert to Judaism were to lose their testamentary rights, and slaves who were converted by force were to be freed. A Jew who converted to Christianity and then returned to Judaism was to lose his or her property to the fisc.[102]

Insofar as it is possible to ascertain the nature of Merovingian Jewish policy, it seems to have been one of nonenforcement of both the secular and canon laws that were enacted to limit the activities of Jews. No positive effort, however, seems to have been made to eliminate restrictive Jewry laws. In internal affairs the Jewish community like other peoples was permitted to use its own law. The failure of secular powers to enforce the laws limiting Jewish activity led to the presence of Jews in important governmental positions and to the conversion of Christians to Judaism. The repeated promulgations by Church councils of canons intended to protect Christians from the proselytizing efforts of Jews seem to testify to the lack of enforcement.

The anti-Jewish policies pursued by Chlotar II and his son Dagobert I seem to have been motivated by a desire to weaken an important group that had supported Queen Brunhild. The obvious failure of Dagobert's anti-Jewish policy, whether it called for general baptism or not, may perhaps have been the result, in part, of the "do-nothing" quality of his successors. The Jews of Gaul like their coreligionists in Visigothic Spain, however, seem to have been too important and to have had too many influential friends and supporters to have been victimized successfully and in a sustained manner by barbarian monarchs who lacked the administrative resources sufficient to the task. When a powerful royal presence developed in Gaul with the Carolingian dynasty, the Jews of the *regnum Francorum*, as we will see in the following chapters, were not a shattered remnant that had been battered by Merovingian persecution but rather an important element in a new Europe.

CHAPTER IV

Jewish Policy in the Early Carolingian Empire and Its Environs

After about a century of prominence as mayors of the palace, the Carolingians finally replaced the Merovingians as kings in 751. It is only in 768, however, when King Peppin I conquered Aquitaine and brought the entire *regnum Francorum* under Carolingian domination that we obtain our first glimpse of the new dynasty's Jewish policy. As part of his efforts to win over the newly conquered inhabitants of southwestern Gaul to the support of the Carolingian house, Peppin continued the policies of previous rulers and issued a capitulary directing that the personality of the law would obtain among the various peoples dwelling within Aquitaine.[1] This policy was of special importance to the Jews of the region because it confirmed for them the traditional *privilegia* of judicial autonomy and religious toleration that they enjoyed under the *Breviary* of Alaric.[2]

Peppin, with the support of his sons Carloman and Charles, went beyond guaranteeing the benefits of the personality of the law to the Jews. The Carolingian rulers issued several edicts (*praecepta*) recognizing the rights of the Jews in the Narbonnaise to the alods that they held by hereditary right and further granted to the Jews the right to employ Christian labor on their lands and in their homes.[3]

These *praecepta* are noteworthy as a guide to early Carolingian Jewish policy because they concern the granting of rights by royal diplomas that previously had not been recognized by any Frankish monarch in

Jewish Policy in the Early Carolingian Empire 67

this region. The Narbonnaise was under Visigothic domination and then under Muslim control, but it never formed a part of the *regnum Francorum* under the Merovingian dynasty. In addition to recognizing the landed rights of people who were newly subject to the monarchy, Peppin and his sons acted contrary to both canon and Roman law by recognizing the rights of Jewish landholders in the Narbonnaise to exercise authority over Christians who were laborers on their estates and in their homes.[4] Thus these *praecepta* serve, in part, as a kind of exemption from those stipulations in the Roman law that prohibited Jews from having authority over Christians.

After Peppin's death in 768, his kingdom was divided between his two sons, Carloman and Charles. The latter inherited Aquitaine where in 769 he was faced with a revolt led by those magnates who had supported the family that had ruled the region before the Carolingian conquest.[5] It is hardly rash to assume that the Jews of the Narbonnaise and probably those elsewhere in Aquitaine as well supported the Carolingians in this conflict. Good relations between Charles and the Jews in the southwest of Gaul are illustrated by his refusal of a request by Archbishop Aribert of Narbonne that he abrogate the pro-Jewish edicts that Peppin had granted.[6]

Archbishop Aribert, however, did not abandon his anti-Jewish position, but wrote to the pope for support.[7] The latter was in a difficult position. The Carolingian house owed to the papacy a modicum of gratitude for its role in helping to establish the legitimacy of the new dynasty, but Rome was dependent upon the Frankish rulers north of the Alps for protection and support against the Lombards. Thus the pope was in the unenviable position of being asked to act against his ally's pro-Jewish policy. That policy of course violated the canons and was perceived at Rome to weaken the Church. Pope Stephen III responded to Aribert's request for help with a flourish of rhetorical anguish over the Carolingian policy, but confined his substantive role to suggesting to the archbishop and the magnates of Septimania and Hispania who were under the latter's ecclesiastical jurisdiction that they encourage the king to reverse his pro-Jewish policy as promulgated in Peppin's *praecepta*.[8]

Charles, however, persisted in his pro-Jewish policy and gave the Jews of Aquitaine and Septimania a discernible role in the creation of a Carolingian presence in Spain. In 778, a decade after Peppin's death, Charles led an army into Spain. This campaign, however, ended ignominiously with the decisive defeat of the Carolingian rear guard at Roncevaux. The failure of this effort highlighted the inadequate support for Carolingian policy in Aquitaine and the difficulties attendant upon sustaining a successful advance into Spain without a firm base. Thus, upon returning from Spain, Charles took several decisive steps to strengthen his position in southwestern France. For example, he removed the counts of Bourges, Bordeaux, Toulouse, Poitiers, Limoges, Clermont, the Velay, Albi, and Périgueux. These men apparently had not provided adequate support for the campaign into Spain. It is important to note that the count of Narbonne, whose military contingent included a substantial proportion of Jewish alodial landholders, apparently served during the Spanish campaign in a satisfactory manner; he was permitted to retain his office.[9]

The setback suffered in 778 by Charles delayed Carolingian penetration of Spain. By 785, however, a portion of the eastern littoral had fallen to Charles's forces; the region extended at least as far south as Gerona.[10] In the period 792-793 the Carolingians suffered a Muslim counterattack, and Narbonne withstood a devastating siege.[11] In 797 the Carolingians once again went on the offensive. Count Burrellus was given charge of occupying a number of deserted places; among these were the city of Vich and the *castra* at Cardona and at Casseres. He was ordered to repair the walls of these places, colonize them, and establish garrisons for their defense. In 800 Louis, Charles's son, led his armies into Spain. They captured and destroyed Lérida and other towns in the region of Huesca. The area around Huesca was ravaged as well. The Muslim governor of Barcelona, a certain Zaddo, moved against Narbonne, but he failed to take the city; instead he was captured. In the fall of 802 Louis launched a massive campaign to take Barcelona. The city was besieged for some seven months and finally fell in April of 803. During the next decade Carolingian armies besieged and ravaged Tortosa and

Jewish Policy in the Early Carolingian Empire   69

Huesca on several occasions and occupied Pamplona. These campaigns, with the exception of the setback in the period 792-793, created the foundation of Carolingian Spain.[12]

The evidence for the role delegated to the Jews of the Carolingian realm in the military operations mentioned above is both specific and circumstantial. For example, in 797 Count Burrellus occupied the city of Vich (also called Ausona) and the strongholds of Cardona and Casseres, colonized these places, and garrisoned them.[13] Contemporary and near-contemporary sources tell us nothing of Cardona and Casseres, but there is material on Ausona (Vich). According to Bishop Idalcarius of Vich (fl. ca. 900) all Christians were driven out of the city during the Muslim conquest. He added that a Christian presence was not reestablished there until the reign of Wilfred the Hairy (ca. 865-898) in the later ninth century.[14] Even if it were assumed that Bishop Idalcarius was exaggerating the suffering endured by the Christians of this part of Spain, it is hardly likely that he made up the story from the whole cloth. He was, after all, discussing an important event—the reestablishment of a Christian community—that took place during his own lifetime and an event that could not have been unknown to his contemporaries.

If Count Burrellus did not occupy the deserted city of Ausona (Vich) in 797 with Christian troops and settlers, then whom did he use? An early tenth-century interpolation into the proceedings of the Council of Narbonne of 788 indicates that it had not been possible to establish an episcopal see at Vich because of opposition from the *pagani* living there.[15] Some idea of the identity of these *pagani* would seem to come from the correspondence of a certain mid-ninth-century Rabbi Natronai of Sura who observed in some of his letters to various Spanish rabbis that Ausona was "a place without gentiles," i.e., a city of Jews. His observation that the market days at Ausona were Friday and Sunday—the Muslim and Christian sabbaths—also seems to indicate Jewish domination.[16] It is not unreasonable to conclude that ca. 850 Ausona was a predominantly Jewish city.

All of these sources taken together seem to indicate that the Christians dwelling in Ausona (Vich) were driven out ca. 712 or shortly thereafter and that they did not return in any significant numbers until the last third of the ninth century. In 797 Count Burrellus repopulated the *civitas* and garrisoned the stronghold. Since the only people known to dwell there during the first part of the ninth century are called in Christian sources *pagani* and in Jewish sources "non-gentiles," i.e., Jews, it seems reasonable to conclude that Count Burrellus occupied, repopulated, and garrisoned Ausona (Vich) with Jews.

As noted earlier, every free male subject of the Carolingian realms who held alodial lands – including many Jews – was obligated to perform military service on a regular basis in a local levy commanded by the count of the *civitas* in which he lived. The rank and file of these levies were comprised of men who, because they commanded considerable wealth and had dependents to work their lands, could afford to serve when called upon regardless of the season of the year. They could supply themselves with food for three months of campaigning and with clothing and arms for six months in the field.[17]

In the campaign against Barcelona that took place from September 802 to April 803 regional levies from Aquitaine, Gascony, Burgundy, Provence, and Septimania took part.[18] Among the local levies that formed the regional levy of Septimania was one raised in the Narbonnaise, where Jewish alodial landholders were prominent and where historically the Jewish community had demonstrated a significant military capability. This was the case not only during the Visigothic period but as recently as 793 when the garrison of Narbonne held out against the invading forces of Abd al-Malik ibn Mughith.[19] In addition to having served in the levy of Narbonne, it may be inferred that Jews were called upon to serve in the regional levy of Provence. Such an inference seems warranted in light of the substantial alodial holdings possessed by Jews in the Lyonnais during this period.[20] The campaign against Tortosa in 805 was probably another instance in which Jewish fighting men were called to serve the Carolingian cause in the establishment of the Spanish March. In this campaign Count Burrellus of Vich (Ausona) played a leading role,[21] and as has already been concluded, the population of his *civitas* was predominantly Jewish.

Charlemagne's Jewish policy for the Spanish frontier, as indicated by the events discussed above, makes it clear that he used military forces raised in the Jewish communities of Aquitaine and Septimania. In order to insure that he would have Jewish fighting men for his military operations Charles continued his father's policy of recognizing the rights of Jewish alodial landholders. These rights included a modicum of power over Christian agricultural and domestic dependents. Such rights were contrary to limitations placed upon Jews by both the canon law and the Roman law. Thus Charles may be seen to have established elements of what we might call Carolingian Jewry law that attempted to eliminate certain disabilities enacted before the new dynasty came to power. Charlemagne's pro-Jewish policy in this regard, it may be pointed out, went considerably further; he did not shrink from establishing an entire *civitas* dominated by Jews. A tangential result of this policy was to keep the Church from establishing a bishopric at Vich during most of the ninth century.

Charlemagne, however, did not restrict his Jewish policy to the utilization of Jewish subjects in military operations and in the control and settlement of frontier areas. In the economic sphere Charlemagne pursued a policy of encouraging Jewish merchant activity. Thus, for example, after the conquest of the Lombard kingdom brought much of Italy under Carolingian domination or influence, Charlemagne is credited with having convinced R. Kalonymus of Lucca to move from Italy and settle at Mainz. Whether Kalonymus's resettlement was brought about to satisfy the demands of an already existing Jewish community for a noted scholar and judge to guide them in this important trading center or whether it was Charlemagne's way of encouraging the establishment of a new Jewish community cannot be ascertained. In either case, however, Kalonymus's move to Mainz should not be dissociated from the growth of an important Jewish community in that city nor from the coincident growth of the city itself throughout the Carolingian era.[22]

Parenthetically it may be observed that the Jewish practice of honoring and recruiting distinguished scholars could not have been viewed unsympathetically by Charlemagne. He not only encouraged learning but sought out scholars and books for his schools and court. In the search for books, Jews seem to have been employed. In addition it is worth noting that Charlemagne made no effort to limit the circulation of Jewish books in his realm even though some of them appear to have been severely critical of Christianity.[23] Archbishop Arno of Salzburg (798-

821), who played an important role in expanding Carolingian influence and trade among the Slavs, was, along with several of his subordinate prelates, friendly with a Jewish physician and scholar. The scholar spoke the Slavs' language and may be assumed to have been useful to Arno not only as a doctor but in economic and political matters as well.[24]

Charlemagne's encouragement of Jewish merchant activity was a successful policy, and the words Jew and merchant became closely correlated in official documents during the Carolingian era.[25] In fact the official policy of encouragement may have led to abuses; Jewish merchants were even known to deal in such prohibited items as church plate. Not only was it against the canons for the clergy to sell such church property, but both Jewish and Christian merchants were foolish enough to brag about their business successes in this area. Charlemagne made an effort to curb this trade in holy ware, but there is no evidence to suggest that secular legislation was any more effective than ecclesiastical legislation in keeping greedy priests from dealing with unscrupulous merchants.[26]

Charlemagne's pro-Jewish economic policy was very probably dictated in large part by circumstances far beyond his control. The Muslim conquest of the eastern Mediterranean had all but eliminated from the scene the many Syrian Christian merchants who previously had dominated trade throughout *Mare Nostrum*. The Jews may be considered to have obtained an increased share in a much diminished trade.[27] Most prominent in long-distance trade were the Radanites, Jewish merchants whose home base was probably in the Rhone Valley and who traveled throughout the Islamic world and beyond in the pursuit of their business.[28]

It is worthwhile to quote in full ibn Kurradadhbah's description of these merchants' activities so the reader may grasp the wide range of their endeavor and gain some insight into their expertise and experience. Ibn Kurradadhbah writes:

> The Routes of the Jewish Merchants Called Radanites
>
> These merchants speak Arabic, Persian, the languages of the Roman Empire, of the Franks, the Spanish, and the Slavs. They go from west to east and from east to west by land and by land and sea. From

Jewish Policy in the Early Carolingian Empire 73

the west they carry eunuchs, female and male slaves, silken cloth, various kinds of furs, and swords. They ship out from Frankish territory on the Mediterranean Sea and head for Farama in the Nile delta. There they unload their ships and put their goods on camels to travel by land to Qulzum at Suez. This trip takes about five days. They then reload their goods on ships and set sail on the Red Sea from Qulzum to al-Jar the port for Medina and then to Jidda the port for Mecca. Then they head for Sind, India, and China. On the return trip from China they carry musk, aloes, camphor, cinnamon, and other goods from eastern lands to Qulzum and on to Farama. From there they cross the Mediterranean again. Some of the merchants sail to Constantinople in order to sell their goods to the Byzantines. Others go to the palace of the king of the Franks to sell their wares.

Sometimes these Jewish merchants take a different route when they leave the kingdom of the Franks and sail on the Mediterranean to Antioch. From there they travel to al-Jabiya. This takes three days. Then they load their goods on a boat that sails on the Euphrates to Baghdad. From Baghdad they sail down the Tigris to al-Ubullah. They leave al-Ubullah and go on to Oman. From Oman they go to Sind, India, and China.

All of these routes are interconnected and links can be made overland. Merchants leaving from the Frankish kingdom or from Spain sail across the straits of Gibraltar to North Africa and then to Tangier. They cross North Africa to the capital of Egypt. From there they go toward Ramla. They stop at Damascus and then go on to Kufa, Baghdad, and Basra. Then they cross to Ahwaz, Fars, Kirman, Sind, and India. Finally, they arrive in China. Sometimes they take the route that passes on the other side of Byzantium and after crossing the country of the Slavs they arrive at Khamlij the capital of the Khazars. From there they take ship on the Caspian Sea and go to Balkh and to Transoxiana. They continue until they reach the region where the camps of the Tughuzghur are established. From there they go on to China.[29]

It is unlikely that these subjects of a Christian ruler could have plied their trade throughout the Islamic world had not some arrangement been worked out, at least, with the caliph. Thus, for example, the embassy sent by Charlemagne to Harun al Rashid may very well have been an element in negotiations between East and West concerning trade in general and the Radanites in particular.[30] It should be remembered in this context that Charlemagne's legates negotiated a trade treaty with King Offa of Mercia at about the same time that discussions were being carried on with the caliph's representatives.³¹ Both these negotiations taken together suggest that Charles and his advisors saw that royal participation in at least some aspects of commercial life was desirable.

In Charlemagne's embassy to Harun al Rashid was a Jew named Isaac. Scholars have hypothesized many roles for Isaac, but there is little solid evidence with which to work.³² It is clear, however, that the two major Christian members of the embassy died during the journey, and that Isaac was in charge of the mission when the group returned home. This would seem to suggest that Isaac was not an unimportant member of the group and that perhaps he was the leader or, at least, one of the leaders from the outset.³³ Whether Isaac acted as an interpreter cannot be ascertained, but if he was one of the leaders of the embassy, it is likely that such chores as acting as interpreter during discussions or translating documents were left to lesser members of the staff. If this picture of the embassy's structure and organization is not inaccurate, then very probably several Jews were called upon by Charlemagne to serve under Isaac. Such men, like the Radanites, may well have spoken "Arabic, Persian, the languages of the Roman Empire, the Franks, Andalusians and Slavs."³⁴ It also should be noted that the Carolingian court considered negotiations with Harun al Rashid to have been a success and that the episode was discussed in the *Royal Annals* in a favorable light.³⁵

It is probably not unfair to suggest that Charlemagne's encouragement of Jewish merchant activity led to the Jews' dominance in Mediterranean trade insofar as the Carolingian empire was concerned. An important text that survives in a later ninth-century collection of anecdotes about Charlemagne is relevant. In this story Charlemagne is depicted as having been resting at a port city in the south of Gaul when suddenly some ships were spotted coming over the horizon. Among the members of Charlemagne's entourage, "some said that they were Jewish merchants, others said that they were Africans [i.e., Muslims] and others said that they were traders from Britain." Charlemagne, however, said that they were Northmen.³⁶ Thus of the four likely possibilities that came to mind, two were enemies, i.e., Vikings and Saracens; they obviously were not bent upon trade. Of the possibilities that appealed to the "popular mind," if such a characterization of anecdotal evidence of this kind is appropriate, Jewish merchants were thought to be the most likely. The only merchants other than Jews who seem to have merited consideration were from Britain, and these quite obviously were not heavily engaged in the trans-Mediterranean trade.[37]

Although Charlemagne pursued a manifestly pro-Jewish policy, he did not give the Jews of his empire carte blanche. For example, although he permitted Jews to serve as mintmasters as had his Merovingian predecessors, Charles did not allow these officials to operate the mints in their homes.[38] By requiring that the mint be in a public rather than a private building (i.e., the minter's home), Charles very probably hoped to encourage confidence in the coinage and to limit abuses.[39]

Charles also sought to control an aspect of the "banking" business within the empire. Jewish lenders were accustomed to accept as collateral for loans the persons of free Christians. If the loan were defaulted upon, the debtor became the dependent and perhaps even the slave of the lender.[40] This is, of course, only one of the many ways that free people became unfree or slaves during the late antique and early medieval periods. The loss of one's freedom meant, however, that the obligations normally incumbent upon a free man no longer obtained. Thus the king could not demand from such a person the performance of duties such as military service in the levy. Charlemagne, in general, sought to retard the process by which a growing number of free men were sinking into serfdom and slavery, and thus prohibited Jews involved in banking from taking persons as collateral for their loans.[41]

Charlemagne also sought to keep Jewish landowners and landholders from forcing their Christian laborers—free, serf, and slave—to work on Sunday. The frequent denunciations of this apparently widespread Jewish practice and the concomitant custom of giving workers Saturday as a day of rest suggest that Charlemagne's officials were little inclined or perhaps unable to enforce the law in this area.[42] Similarly it seems that the authorities were unable to enforce the laws that prohibited merchants, Jews and Christians alike, from dealing in church property.[43]

In his efforts to control commerce throughout the empire, Charles emphasized the importance of the local market where his officials could oversee weights and measures, collect taxes, and monitor prices.[44] Some Jews in the Carolingian realm seem to have found it more profitable to

76   Jewish Policy in the Early Carolingian Empire

do business from their homes away from the government's watchful eye. Charlemagne therefore issued an administrative order forbidding Jews from storing commodities intended for sale such as grain and wine in their homes and thus hoped to stop business from being done outside of the market place.[45] By and large the legislation discussed above was not motivated by religious zeal but rather by Charles's desire to control commerce within the empire.[46] Jews are mentioned specifically in these edicts when their national law (*lex Judaeorum*) or their self-interest apparently did not restrict them from business practices that Charles found inimical to his economic policies.

It is clear that the Jews were a people within the empire as were, for example, the Salian Franks, the Ripuarian Franks, Bavarians, *Romani*, Saxons, and Lombards. It seems that during the early ninth century Charlemagne's legal advisors (some of whom may have been Jews)[47] were beginning to make a serious legal distinction between *Romani* who were Jews and *Romani* who were Christians. This distinction from the legal point of view is a logical one because Jews though *Romani* lived essentially according to the Jewish law (*lex Judaeorum*) and were subject to the various epitomes of the Roman law (see below) only in relation to non-Jewish *Romani*. In short, the Jewry law provisions of the *lex Romanorum* concerned relations between Jewish and non-Jewish *Romani* but were of no standing in relations between Jews and the various barbarian peoples each of whom had its own law. Thus it was necessary for the Carolingians to deal with the important problem of the legal relation between the Jewish law and the various barbarian law codes.

In general Charlemagne was very much concerned with the national laws of the various peoples living within the empire, and he saw to it that each people's code was written down if this had not been done previously. In addition Charles found it necessary to emend the various law codes from time to time and, even more important, he arranged for procedures to be established in cases that concerned relations between persons subject to different national laws. Thus Charlemagne established regulations for the various Germanic peoples in regard to their legal relations with one another.[48] In cases involving litigation between Jews and barbarians, the emperor's problem was somewhat simplified because all the non-Jews were Christians—at least nominally.

Jewish Policy in the Early Carolingian Empire 77

In 809 Charlemagne established the procedures concerning the number and the legal personality of the witnesses necessary in cases involving Jews on one side and non-Jews on the other side.[49] The latter, such as Franks, Lombards, and Saxons, are described in the text by the shorthand term *Christiani*. The most important point here, however, is that the limitations stipulated under the Roman law that curtailed Jewish participation as witnesses in legal proceedings with and against Christians were eliminated by this legislation. Thus Charlemagne established Jewry law which arranged certain legal relations between Jews and non-Jews and which eliminated disabilities that had existed in Roman Jewry law.

When acting as a witness or appearing in a law suit it was customary during the Carolingian era for the parties involved to swear oaths. Obviously the various oaths sworn by Christians would have been unsuitable for Jews, and thus Charlemagne's legal advisors worked out the following formula for Jews: "So God may help me, the God who gave the law to Moses on Mount Sinai, and so that the leprosy of the Syrian Naamen may not come upon me as it came on him, and so that the earth may not swallow me up as it swallowed up Dathan and Abiron, in this case I have done no evil against you."[50]

According to Charlemagne's directive, when a Jew prepared to recite the above-quoted formula, he was to wrap himself from head to foot in his cloak. Then "according to his law [i.e., Jewish law] he was to take the five books of Moses [i.e., the Torah] in his right hand" and pronounce the formula quoted above. Charlemagne also indicated that the Hebrew version of the Torah was to be preferred for the ceremony but that if one were not available a Latin translation could be substituted.[51]

The stipulated use of the Torah rather than of some other religious writing or relic and the emphasis upon the Hebrew text as the preferred one would seem to suggest that Charles was advised by men learned in Jewish customs and law. This impression is strengthened by the fact that holding or touching the Torah was in accordance with the Jewish law.[52]

Charlemagne's concern to organize the judicial apparatus of the Carolingian empire to facilitate legal concourse among the many different peoples of his realm should not be understood to mean that the Jews' status as *Romani* was overturned. As noted in chapter III above, the diminution of legal education and expertise during the early Middle Ages gave rise to the need for epitomes of the Roman law codes so that jurists would have concise and easily understood materials at their disposal. From the period under discussion no less than five such epitomes have survived: the *Scintilla* also known as *Epitome Codicis Guelpherbytani*, the *Monk's Breviarium*, the *Epitome of Lyons*, and the *Saint Gall Epitome*.[53] These epitomes are assumed to have enjoyed authority in various local contexts, but it is not possible at present to ascertain the boundaries of their use within the *regnum Francorum*. Parenthetically it should be noted that the *Lex Romana Curiensis*, discussed in chapter II, though not an epitome of Alaric's *Breviary*, was also current in a part of the Carolingian empire during the period now being considered.

From the epitomes it is clear that the Roman law was of substantial significance in the Carolingian world.[54] It is also clear that the Jews of the Carolingian empire were *Romani*.[55] As noted in chapter II, the distinction between Jewish and non-Jewish Romans was substantially diminished in the Roman law of Chur. In the epitomes based upon Alaric's *Breviary*, however, special legislation concerning the Jewish *Romani* followed the direction set out in the *Breviary*. The basic lines thus tended to insure Jewish rights and *privilegia* while attempting to protect Christians from Jewish missionary activity. Thus Jews continued to enjoy the privilege of using Jewish law in cases among themselves and of having Jewish law used in cases with non-Jews if the latter agreed. Also, Jewish religious rights were protected.[56]

The basic principle that was employed in protecting Christians focused upon keeping Jews from having power over them. Thus Jews continued to be prohibited from owning Christian slaves and from holding offices in which they exercised governmental authority over Christians. Any Christian who converted to Judaism for the purpose of marriage to a Jew was considered to be engaged in adultery. Any convert from Christianity to Judaism was to lose his or her testamentary rights and/or property.[57] There are, however, some variations worthy of note. For example, in the *Breviary* of Alaric a Jew who converted a slave to Juda-

Jewish Policy in the Early Carolingian Empire 79

ism not only lost the slave but was also subject to capital punishment.[58] In most of the epitomes, by contrast, capital punishment was eliminated and the Jewish proselytizer was forced only to give up the slave.[59] It should be emphasized that in the epitomes the Jews were forbidden only to own Christian slaves; they were permitted to own non-Christian slaves. The Jewry law provisions in the epitomes seem in general to have coincided with the efforts of the early Carolingians to insure Jewish privileges and to encourage the Jews to develop as a productive element in the empire.

The Christian polities in the environs of the Carolingian empire during the period under discussion were to varying degrees influenced by Charlemagne's policies and programs.[60] Among the various political agglomerations that flourished in the British Isles, the most prominent was the Mercian kingdom of King Offa who formalized trade relations with Charlemagne. It can be assumed that Jewish merchants who were so important to Carolingian commerce took part in the transchannel trade. However, positive evidence for Jews in Britain during the period under discussion is lacking; thus Anglo-Saxon Jewish policy very probably did not exist.[61]

We have seen that in Christian Spain Jews were used by Charlemagne in the establishment of the Spanish March. It is probable that Charlemagne encouraged the settlement of Jewish émigrés from Muslim lands in this region and especially at Barcelona. This, however, will be discussed in detail in chapter VI because the evidence for Carolingian encouragement of such settlement is much more abundant during the mid-ninth century.

In the Christian kingdom of Asturias which was both poor and weak there were probably very few Jewish settlements at this time.[62] According to Einhard, the Asturian monarch was a *vassalus* of Charlemagne. However, Einhard's claim has often been attacked. Whether we see King Alfonso as having done homage to Charles or we merely recognize the fact that Asturian dependence upon Carolingian military might was a strategic reality, it is not unreasonable to infer that Jews in this part of Christian Spain were not treated very differently from Jews in Carolingian-dominated areas of Spain.⁶³ Some support is given to this inference by a letter written in 785 by Pope Hadrian I to the bishops of Spain. In this letter the pope voiced his consternation at the close friendly relations enjoyed by Jews and Christians throughout Spain.⁶⁴ It is more than likely that he intended his criticism primarily for the situation in Christian Spain rather than for the Muslim areas because the pope might be expected to have had greater influence over bishops dwelling in the former than in the latter.⁶⁵ This letter may be viewed as suggesting that close relations between Christians and Jews were the result either of an active or at the very least of the tacit policy of those in power.

In Rome and those parts of central Italy where the pope exercised some degree of political power, the Jews seem to have been treated in much the same manner as they had been in the days of Gregory I whose writings and decisions provided an influential example to subsequent popes.⁶⁶ The example of Gregory's pro-Jewish policy was certainly reinforced by Charlemagne's stance in the matter since as both king and emperor he exercised great power over the pope. Therefore, it is worth noting that Pope Hadrian I who personally seems to have harbored strong anti-Jewish feelings was unable or unwilling to pursue an active anti-Jewish policy.⁶⁷ As mentioned earlier Hadrian's predecessor Stephen also seems to have had anti-Jewish sentiments, but was restrained by political reality—Carolingian power—from doing more than advocating a reversal of the dominant pro-Jewish policies pursued by Charlemagne and by his father.⁶⁸

Much of the south of Italy, scattered enclaves in the north of the peninsula, and Sicily were in Byzantine hands during the period under discussion. From a legal point of view, the Jews in Byzantine Italy were subject to the policies formulated by the emperor at Constantinople. It is difficult, however, to characterize Byzantine Jewish policy during this period and even more difficult to estimate its effectiveness either throughout the empire or specifically in Italy. Emperors from Leo III (717-741) onward, whether iconoclast or iconodule, blamed the opposition for being influenced by the Jews.⁶⁹ At the council of Nicaea in 787, however, the Byzantine church which was an organ of the government stated specifically that Jews should not be harassed and that they should be permitted to live according to their own customs. It was stipulated that the Jews should neither buy nor possess slaves.[70] Under the Empress Irene (797-802) a selection of laws was published. These *Ecloga* were not meant as a full code but were merely a compendium of laws intended to deal with contemporary problems. The laws chosen for publication in the *Ecloga* that concerned Jews were based essentially upon Justinian's *Code* and were appended to the earlier compilation made under Leo III.[71] From the *Ecloga* it seems that Irene's legal advisors were concerned with problems associated with Jews who attained high rank, held public offices, and served in the military. Thus the *Ecloga* restated prohibitions found in earlier legislation on the above-mentioned matters and stipulated that a fine of thirty pounds of gold was to be paid by anyone who broke these laws. Jewish proselytism seems to have also been a continuing problem, and Irene's *Ecloga* mandated that any Christian who converted to Judaism was to lose his property and that any Jew who was successful in converting a Christian to Judaism was to be decapitated and have his property confiscated. A Jew was to be executed for circumcising a slave and the circumcised slave was to be freed. In fact Jews seem to have continued to own and possess slaves contrary to earlier legislation. In Irene's *Ecloga*, Jews were prohibited from owning or possessing slaves. Malefactors were to lose their slaves and pay a fine of thirty pounds of gold to the treasury.[72]

The above-mentioned legislation was intended to deal with contemporary problems. The question remains, however, was it successful? Irene's *Ecloga* make it clear that the anti-Jewish policies of previous emperors: Justinian I, Heraclius, and Leo III, failed to keep Jews from practicing their religion, proselytizing, attaining high ranks, and owning Christian and non-Christian slaves.

While past imperial failures to enforce anti-Jewish legislation may well point to the general difficulty of carrying out an anti-Jewish program, these failures cannot be regarded as conclusive evidence that Irene's anti-Jewish efforts did not succeed in Byzantine Italy. The empire during the early ninth century was subject to circumstances that no previous Byzantine ruler had faced. Within the empire factional struggles combined with the iconoclastic controversy to disturb the effectiveness of government throughout the period. The internal weaknesses of the Byzantine empire were compounded by the extensive Muslim advances into the western Mediterranean that made communication between East and West more difficult. Finally, the accession to the throne of the Empress Irene whose right to rule was widely challenged further disturbed the empire.[73]

While the Eastern Empire was thus suffering from both internal and external woes, the Carolingians were conquering most of northern Italy and making serious inroads south of Rome. King Peppin became the protector of the papacy, and on Christmas Day 800 Charlemagne was proclaimed emperor. The latter emphasized his power in Italy by seizing control of Venice from the Byzantines.[74]

The fundamental question that must be answered focuses upon the effectiveness of imperial Jewish policy in Byzantine Italy. Were the Jews in the Byzantine parts of Italy subject, in fact, to the harsh policy stipulated in the *Ecloga* of Irene and advocated by Nicephoras the patriarch of Constantinople (811-813) or did Charlemagne's pro-Jewish policy dominate even beyond the borders of his empire? From what little we can ascertain about Byzantine Italy during the period under discussion it seems clear that Jewish life was flourishing. The amazing series of tombstones surviving from Venosa attests to a rich and flourishing Jewish community in that city. Centers of learning produced important works even in such relatively unimportant places as Oria and Venosa. A renaissance in the use of Hebrew seems to have begun late in the eighth century, and both Greek and Latin can be seen to have been replaced to some extent in the Jewish communities of Byzantine Italy.[75]

Parenthetically, it should be noted that those officials who helped administer the law to those of the Lombard nation dwelling throughout Italy seem to have been progressively influenced by men knowledgeable in Jewish law.[76] More to the point, however, it seems reasonable to hypothesize that the Jews living in Byzantine Italy were more likely to have been under the influence of Carolingian policy than subject to the harsh Byzantine policy. This hypothesis rests upon four points. First, traditionally the Byzantine emperors who chose to follow an anti-Jewish policy during the early Middle Ages failed to accomplish their ends. Second, during the early ninth century the Byzantines had great diffi-

Jewish Policy in the Early Carolingian Empire 83

culty in carrying out any policy in the empire due to internal upheaval and external problems with the Muslims. Third, Charlemagne held the dominant position in Italy from a political and military point of view. He also was a crowned emperor while Irene was considered to be a usurper. Fourth, the positive evidence from the Jewish communities of Byzantine Italy indicates that they were flourishing. In addition, not a word about persecution is to be found in the Jewish sources from this area.

The early Carolingians pursued a vigorous pro-Jewish policy in the empire, and Charlemagne's position very probably influenced the policies of Christians in the environs of his realm. Carolingian Jewish policy recognized the Jews as a people in the same way that Lombards or Saxons or Bavarians were given recognition. In his efforts to regulate relations among the many peoples of his empire, Charlemagne saw to the creation of a body of Jewry law. But like other nations the Jews were permitted to live according to their own law when it was applicable and to practice their national customs including their religion. With respect to religious practices, it is important to note that Jews were the only people to be given such an exemption. In addition to the basic legal policy of national parity, the Carolingians actively encouraged Jewish merchant activity. Jews were also used for the settlement and garrisoning of frontier towns, for service in the military, and as diplomatic envoys. Early Carolingian Jewish policy resulted in the elimination of many social, legal, and economic restrictions that had been enacted to hamper Jewish activity during the preceding three and one-half centuries.

CHAPTER V

Jewish Policy under Louis the Pious (814-840) and in the Environs of the Empire

When Charlemagne died on 28 January 814, he was succeeded by his son Louis the Pious. The new emperor whom scholars have credited with having noteworthy administrative talent followed his father's pro-Jewish policies. Louis, however, tended to systematize and organize governmental institutions in the empire. Among the new administrative offices that he created were the *magistri*, and among these was the *magister Judaeorum*.[1] Although there is no document that describes in full the powers of the various *magistri*, it is clear from a wide variety of sources that all of these officers were closely associated with the royal court. The *magister ostiariorum*, for example, directed the palace staff and controlled access to the king; there was also a *magister* in charge of the merchants who dealt with the court.[2]

It is less clear, however, what exact role the *magister Judaeorum* played in Louis's administration. We do know that he held the power to adjudicate disputes between Jew and non-Jew. The latter might even be so high ranking a personage as an archbishop. In such a case the *magister Judaeorum* had the power delegated from the emperor, the *bannum*, to declare that even an archbishop was in the wrong and, further, to command the wayward ecclesiastic to act correctly or to face punishment. The *magister Judaeorum*, however, did not have the resources at his command to enforce obedience to his decisions. Thus, he engaged in the *missi dominici* in whose *missaticum* he was operating to enforce his decision.³ The fact that the *magister Judaeorum* employed royal *missi* rather than the count of the *civitas* or the viscount to carry out his order makes clear that these activities were closely connected to the central government and not to the local government.

Scholars have often debated whether the *magister Judaeorum* was himself a Jew.⁴ The clear injunction in both the Roman and canon law prohibiting Jews from exercising power over Christians would seem, *prima facie*, to make it unlikely that Louis would have appointed a Jew to this powerful position. Nevertheless it should be noted that the office of *magister Judaeorum* seems to have been constituted so that it had to call upon the *missi dominici* to carry out its decision. Such subtlety in the division of labor intended to prevent abridgements of the law was certainly not unknown during the Middle Ages. For example, the Church would sentence a heretic to burn, but for theological reasons the secular power would execute the decision. Whether this example is relevant to conclusions concerning the religion of the *magister Judaeorum* may be of little consequence since, as will be shown below, Louis employed Jews in governmental posts in which they exercised power over Christians.

We know the name of only one *magister Judaeorum*, a certain Evrardus, and from this information alone we certainly cannot ascertain his religion.⁵ From the activities of the *magister Judaeorum*, however, it is clear that he was asked to make decisions concerning the validity and applicability of the *lex Judaeorum* in various cases.⁶ Thus if the *magister* himself were not a learned Jew, it was necessary for him to have in his entourage, perhaps as members of a permanent staff, men who were experts in the Jewish law. It is more than likely that few, if indeed any, Christians could have been found with such credentials during this period.

It is reasonable to assume that the *magister Judaeorum* whom Louis appointed was charged primarily with the implementation of the emperor's Jewish policy. The welter of laws, practices, and problems that impinged upon Evrardus and his predecessor (whose name has been lost to us) needed organization and systematization. For example, Louis followed his father's policy of encouraging Jewish merchant activity and settlement. The establishment of a flourishing Jewish community necessitated a synagogue. Unfortunately the Roman law to which Jews were subject in this regard prohibited the building of new synagogues.[7] Enterprising Jews might have avoided this restriction for a time, at least, by worshiping in private homes; but when the Carolingians sought to encourage the growth of Jewish immigration and recruited celebrated scholars like Kalonymus of Lucca to go to Mainz, the prohibition against building new synagogues very probably was lightly regarded. Thus it is not surprising to find that Louis permitted the building of new synagogues and, in effect, abrogated that particular restriction of the Roman law within the lands under his control.[8]

Other elements of the various Roman law codes used in the Carolingian empire also threatened to place difficulties in the way of Louis's Jewish policy. For example, some legislation deprived the Jews of the right to employ Christian labor.[9] This made it difficult for Jewish landowners and merchants to carry on their business, and Louis ordered that Jews could use such labor.[10] Thus he permitted Jews to exercise power over Christians although this was prohibited by the Roman law and also by the canon law.

Restriction of Jewish purchase, possession, use, and sale of slaves was another problem created by the Roman law. Therefore the emperor eliminated all restrictions on Jewish dealings in pagan slaves that existed in the Roman law.[11] Louis's actions in this area had far-reaching consequences because under Jewish law by which the internal affairs of the Jewish community were governed no Jew might own a non-Jewish slave for more than twelve months. To keep the slave for longer than the twelve-month period it was necessary to convert the slave to Judaism. This, of course, meant that males were to be circumcised.[12] Under the Roman law to which Jews were subject in these matters the conversion and/or circumcision of a slave meant the loss of the slave by the owner. The owner was himself subject to capital punishment (or a lesser punishment depending upon the epitome) for having converted his slave.[13] It is clear, however, that in Louis's reign Jews were permitted as a matter of course to convert their pagan slaves to Judaism and to do so without governmental interference.[14]

The great importance of slaves to the Carolingian economy and to the well-being of the Jewish minority in the empire led Louis to protect

Jewish-owned slaves from conversion to Christianity. Pope Gregory the Great (590-604) had worked to baptize Jewish-owned slaves and to gain freedom for those who converted to Christianity. The example of this esteemed Church father was not lost upon pious Carolingian churchmen; the emperor, however, refused to tolerate such a threat to his pro-Jewish policies and decreed that no Jewish-owned slave might be baptized without the consent of its owner.[15]

Louis's policies also led him to appoint Jews to governmental positions in which they exercised power over Christians. Jews held the key positions of *judex* and *tellonarius* and in general were denied neither the *dignitas* of performing governmental *militia* nor the possession of *honores*.[16] Louis's practices in this regard were contrary to the Roman law, and it should be pointed out that, by and large, the restrictions in the Roman law that limited Jewish activities were also to be found in the Church canons. These Louis seems to have ignored as well.[17]

In the previous chapter we saw how Charlemagne's legal advisors had begun to work out some of the procedural problems of cases that involved Jews on one side and Christians who were not *Romani* on the other side. Louis saw to the continuance of his father's work and addressed himself to eliminating those restrictions upon Jews that existed in the Roman law. The above-mentioned policies enacted by Louis to protect Jewish slave owning, to provide for new synagogues, and to place Jews in public office made Jewish and non-Jewish *Romani* virtually equal. The Jews, however, still enjoyed the privileges as *Romani* of living under the *lex Judaeorum* in matters concerning the Jewish community and of having their religious liberties protected. In the latter area Louis made no effort to stop Jews from proselytizing among free people through preaching in public, through disputation, and through the dissemination of literature hostile to Christianity.[18] For example, the *Toledoth Jeshu*, a bitingly satiric account of Jesus's life was circulated, and its contents were actively made known to Christians.[19]

Louis the Pious is known to have issued several *capitula* that are not extant; some of these concerned Jewish matters.[20] Although historians have been intrigued by these lost documents, there is no scholarly consensus concerning what may have been contained in them.[21] It was common practice for the Carolingians to issue capitularies for dealing with administrative problems and for adjusting the various national *leges* to meet contemporary needs. It seems reasonable to suggest that the above-mentioned changes in the Roman law as it applied to the Jews were the subject of at least some of Louis's *capitula* that no longer survive.

In accordance with the usual form of such *capitula* it may not be too fanciful to suggest that Louis enacted Carolingian Jewry law in the following manner:

1. Let no one presume to keep a Jewish community from building a new synagogue.[22]
2. Let no one presume to deprive a Jew of the right to purchase, possess, employ, or sell pagan slaves.[23]
3. Let no one presume to punish a Jew for converting a pagan slave to Judaism.[24]
4. Let no one presume to punish a Jew for circumcising a pagan slave.[25]
5. Let no one presume to baptize a Jewish-owned slave without the owner's permission.[26]
6. Let no one presume to stop Jews from employing Christian laborers.[27]
7. Let no one permit a market to be held on the Jewish Sabbath.[28]

A skeptical reaction to the idea that Louis pursued such a policy and issued such pro-Jewish capitularies orally before his assembled courtiers[29] might be warranted if it were not clear that Jews played a prominent role at his court. For example, the dominance of Old Testament motifs at the Carolingian court was probably the result, in part, of the influence exercised by learned Jews in the emperor's entourage. Thus the Alaman noble Bodo, who was Louis the Pious's friend, was converted to Judaism through contacts with Jewish scholars.[30] The celebrated theologian and liturgist Amalarius of Metz was a recognized Judeophile,[31] and even Rabanus Maurus carried on productive scholarly relations with educated Jews.[32] Among Carolingian artists who were patronized by the court and the magnates, Old Testament themes were prominent, and the Synagogue was depicted as co-equal with the Church.[33]

In this intellectual and artistic atmosphere the Jews of the empire also enjoyed the advantage of having powerful friends at court.[34] For example, Helisacher the abbot of Saint Riquier and Louis's cousins, Adalard, abbot of Corbie, and Count Wala supported the Jewish position. The humiliating treatment they meted out at Aachen to Archbishop Agobard of Lyons when he tried to press an anti-Jewish campaign highlights this point.[35] Jewish community leaders were held in high esteem at court,[36] and presents were frequently exchanged not only between Jewish and non-Jewish courtiers but between Jews and members of the royal family as well.[37]

The treatment of Jews at Louis's court was fundamentally consistent with the emperor's personal beliefs in the matter. A royal charter issued by Louis for a group of Jews in Septimania illustrates the emperor's position: "Although apostolic teaching reminds us especially to do good for our brethren in the faith, it does not prohibit us from doing kindnesses also to all the rest. But it exhorts, rather, that we pursue humbly the course of Divine mercy."[38]

Louis's aim of pursuing actively a pro-Jewish policy is also evidenced in his one surviving *capitulum* concerning the Jews. In the previous chapter we saw how Charlemagne with the help of his Jewish legal advisors worked out an oath for Jews to take in cases involving litigation with non-Jews.[39] Louis also consulted with his advisors on this matter and saw to the establishment of a formula that was even more thoroughly Jewish in spirit than the one instituted by his father.[40] Thus during Louis's reign, Jews took the following oath:

> I swear to you by the living and true God and by the holy law that the Lord has given to the blessed Moses on Mount Sinai, and by the good Lord, and by the pact of Abraham that God gave to the children of Israel, and so that the leprosy of Naamen the Syrian may not cover my body, and so that the land may not swallow me up alive as it did Dathan and Abiron, and through the arc of the alliance that appears in the heavens to the children of man, and the holy place where holy Moses stood and where the blessed Moses received the holy law, I am not guilty in this case.[41]

Although Louis's pro-Jewish policy can be said to have had a philosophical and religious impetus, it would be unfair to claim that these were his exclusive reasons for treating his Jewish subjects in a tolerant manner. Louis's predecessors had seen the advantages of fostering Jewish immigration into the empire, of establishing Jewish frontier settlements, and of encouraging Jewish merchant activity. Thus with his accustomed flair for administrative detail, Louis saw to the systematization and organization of his father's policies in these areas.

Many of the documents of the Carolingian government were produced in imperial writing offices. These offices operated through the use of formularies, i.e., models of various kinds of diplomatic instruments that in their essentials had a fixed form.[42] Under Louis a formulary for the protection of important Jewish merchants was developed.[43] The charters based upon the model as will be seen had several elements of significance, and the inspiration for the various parts of the document derived from different sources.

The section of the formulary that makes it clear that Jewish merchants rather than, for example, Jewish artisans were the beneficiaries of the document is found in the exemption clause: "neque teloneum aut paravereda aut mansionaticum aut pulveraticum aut cespitaticum aut ripaticum aut portaticum aut pontaticum aut trabaticum aut cenaticum a praedictis Hebreis exigere praesumat."[44] A merchant doing business over a wide area who was subject to the tolls, services, and taxes enumerated above would have found it very difficult to carry on his commercial activity. Thus the above-quoted exemption went to the very heart of merchant life and had as its inspiration the desire to encourage commerce. Such an exemption would have been of little value to a farmer or an artisan.

Parenthetically it should be noted that the long list of tax—toll—and service exemptions found in the formulary for Jewish merchants is also found in the formulary *Praeceptum negotiatorum* that was developed for the benefit of non-Jewish merchants.[45] It is perhaps of some significance in assessing the importance of Jewish merchants that the *Praeceptum negotiatorum* was partially based upon the formulary established for Jewish merchants, i.e., in part the exemption clause is modified by the words "sicut Judeis."[46]

In addition to the exemption clause there were three elements of protection built into the formulary for Jewish merchants.[47] In the first of these, the protection clause proper, the emperor indicated that he had taken the Jewish merchant or the group of Jewish merchants listed therein under his protection and would keep them under his protection as long as they remained faithful to him.[48] He also placed their property under his protection. The second element of protection, scholars have termed the peace clause. In this the emperor warned everyone to permit the beneficiary of the charter to live in peace, do business in peace, and to have his property left in peace.[49] Finally in what has become known as the reclamation clause, the emperor enumerated the penalties that would be incurred by those who thwarted his will in these matters, and further he made clear that the palace court would make the ultimate decision in any case that the charter's beneficiary might feel necessary to appeal.[50]

The exemption and protection clauses discussed above are basic to documents designed for merchants whether they were Christians or Jews.[51] Several other aspects of the formulary for Jewish merchants, however, seem to have been included because the Carolingians had made substantial changes in the laws relating to Jews, and these alterations could be reiterated profitably not only because they were novel but because they were controversial and subject to occasional attack.

For example, as noted in the previous chapter Charlemagne issued a capitulary regulating the procedure to be followed concerning witnesses in cases involving Jews on one side and non-Jews on the other side. This legislation was substantially different from the Roman law that previously had governed such procedures.[52] Thus in developing the formulary for the protection of Jewish merchants, Louis reaffirmed his father's procedures by having the following clause included: "If a Christian has a case or litigation against them [the Jewish beneficiaries of the charter], he is to bring three worthy Christian witnesses and three worthy Jewish witnesses also in his support and with these witnesses he may pursue his case successfully. And if they [the Jewish beneficiaries of the charter] will have a case or litigation against a Christian, they must bring Christian witnesses to testify in their behalf and with these they may pursue their case successfully."[53] This procedure as indicated by Charlemagne's capitulary mentioned above was not reserved solely for Jewish merchants, but rather was intended for all Jews in the empire with regard to their dealings with non-Jews in public courts.

Louis also included in the formulary a statement of the basic principle of personality of the law that affirmed to the Jews the right to live by their own law,[54] to receive punishments stipulated only by their own law,[55] and to give evidence in accordance with their own law.[56] These rights had been established in part by the Roman law to which Jews were subject in a formal sense; by Charlemagne's *capitulum*, later modified by Louis the Pious, that set out the formula and procedure by which Jews affirmed their guilt or innocence in cases that involved a Christian on one side and a Jew on the other side; and by several *capitula* that are not extant but which guaranteed to the Jews of the empire, and not simply to Jewish merchants, specific rights concerning punishments and interrogation. Thus, Louis set out in a systematic manner in the Jewish merchant formulary much previous legislation that obtained to all Jews of the empire with regard to both the subject of legal personality and judicial procedure.

Also included in the Jewish merchant formulary was an unambiguous statement of the right of Jewish merchants to buy and sell pagan slaves.[57] Some versions of the Roman law that circulated in the empire during the early ninth century prohibited this practice (see ch. IV above), and it is probable that in one of the lost *capitula* either Louis or perhaps even Charlemagne had established this right for Jews. It seems reasonable to suggest that the right was reiterated in the merchant formulary because like the other rights discussed above it was probably newly guaranteed, in conflict with both Roman and canon law, and thus subject to opposition.

On occasion we find in a charter that is based upon the Jews' merchant formulary a clause that illustrates an immediate problem. Thus in a diploma granted to a certain Rabbi Domatus and his nephew Samuel there is evidence to suggest that local officials had been denying the right of Jewish slave owners to prohibit Christian proselytizing among Jewish-owned pagan slaves. Also the right of Jewish slave owners to refuse permission to their slaves to be baptized seems to have been violated. Therefore Louis took the opportunity in having the above-mentioned charter drawn up to augment the list of exemptions, rights, and protections found in the formulary.[58]

Jewish Policy under Louis the Pious   93

The augmentation of the Jewish merchant formulary as seen in the charter issued by Louis for Domatus and Samuel began with a report of the violation of the law: "Indeed, these same Jews brought to the attention of our highness that certain men contrary to the Christian religion are persuading Jewish-owned slaves under the guise of the Christian religion to condemn their lords and to be baptized. They argue that if baptized they [the slaves] will be freed from service to their lords."[59] The emperor then indicated that "the holy canons in no way support this practice and they adjudge on the contrary that those who perpetrate such acts deserve the severe sentence of anathema. Therefore we wish that none of you [the officials to whom the charter is addressed] dare to do anything more like this to the above-mentioned Hebrews or that you permit your subordinates to do anything of the kind. You may be sure that whomsoever might perpetrate this and we learn about it, the person will find himself personally in danger and he will not be able to escape the loss of his property."[60]

It is clear that Louis emphasized the violation of canon law in the case above, but there can be little doubt that the emperor interpreted the Church law as consistent with the secular law of the empire in this situation. Louis may have chosen to dwell upon the canonical precedent for his law because clerics were the most likely people to violate it. The one documented instance of such illegal activity concerns the efforts of Archbishop Agobard of Lyons.[61] A second and more subtle reason for emphasizing the precedent of canon law concerns the nature of early medieval authority. It would serve Louis well to have had a legal precedent for his action in this matter rather than to have had the law established solely upon his own *auctoritas*. Indeed no less a figure than Pope Gregory I had lent his efforts to encouraging the baptism of Jewish-owned slaves. In fact a strong Church tradition in the West supported efforts to baptize Jewish-owned slaves.[62]

It should be emphasized, however, that after Rabbi Domatus called to Louis's attention the above-mentioned violation of imperial and canon law, the emperor saw to it that his position in the matter was made unambiguous despite the teaching of Gregory and those who followed him in this matter. Further Louis went on to systematize imperial policy and had placed in the Jewish merchant formulary the following clause: "et nemo fidelium nostrorum praesumat eorum mancipia peregrina sine eorum consensu ac voluntate baptisare."[63]

In the foregoing pages we have seen how Louis lent his administrative talents to the systematization and organization of Carolingian Jewish policy. The dual aims of this policy were the elimination of the legal disabilities that previous enactments had placed upon the Jews in the empire and the establishment of institutions for the productive functioning of his Jewish subjects. The formularies and *capitula* discussed above illustrate his success in creating an administrative-legal structure to support his policy. It remains to assess the practical social and economic consequences of this policy.

If the nature of the surviving evidence can be understood to indicate something positive about Louis's priorities, and such an assumption is by no means indisputable, then it seems that the emperor had a substantial interest in seeing Jewish commercial activity flourish. In light of the extant data it is possible to suggest that Louis's policies aided Jewish merchants at three distinct though not unrelated levels of their business: on the local level, within the empire, and beyond the borders of the empire.

By imperial order it was established that markets were not to be held on Saturday, the Jewish sabbath.[64] This was particularly important because local markets in the towns and cities of the Carolingian empire tended to be held only once during the week. Thus Christians who might have tried to keep Jewish merchants from doing business were frustrated. In the Lyonnais, for example, Jewish wholesale and retail dealers in meat and in wine dominated the local markets. The wine merchants also seem to have played a role in supplying the imperial court at Aachen with their wares. These businesses, according to a contemporary report, were very profitable.[65]

The success of the above-mentioned Lyonnais Jewish merchants on both the wholesale and retail levels raises questions concerning their supply of goods and Louis's policies toward Jewish landholding. With regard to the latter, it is clear that Louis continued the policies established by his grandfather and father when they granted to the Jews of Aquitaine and Septimania the right to possess alods, to employ Christian and non-Christian labor—free, non-free, and slave.[66]

Despite the existence of charters that illustrate Jewish landholding during this period, the few land records that survive generally do not permit statistical evaluation.[67] Therefore no firm conclusions may be drawn concerning the possibility that Jews were engaged in significant vertical economic operations, i.e., the movement of goods on a large scale from Jewish-owned or held estates to Jewish wholesale merchants to Jewish retail merchants and also to Jewish commercial adventurers who operated in long-distance trade. The existence of Jewish owned estates and imperial support for them made it possible that such vertical operations did exist, but in lieu of conclusive evidence it should be surmised that Jewish merchants at all levels dealt with Christian producers.

Any examination of empire-wide Jewish trading activity should begin by noting that a Jewish community was well established at Louis's capital, Aachen, by 820 if not earlier. There, Jewish merchants stored goods and did business with the court.[68] Although commercial connections with the court were profitable both economically and politically, it was the ability of Jewish merchants who enjoyed imperial favor to move their goods throughout the empire freely that resulted in substantial advantages.

The formulary that provided the model for charters of protection and privilege granted to Jewish merchants by Louis listed exemptions from all general road tolls, from mooring dues at ports, from dues that were demanded of merchants to enter the gate of a town or city, from bridge tolls, from imposts charged against those who damaged fields by their transit, from the payments due to support the food and lodging of governmental officials, from the right of imperial officials to requisition horses, from the taxes demanded for the right to fish, and from the duty to perform work in support of public services.[69]

The significance of most of the exemptions listed above is obvious. In some cases it is less so. For example, if local officials could requisition a merchant's horses (*paravereda*), the merchant's ability to do business and travel might be destroyed. Similarly, if a local official could demand an impost for the damage done to crops by traveling merchants (*cespitaticum*), the latter might be severely restricted in the routes that they might choose. The right granted to Jewish merchants to fish freely (*cenaticum*), however, seems to be the most obscure of the above privileges and may perhaps have resulted from the problems encountered in obtaining suitable meat, i.e., ritually acceptable meat. Thus the Jewish merchant while on the road or while visiting towns that had no Jewish community could supplement his diet with freshly caught and ritually acceptable fish.

Most significant about the Jewish merchant formulary, however, is its very existence. The creation of such a model is generally understood by scholars to indicate its wide usage and frequent employment. Therefore, we may perhaps surmise that Louis issued to Jewish merchants many charters that granted the important legal and economic privileges discussed above as well as imperial protection.[70]

The importance of slaves to the Carolingian economy necessitated the importation of new stock from beyond the eastern frontier.[71] Louis, as noted above, strongly supported Jewish slave traders by emphasizing their right to buy and sell pagan slaves and by protecting these merchants from the unwanted missionary efforts of meddlesome churchmen. It should be recalled that Louis tried to keep slave traders from dealing with the Muslims and restricted Jewish merchants trading in Christian slaves. In some areas, if not generally throughout the empire, the above-mentioned restrictions were poorly enforced by imperial and local officials. Thus there are contemporary reports that Jews purchased Christian slaves from Christian owners and sold the former to the Muslims in Spain.[72] Jews also apparently castrated some slaves especially for the foreign market[73] and even kidnapped Christian youths for sale abroad.[74] It is impossible, however, to develop a quantitative estimate of such illegal activity.

It is clear that Christian slave owners, despite the law and despite the attempted intervention of clerics, cooperated with Jewish traders in buying and selling Christain slaves. Further, Jews were employed as *tellonarii*[75] and thus were in certain instances the very officials responsible for dealing with merchants who traded beyond the frontiers. In addition privileged Jewish merchants were by and large exempt from governmental interference, and officials may very well have paid little attention to their activities. Thus only concerned churchmen are found to have complained about the situation.[76]

The reference to Jewish merchants dealing with the Muslims leads us to an examination of commercial activity beyond the borders of the empire. In the previous chapter the Radanites were discussed in some detail. From the little information available, it seems that these men continued to flourish in their far-flung trading operations at least until the last decade of the ninth century.[77] Louis also seems to have been interested in fostering trade somewhat closer to home. For example, the city of Saragossa stood on the southwestern frontier of the Carolingian empire and was at least nominally in Muslim hands. Saragossa, however, had an important Jewish community with its own armed forces. A prominent Jewish merchant from Saragossa, a certain Abraham, was granted a charter by Louis that guaranteed him protection and provided him with extensive immunities and privileges for commercial purposes within the empire. Among the latter was the right to buy and sell pagan slaves within the empire.[78]

Louis's policy of integrating his Jewish subjects into the mainstream of imperial life had social and political results as well as economic and legal ones. We have seen above that Jews held government positions such as *judex* and *tellonarius* and that they also possessed *honores*. Socially Jews and Christians seem to have had close relations. It was not uncommon for Jews and Christians to dine together on kosher food, nor for the latter to adopt Jewish customs such as working on Sunday and resting on Saturday. Christians celebrated Jewish holidays and ignored their own; clerics were particularly disturbed by the growing practice of Christians feasting with Jews and eating meat during Lent.[79] These local contacts in the towns and *civitates* of the empire seem to highlight the closeness of Jewish-Christian relations at the imperial court. Jewish and Christian scholars exchanged ideas and information, Jewish books circulated, Jewish courtiers were well received by the royal family and exercised substantial influence according to contemporary Christian sources.[80]

Louis's vigorous pro-Jewish policy and its manifest success are startling because the emperor had many enemies who could have used a "Jewish issue," had there been one, to their advantage. The efforts by Archbishop Agobard of Lyons to pursue an anti-Jewish policy illustrates the political dynamics of the situation.[81]

In his letters Agobard indicated the nature of his own Jewish policy. He recounted that he preached sermons to encourage Christian slave owners not to sell their Christian slaves to Jews, that he alerted officials to the actions of Jewish slave traders who were selling Christian slaves to the Muslims in Spain, and that some of these slaves had been kidnapped in various parts of Gaul. Further he mentioned that he preached against Jews employing Christian labor, against Christians working on Sunday and resting on Saturday, against feasting with Jews during Lent, and against Christians eating meat and wine that were processed and sold by Jews. These were, as he saw them, evils that flourished in his diocese,[82] and he was determined to use his power as bishop and his talents as a preacher to wipe them out. He also indicated that he felt compelled to carry on missionary work among the Jews and especially among their slaves.[83]

Agobard's program seems at base to have called for the enforcement of the canon and secular laws that had been enacted during the later Roman empire and that for various reasons might have been considered to have application in his diocese. For example, both Roman and canon law restricted Jews from possessing or owning Christian slaves.[84] Imperial law prohibited the sale of slaves outside the empire.[85] Kidnapping was illegal under all of the many *leges* that had currency in the empire. Jewish use of Christian labor was contrary to both canon and some versions of Roman law because it gave Jews power over Christians. (Louis, however, had made it legal for Jews to employ Christians if the latter were permitted to celebrate their feast days and to observe Sunday as their sabbath.) Agobard's efforts to keep Christians from using wine and meat processed and sold by Jews seem also to have had religious overtones. Both of these products were processed according to what might be perceived to be religious ritual. Agobard was aware of this, and it is probable that he believed that the consumption of these Jewish-processed foods involved Christians in Judaizing acts.[86]

On the whole Agobard seems to have seen himself as a *miles Christi* battling for the souls of Christians and pagans who were Judaizing and being converted to Judaism through the persuasive preaching, generous hospitality, economic prosperity, and coercive powers of the Jewish community in the Lyonnais.[87] As a part of this struggle, Agobard saw it as his duty to convert to Christianity the pagan slaves owned by Jews before the latter converted them to Judaism. Agobard saw this endeavor not only as a spiritual imperative but believed that he had canonical warrant for it.[88]

Agobard, nevertheless, professed that "since they [the Jews] live among us we should not be hostile to them or injure their life, health, or wealth." It is clear, however, that his policies if successful would have deprived the Jews of labor to work their lands, forced them out of the slave trade, and eliminated their markets for wine and meat.[89] The emperor sought to encourage the economic development of his Jewish subjects; thus the imperial court and the Archbishop of Lyons were on a collision course.

Agobard's policies came to the attention of the emperor ca. 822. It seems that the archbishop succeeded in baptizing a Jewish-owned slave. The slave originally had been a pagan who had been converted to Judaism by her owner.[90] The latter refused to accept the validity of the subsequent baptism and resisted Agobard's efforts to obtain the slave.[91] The prelate complained to the imperial court, and the official who was designated to handle such matters, the *magister Judaeorum*, was sent "with instructions" to Lyons. The *magister* supported the Jews, and Agobard blamed him for failing to act reasonably and for not showing proper respect to a prince of the Church. Agobard conveyed the impression that he was convinced that the *magister*, in fact, had violated his instructions by finding in favor of the Jews. Upon failing to obtain satisfaction from the *magister*, Agobard seems to have seized possession of the slave; it was then the owner's turn to complain to the court. Agobard attributed the discord and contention brought about by this litigation to the unreasonable manner in which the *magister* handled the first phase of the case.[92]

At the palace court the Abbot Helisacher of Saint Riquier, Abbot Adalard of Corbie, and Count Wala heard the case. The Jews, according to Agobard, were forcefully represented by a powerful advocate. They also had influential friends at court. The prelate, himself, said that he felt intimidated by the circumstances in which he was involved. He indicated that he was unable to present his case as vigorously as his afterthoughts on the matter led him to believe he was capable of doing, and he blamed the injuries to his cause and position on the cross-questioning of the court and on the initial failure of the *magister Judaeorum* to handle the matter reasonably. The court not only found against Agobard, but the emperor added the personal humiliation of dismissing him from the palace in a preemptory manner.[93] Louis provided the Jews with a *diploma* bearing the imperial seal that bore witness to their victory.[94]

Despite the unfavorable judgment of the palace court and the emperor's obvious displeasure with him, Agobard continued to pursue his anti-Jewish policy. The Jews reported his behavior, and the imperial administration took a series of actions designed to enforce Louis's pro-Jewish policy.[95] Writs were issued by the imperial court and served on both Agobard and on the viscount of Lyons. The former was ordered to cease and desist in his anti-Jewish actions, and the latter was instructed to enforce the government's policy. The viscount, in fact, published the writ so that all people in the region might know the emperor's will.[96] The *magister Judaeorum* was sent to Lyons to support the viscount and to convey personally to Agobard the great displeasure of the emperor and of his advisors.[97] Finally, the *missi dominici* Garic and Fredric, in whose *missaticum* the Lyonnais was located, arrived on the scene with additional documents; these, in effect, seem to have outlined Louis's Jewish policy.[98]

Agobard's response to the cumbersome processes of imperial administrative machinery was evasion and resistance. He kept to his anti-Jewish efforts for the most part while at the same time inundating the palace with letters. In general, he tried to convince whomever might listen that Adalard, Helisacher, Wala, and other highly placed court dignitaries had provided the emperor with inaccurate information on the dangerous situation in the Lyonnais. Further, he intimated that the diploma that the Jews received from the court was not authentic. In addition he implied that imperial officials in the field such as the *magister*

Judaeorum and the *missi dominici* as well as some at court were either pawns of Jewish interests or acting from a misunderstanding of the situation. Finally as the *missi dominici* were about to descend upon Lyons with a plethora of pro-Jewish documents and a plenitude of power to enforce government policy, Agobard fled.[99] Thus after some five years of contention the weight of imperial bureaucracy ground the archbishop into defeat.

Agobard noted that of those Christians who supported him in his policy against the Jews, some went into hiding and others were punished by imperial officials. He lamented that the cause of Christianity suffered greatly because the mass of the people saw the Jewish victory. According to Agobard the Jews, by contrast, were elated over their success; they pursued their missionary efforts vigorously and attacked Christianity vehemently.[100]

By 827 Agobard seems to have been convinced that the emperor and his advisors were determined to pursue a pro-Jewish policy and that nothing he might do or write would turn them from their course. However, the archbishop did have supporters—men like Bernard and Faof, the bishops of Vienne and Châlons-sur-Sâone, respectively, who collaborated with him in writing the vigorously anti-Jewish polemical tract *On Jewish Supersititions*.[101] Also among Agobard's supporters was Bishop Nibridius of Narbonne. Agobard wrote to him with a new scheme for pursuing an anti-Jewish policy. Basically this approach called upon the clergy and especially the bishops to enforce canon law by punishing their Christian subjects who violated it. Through enforcement of canon law and preaching, the bishops were urged to enforce a policy that aimed to curtail Judaizing and to isolate the Jewish and Christian communities from each other.[102] It is important to note that this new policy was to focus upon Christians, and it is clear evidence that Agobard realized that nothing serious could be gained by trying to oppose imperial policy overtly or by attacking the Jews directly.

The general failure of Agobard's "new approach" not only is underscored by the continuing complaints registered by later contemporaries on the very issues of Judaizing and fraternization[103] but is suggested by Agobard's active role in the revolt against Louis that took place in 833.[104] It is probably not coincidental that Louis, after regaining power and sending Agobard into exile, replaced him as the ecclesiastical administrator of the Lyons diocese with the pro-Jewish Amalarius of Metz, former archbishop of Trier, imperial ambassador, and renowned scholar.[105]

Scholars have been intrigued by Agobard's persistent anti-Jewish policies. Although many explanations have been offered,[106] none of these seems to emphasize sufficiently how Agobard's experiences as a youth may have affected the formulation of his views. It should be noted that Agobard was born and raised in the Spanish March and Septimania where the Jews were exceptionally powerful.[107] He very probably knew about such Jewish *civitates* as Ausona and was aware of the power that the Jews of the Narbonnaise had exercised for centuries. In short Agobard came from that very region that Archbishop Julian of Toledo had characterized as a "brothel of blaspheming Jews."[108] In the Lyonnais where he served as priest, *chorespiscopus*, and archbishop, Agobard encountered a Jewish community not very different from the ones he had known as a boy. He seems to have believed, and he was correct, that compromise with the militant, aggressive, and powerful Jews of Lyonnais would have meant defeat for the Church. As a religious churchman deeply committed to the spiritual health of his flock he had little choice in his course of action; he fought and lost.

The significance of Agobard's anti-Jewish policy in the present context is that it ended in ignominious failure. Despite the vast resources that a prince of the Church might mobilize in an important diocese, he was clearly no match for the imperial government. The administration gound him down, and Louis's pro-Jewish policy prevailed. If a man of Agobard's commitment and ability could do nothing lasting against the Jews, we may perhaps be permitted to speculate that men of lesser motivation and talent would also have been unsuccessful had they attempted to oppose a determined emperor. In short, on the Jewish issue at least, imperial policy under Louis the Pious was motivated by secular concerns, and it prevailed despite the determined opposition of at least one high-ranking and powerful ecclesiastic. The lesson that was taught to Agobard may well have deterred others.

Among the Christian polities in the environs of the Carolingian empire during this period (814-840), Jewish communities functioned in Byzantine Italy and in northern Spain. We are not well informed about the latter area. Later medieval chroniclers were wont to praise early ninth-century Asturian monarchs for destroying synagogues, murdering Jewish community leaders and burning Hebrew books.[109] The likelihood that such anti-Jewish policies were pursued as part of a governmental program is very remote. In the Muslim lands that bordered Asturias pro-Jewish policies were the general rule; and as we have seen, this was the case in Carolingian Spain too. Thus if Jews in Asturias were harshly treated, they could find a far better home either among the Muslims in places like Saragossa or among the Carolingians in cities like Barcelona or frontier Jewish-dominated settlements like Ausona.

In Byzantine Italy which, unlike the Asturian kingdom, was a rich and desirable place to live, the Jews were well treated during this period. The Emperor Michael II (820-829) pursued a vigorously pro-Jewish policy. He eliminated the religious tax that Jews were required to pay, and according to one source he is alleged to have made Jews free of all taxes. The often debated and somewhat confusing question of the "Jewish tax" in the Byzantine empire may perhaps be elucidated for this period if we grant that Michael did, in fact, eliminate the tax owed by Jews because of their religion. This tax had been levied in addition to that demanded of them as imperial subjects.[110] The notion that the Jews of the Byzantine empire were freed of all taxes simply cannot be sustained. It is not impossible, however, that the sources which condemned Michael for such an action were referring obliquely to special privileges granted to Jewish merchants. If this were the case, then Michael's legislation could be seen to have paralleled Louis's efforts to eliminate some of the more obvious disabilities that weighed upon Jews, in general, and, more specifically, to encourage the economic development of Jewish merchants. It is clear that in Italy there was noteworthy contact between Jewish merchants in the Byzantine regions and those in the Carolingian dominated areas.[111] Similarly Jewish merchants from the Carolingian empire traveled through the Byzantine empire and are known to have traded in the Jewish-ruled Khazar land on the imperial border.[112]

104 Jewish Policy under Louis the Pious

Michael's pro-Jewish policy was reflected in the flourishing of Jewish communities in Byzantine Italy. At Venosa the renaissance of Hebrew study mentioned in the previous chapter moved along rapidly. A Hebrew academy was well established in Venosa during the period, and its dean, a certain Nathan ben Ephraim, was revered as a sage.[113] Jewish prosperity at Venosa is also evidenced by the tombstones surviving from this period.[114] A collation of statistics from a sample of these suggests that the average Jew in Venosa during this period lived to the age of forty-five years and about five months. The age at death in the sample ranges from seventeen to seventy-four years. The distribution of dates and the contents of the inscriptions make it clear that neither war, nor pestilence, nor privation struck the community.[115]

At Oria there was yet another Jewish community that benefited both from Michael's pro-Jewish policy and from the proximity of the Carolingian empire. Trade between Jewish merchants of Oria and the Carolingian empire flourished.[116] The community was so rich that it or, more exactly, individual families could send large sums of gold to Jerusalem for the support of scholarly work. In addition we have evidence that Jews of Oria made pilgrimages to Jerusalem, and one man is known to have made three voyages to the Holy Land.[117] Jewish communities also flourished at Taranto, Bari and throughout Sicily. In the last area, however, Muslim attacks beginning in 827 had a harmful effect.[118]

Louis the Pious systematized the pro-Jewish policy pursued by the early Carolingians. His work led toward the elimination of or the disregard for previous legal disabilities that had restricted Jewish activity and life in general. To accomplish his aims, Louis enacted laws that protected Jews and developed an administrative apparatus to enforce his policies. Louis also followed the earlier Carolingian policy of encouraging Jewish merchant activity; in this area he saw to the development of a formulary for charters that contained protections and exemptions so that Jews involved in commerce might prosper. The emperor also protected Jewish landholders and landowners from harassment.

Louis brooked no opposition to his Jewish policy. Thus he humiliated and beat down Archbishop Agobard of Lyons who sought to pursue an anti-Jewish policy in his own diocese and to encourage the emperor to alter the government's stance in this area. Louis's officials, perhaps taking their lead from the emperor's vigorous pro-Jewish posture, apparently ignored gross violations of the law by Jewish slave traders who bought and sold Christian slaves and kidnapped and castrated Christian youths for the Muslim markets in Spain. In the environs of the Carolingian empire during this period the Byzantine Emperor Michael II also pursued a pro-Jewish policy. The prominence of Jewish merchants within the Carolingian empire and throughout the East highlights the success of Louis's pro-Jewish policies.

CHAPTER VI

Jewish Policy in the Carolingian Empire and Its Environs during the Period of Dissolution (840-877)

When Louis the Pious died in 840, the discord within the empire that had become manifest during the previous decade was exacerbated. Louis's three principal heirs, Lothair, Louis the German, and Charles the Bald, went to war. For three years alliances shifted and the balance of power swung from one faction to another. Finally, a bloody battle was fought at Fontenoy which was decisive not because one side was clearly victorious but because immense losses were sustained by everyone involved. The single most important result of the battle of Fontenoy was that it turned the interests of the nobles from civil war which they had previously encouraged toward peace. After protracted negotiations in which the magnates played an important role, Louis's sons finally assented in 843 to the Treaty of Verdun. This agreement created three *Teilreiche*: *Francia Occidentalis* ruled by Charles the Bald, *Francia Orientalis* ruled by Louis the German, and the Middle Kingdom which extended from the North Sea to northern Italy and was ruled by Lothair who also held the imperial title. The Treaty of Verdun gave legal status to and demonstrated extensive aristocratic support for the dissolution of the Carolingian empire. Previously the empire had survived as a unified whole more by fortune than by design; in 843 that luck ran out.[1]

The three years of civil war that tore apart the empire after Louis's death sapped the power of his sons and encouraged various elements in the society to pursue policies that earlier had proved fruitless. Among

Jewish Policy during the Dissolution 107

the problems faced by Charles the Bald in his newly legitimized kingdom of *Francia Occidentalis* was the resurgence of an emboldened clerical party. That party was headed by Hincmar, the exceptionally able and ambitious archbishop of Rheims who assumed power over that see in 845. The ecclesiastical magnates presented a program based upon three fundamental *desiderata*: 1) laymen must be kept from controlling ecclesiastical establishments; 2) laymen must return to Church possession lands that had been granted previously under precarial tenure or that had been usurped; and 3) the Jews must be crushed.[2] As a retrospective gauge of the success of Louis's Jewish policy it is important to note that the Church party established as a basic tenet of its program the reversal of that policy.

In a series of Church councils culminating at Meaux-Paris in 846, the ecclesiastical magnates established their program for destroying the Jews. Thus it was advocated that Jewish children should be removed from their homes and placed in monasteries or in the households of God-fearing Christians who would raise them in an appropriate manner.[3] The policy makers, however, labored under no illusions, and they probably were aware that even if this canon were approved by royal authority and enforced, it would take many years for it to have the desired effect. More practical legislation therefore was also enacted. For example, the building of new synagogues was prohibited and if this law were broken, the edifice was to be turned over to the Church and the builders fined fifty pounds of gold.[4]

The new synagogues built during Louis's reign surely irked the churchmen assembled at Paris. Much practical as well as symbolic value could be attached to such buildings. There were, however, more pressing day-to-day problems with which these ecclesiastics had to deal. The assembled clerics made it clear that Jews were to be ousted from all governmental positions in which they exercised power over Christians. Particularly, the offices of *judex* and *tellonarius* were to be kept out of Jewish hands. In general, Jews were not to possess any *dignitates* or *honores*. Jews who obtained such *beneficia* were to lose them and, in addition, were to pay a fine of fifty pounds of gold.[5]

The ouster of Jews from governmental positions was but a prelude to depriving them of the protection and benefit of the laws established by Louis the Pious. Thus Jews were to be prohibited from pleading their cases in Christian courts. At the same time Jewish law, Jewish courts, and Jewish judges were to be employed only in cases involving Jews. Christians were in no way to be ensnared by the Jewish legal system. The intent of this legislation was the segregation of Jews and Christians. Although the implementation of this canon would probably have been impractical, at least for a time, its theoretical basis was clear.[6]

Other enactments also pointed to the effort to segregate Jews and Christians. For example, strict penalties were to be meted out to Christians who dined with Jews or associated with them too closely. Christians were warned sternly and threatened not to do favors for Jews even if the latter offered money in return. During Easter week Jews were prohibited from mixing in public with Christians, and "mixed marriages" were vigorously forbidden.[7] Such liaisons were considered to be adulterous.[8]

Perhaps the most immediate problem faced by the council was the prevailing government support of Jewish slave traders and slave owners. Thus it is not surprising that a substantial number of enactments were addressed to this situation. The churchmen established that under no condition were Jews to own Christian slaves. Jews who bought Christian slaves in error (i.e., not knowing that they were Christians) had to resell them within forty days or lose them. Jews, however, were required to sell these Christian slaves to Christians who dwelled within the empire. Slaves who were converted to Christianity while owned by Jews were to be sold to Christians for twelve *solidi*. A Jew who converted either a Christian or a pagan slave to Judaism with the assent of the latter was to lose the convert who was then freed. Jews who persisted in such successful proselytism were to be banished from the region. Jewish owners of either Christians or pagans who converted these slaves against their will were to be executed and to have their property confiscated. The slaves were to be freed. It should be noted, in addition, that Jews who converted free men or women against their will were also to be executed, and their property was to be confiscated.[9]

The policy makers of the ecclesiastical party showed traditional respect for authority as they formulated their program. They carefully selected the canons discussed above from a vast corpus of anti-Jewish leg-

Jewish Policy during the Dissolution 109

islation that had been enacted previously by popes, Roman emperors, and Church councils. The choice of canons they made for the Paris program clearly was influenced by contemporary problems and future *desiderata*. Thus the assembled churchmen bewailed the contemporary state of affairs in order to emphasize the great need to reverse the effects of Louis's pro-Jewish policy. They claimed that they were compelled to act because "now ... throughout the cities and towns ... so much [Jewish] arrogance and oppression have burst upon the scene."[10] In light of Agobard's continuous complaints and humiliating defeat two decades earlier, it seems reasonable to suggest that the "Jewish threat" had escalated substantially.

Agobard's successor at Lyons, Amulo, presented to his fellow prelates and to King Charles a defense of the council's position. In a document entitled *Liber contra Judaeos* Amulo elaborated not only theological arguments in support of the program but catalogued large numbers of abuses inflicted by Jews upon Christians. For example, he called the king's attention to and attacked the vigorous proselytizing efforts of the Jews. He noted that Jewish tax collectors took advantage of their positions as governmental officials to bring about the conversion of Christians to Judaism. He emphasized that this abuse was especially prevalent in rural areas where the people were unsophisticated and where there were few learned clerics to defend the flock.[11] It seems a reasonable inference from Amulo's remarks that Christian government officials had done nothing to stop the Jews in their coercive missionary activity.

Amulo, however, condemned too one-sidedly the innocence and vulnerability of the rustics. In the cities where there were many educated priests, the Jews were also successful. Thus the unhappy prelate lamented that Christians preferred to listen to the sermons of Jewish preachers and to neglect those of their own clergy.[12] In this competition, according to Amulo, the Jews did not hesitate to blaspheme Jesus and to popularize the scurrilous *Jewish Life of Jesus* (*Toledoth Jeshu*).[13] Amulo noted that the Jews were willing to admit that Jesus existed, but they maintained with a plethora of "erroneous" arguments that he should not be considered God. The subtleties involved in this and other arguments elaborated by Amulo seem to suggest that the Jewish community of Lyons was strong and secure. Simultaneously, it would appear that the Christian population was highly sensitized to theological disputation and debate and was vulnerable to Jewish proselytism.[14]

Amulo also lamented the close relations between Christians and Jews, the popular custom of feasting together, the prevalence of Christians who rested on the Jewish sabbath and worked on Sunday, and the large numbers of Christians who were employed by Jews. In this context it may be added that Amulo characterized the Jews as wealthy and noted that as in Agobard s time, they flourished in the wine business. He added that Christians continued to use both wine and meat processed by Jews according to religious rituals.[15]

In this document Amulo remarked that he had begun to put into practice certain elements of the Church's anti-Jewish program. He indicated that he had preached several times that Christians should avoid all social contact with Jews and that free Christians should not work for Jews or buy from them. In this he emphasized the avoidance of "tainted," i.e. Jewish processed meat and wine.[16] This program, of course, was much milder than that advocated by the council. Before the canons were enacted by the king and received royal support, however, Amulo could only try to influence Christians; he could not act directly against the Jews. In this regard he was following the policy outlined almost twenty years earlier by Agobard in his letter to Nebridius. This letter had been written only after Agobard realized that imperial opposition could not be overcome.[17]

In June of 846 representatives of the clerical party presented their program to King Charles at Épernay. Charles approved several canons that implied that some reforms would be made in regard to Church lands. On the whole, however, the king refused to be influenced by Hincmar and his supporters. This is especially clear with regard to their anti-Jewish program; Charles rejected it completely.[18] Not a single anti-Jewish measure was enacted by the king! Despite the diminution of royal power that had resulted from the conflicts of the preceding five years, Charles made it unequivocally clear that he intended to continue the pro-Jewish policy that his father had so successfully fostered.

Thus Charles refused to condone efforts that were aimed at driving Jews from governmental office and refused to take action against the economic and religious institutions of the Jews in *Francia Occidentalis*. There seems no reason to believe that the conspicuous role that Jews played at court during Louis's reign was diminished by Charles. In fact the latter is reputed to have retained a Jew as his personal physician and to have had at least one Jewish *fidelis* in his entourage.[19]

Of far greater significance as a positive demonstration that Charles continued to pursue what may perhaps be termed "traditional" Carolingian Jewish policy was his employment of Jewish mintmasters. When Charles acted to reform the legislation through which the coinage was controlled, he noted that those minters who lived under the Roman law were to be regulated in this activity by Roman law but that all others, including Jews, were to be regulated by his capitulary.[20] Thus Charles was aware that under the Roman law to which Jews would normally be subject in this matter they were not permitted to perform the governmental *militia* of mintmaster. Therefore, Charles indicated that Jews were to be treated according to his capitulary and in the same manner as any other free person. In this act Charles negated the restrictions of the Roman law. He recognized the free and unencumbered status of the Jews with regard to minting and established an important element of Carolingian Jewry law.[21]

The employment of Jews in minting activities by the Carolingians sustained a pattern of administrative policy that also had been followed by the Merovingians.[22] Among those policies that were pursued by both dynasties we may also include the employment of Jews as tax collectors.[23] It appears that an obvious inference might be drawn concerning the economic success of Jews in the *regnum Francorum* who were active in both minting and tax gathering. Thus we cannot be surprised to find that contemporaries of Charles the Bald noted the wealth of the Jews and recognized their value to the monarchy. Amulo, the archbishop of Lyons, was fundamentally aware of this situation. Thus he took the bold but naïve step of suggesting to Charles that he not let the substantial taxes paid by the Jews to the treasury and the gifts they made to the crown inhibit him from doing what was best for the souls of his subjects, i.e., enacting an anti-Jewish policy.[24]

The interrelation of minting and tax collecting in the governmental sphere of economic life had an analogue in medieval business. It was not uncommon for merchant activity and banking, of which money lending was (and is) an integral part, to be closely connected during the Middle Ages. Jewish involvement in banking was, as we have seen, the subject of legislation by Charlemagne. Under the latter's grandson and namesake, Jews continued in this business. Although it is impossible to obtain any quantitative data concerning the transactions of Jewish bankers during this period, some bits of evidence survive to suggest the nature of their activities. For example, some remarks by the Countess Dhuoda indicate that she borrowed noteworthy sums of money, perhaps on a regular basis, from Jewish sources.[25] It is particularly important, especially in light of previous scholarly and popular treatments of usury, to note that the countess attached not a word of obloquy to the Jews in her discussion of this business and its practitioners. Rather, her tone is one of gratitude and obligation.[26]

In the area of trade, Jewish merchants were specifically recognized by Charles in his legislation. Among the taxes collected by Charles from the Jews living or trading in his realm were levies on the profits earned by the merchants. Of these profits the royal treasury received eleven percent.[27] It should also be remembered that during the reign of Charles the Bald the Radanite merchants who based their activities in southern Gaul flourished. Lack of data makes it impossible to gauge the economic impact of the Radanite merchants on the *regnum Francorum*. Their extensive activity in Muslim lands, however, emphasizes the cooperation practiced among the Carolingian dynasty, the Abbasids, and the Jews. The last benefited both groups as intermediaries while helping themselves more than a little.[28]

The trans-Mediterranean aspects of Carolingian Jewish policy are apparent in the encouragement of Jewish settlement in the *regnum Francorum*. For example, R. Natronai, Gaon of Sura, who flourished (853-858/863) during the middle years of the reign of Charles the Bald provides information on the immigration of Jews from Kairouan to the Spanish March.[29] Throughout the ninth century contacts were maintained between the Jewish communities of the Muslim east and Carolingian Spain, but in the reign of Charles the Bald the intellectual and legal correspondence alone assumed gigantic proportions. R. Tsemah, Gaon of Pumbeditha (fl. 872-890), indicates that the volume was so great

Jewish Policy during the Dissolution 113

that many pack animals had to be used to transport the correspondence during any given period of exchange.[30]

Aside from the immigration of Jews to Charles's realm and the growth in the amount of correspondence, another index of the success of the king's pro-Jewish policy would seem to be the explosive growth in the number of rabbis in Carolingian Spain. Evidence of numerous letters survives from the 850s. These were addressed to a large number of rabbis in Barcelona. For example, in 858 one text mentioned R. Meir ben Joseph and "the sages of Barcelona," and another was addressed to all the rabbis of Barcelona and their disciples.[31] The numerous sages and disciples may perhaps suggest the existence of an academy at Barcelona such as the one in contemporary Venosa.

Barcelona may well have been the continuous home of a substantial and periodically powerful Jewish community from the late Roman period onward. Barcelona has received the greatest amount of attention as rightly befits an important city; we should not forget, however, less populous places like Ausona which also had a prominent Jewish community. In chapter IV we discussed Charlemagne's policy of establishing Jewish settlers in frontier communities such as Ausona for both military and economic purposes. The survival and development of Ausona through the first half of the ninth century and, indeed, later, as a Jewish stronghold are evidenced not only by the failure of the Church to establish a bishopric there but by the presence in the town of a rabbi, Joseph, the father of R. Meir of Barcelona.[32] It might also be noted as evidence both of Jewish prominence in Ausona and of the enforcement of Carolingian policy that Saturday was not a market day; the market days there were Friday and Sunday. Conspicuously then, the Jewish sabbath was not a market day at Ausona, but both the Muslim and Christian sabbaths were used for business.[33]

All the available evidence strongly suggests that Charles the Bald pursued the traditional pro-Jewish policy of the Carolingian dynasty. We are given to believe from contemporary evidence, however, that Jewish communities in *Francia Occidentalis* and in Carolingian Spain actively pursued both military and political policies that were inimical to Charles's interests. For example, in 847 Bodo, the Alaman noble who converted to Judaism in 838-839 and abandoned the garb of a cleric for that of a fighting man, was accused of stirring up the Muslims against the Christians in Spain. Bodo, who made his home in the Jewish town of Ausona, is said to have mobilized the enemy and forced Christians to choose between Judaism or Islam and death. The Christian victims of Bodo's alleged persecution are reported to have appealed to King Charles for aid and protection.[34]

It is charged that in 848 the Jews of Bordeaux sided with Viking raiders and turned the city over to the enemy. As a result of the alleged Jewish cooperation with the Vikings, Duke William who had been in control of the city was captured, and the city itself was depopulated and then burned.[35] According to the *Annals of Saint Bertin*, the Jews of Barcelona handed over their city to the Moors in 852. It is said that Barcelona was devastated, that the Christian population was virtually annihilated, and that the Muslims slipped away without suffering serious losses.[36] Finally, in 877 the Jews are seen to have taken their ultimate revenge on Charles the Bald. The monarch's Jewish physician Sedechias was accused of administering a fatal dose of poison to his patient.[37]

It should be emphasized that extreme violence is involved in all of these incidents in which the Jews of Charles's kingdom stand accused. In three of the four instances mentioned above military or paramilitary action was indicated or strongly implied. This military capability as we have seen in previous chapters is a frequently noted aspect of Jewish community organization. Thus it is apparent that the Jews of Charles's realm had both the ability and the opportunity to carry out the acts with which they are charged. Yet it is questionable whether they, in fact, stripped their benefactor of two important cities, attempted to convert his loyal subjects and co-religionists at the point of a sword, and finally murdered him.

An examination of the source of these anti-Jewish charges provides some perspective. All the accusations appear to be based on a single source, the *Annals of Saint Bertin*, which during the period under discussion were authored by Bishop Prudence of Troyes and Archbishop Hincmar of Rheims.[38] The latter, one of the leaders of the anti-Jewish party which presented the Paris Program to Charles in 846, may also be considered to have been the guiding spirit behind the *Annals*. It is certainly tempting to conclude, with most scholars, that in writing about Jewish cooperation with the Vikings and Muslims the aim of the *Annals* was to spread anti-Jewish propaganda.[39] Perhaps there was an additional aim, i.e., to embarrass Charles or perhaps even to sway him from his pro-Jewish policy. The account of Charles's poisoning very probably was intended to convince his son and successor that he should pursue an anti-Jewish policy to revenge his father's death.

Despite the obvious *parti-pris* of the *Annals of Saint Bertin* in these cases, it seems unlikely that these stories were pure fantasy. There is substantial documentation for the Viking attack on Bordeaux in the years 847-848, and there is also reason to believe that there was a Muslim attack on Barcelona some time later.[40] Similarly it is not unreasonable to believe that Bodo, with the zeal of a new convert, harassed his former co-religionists. The question, thus, is whether the Jews of *Francia Occidentalis* and Carolingian Spain who had clearly benefited from Charles's pro-Jewish policy played a key role in events that seriously compromised the king's position.

A close examination of the situation at Bordeaux in 848 suggests a possible answer. In June of 844 Charles the Bald lost control of the greater part of Aquitaine to his nephew and enemy Peppin. With the aid of William, son of Bernard of Septimania (Charles had executed Bernard in May of 844), Peppin defeated Charles's forces decisively in June 844.[41] During the Viking attacks on Bordeaux in the years 847-848, William was in control of the city. Peppin seems to have been unable to bring support to William and to relieve the city. Charles then led a contingent of his forces to Bordeaux. We must presume that he intended not only to drive the Vikings away but to gain control of the city for himself and to capture William who was Peppin's ally. Charles, however, also failed.[42] Is it unreasonable to suggest that Charles, who had dealt with the Vikings frequently,[43] prevailed upon the Jews toward whom he had already demonstrated his good will in 846 to act in concert with the Northmen and to seize the opportunity to drive William from the city? We do know that in the wake of the Jewish-Viking victory at Bordeaux, William was captured, the city was ultimately restored to Charles, and Charles's fortunes in Aquitaine improved markedly.[44]

116 Jewish Policy during the Dissolution

In turning to the alleged Jewish role in the capture of Barcelona by the Moors, we are faced with a paucity of information. Only one source provides corroboration for such an attack. It dates the event in the year 850 and not in 852 as indicated in the *Annals of Saint Bertin*. In searching for a reason why the Jews of Barcelona may have cooperated with the Moors we once again encounter Charles's sworn enemy William whom the Jews of Bordeaux seem to have helped to drive from their city. By 849, however, William had escaped from captivity and had fled into Carolingian Spain. In 850 he won a victory over Charles's forces, but the latter defeated him later in the same year. Following this defeat, William ensconced himself at Barcelona. Shortly thereafter William was captured at Barcelona and handed over to Charles's forces who executed him.[45] It is possible that it was the Jews of Barcelona, with the support of a group of Muslim allies, who seized William. In such an encounter Christians who supported the rebel probably were killed. Thus once again we would have an incident in which Charles's Jewish subjects supported their benefactor's interests with the help of an "unpopular" ally. Such incidents in which Christians were killed by Muslims or Vikings and their Jewish allies could easily be manipulated, and apparently they were by clever and biased clerics.

Regarding the case of Bodo, it is indeed tempting to see him as a zealous proselytizer carrying on vigorous missionary efforts. But his presence at Ausona, the Jewish dominated town which was part of Charles's realm may make us reconsider. From the evidence concerning Bodo's anti-Christian activities (844-847) it seems that he was acting against Charles's apparent interests in Carolingian Spain. We must ask, however, would Bodo, despite his zeal, have knowingly acted against Charles's interests especially after the latter's pro-Jewish stand at Épernay in 846? After June 844 Peppin, Charles's enemy, held sway throughout much of Aquitaine and Carolingian Spain; many Christians, in fact, recognized him as their legitimate ruler. Thus Bodo may perhaps be seen to have attacked Christians who supported Peppin. As with the Bordeaux and Barcelona incidents, the *Annals of Saint Bertin* provide a "version" of what happened with the aim of placing the Jews in a bad light. In short, it is more reasonable to assume that the Jews remained

Jewish Policy during the Dissolution 117

loyal to Charles than to believe that while he was pursuing a pro-Jewish policy, the beneficiaries of that effort were attacking his interests.

A letter written by Charles the Bald in 876 might be seen to cast some further light on his relation with the Jews of Barcelona:

In the name of the holy and undivided Trinity. Charles emperor and augustus by the mercy of almighty God [sends] greeting to all our own Barcelonians. Know that we thrive in seemly prosperity as a gift from above. We wish greatly that it may also remain among you. We send to you, moreover, very many thanks because always and in all ways you have extended [yourselves] in faithfulness to us [literally "in our faithfulness"]. Accordingly, Judah the Hebrew, our *fidelis*, comes to us and has described in detail your faithfulness to us. Thence, for your faithfulness we are ready to send proper remuneration and worthy reward. Therefore, concerning our steadfast faithfulness do not in any way hold back, but in this, accordingly, know and be more powerful. Continue extending [yourselves] in all things just as you have done thus far. Farewell. And know that I am sending ten pounds of silver to Bishop Frodo for the repair of his church by my *fidelis* Judacot.[46]

From the letter it is clear that Charles had at least one important loyal Jewish supporter who was knowledgeable about affairs in Barcelona and who may even have been from that city or region. Judah's report led Charles to write the above-quoted letter thanking his "own Barcelonians." It is clear from the last sentence that Bishop Frodo of Barcelona was not one of the king's own. Yet it is also apparent that the prelate was not out of royal favor. The absence from the letter's address of any reference to royal officers such as the count or viscount is curious and has suggested to some scholars that the addressees were a defined (or corporate?) group of some kind.[47]

The use of the word "peculiaribus" to modify "omnibus Barchinonensibus . . . nostris" is very peculiar indeed. The most common meaning of *peculiaris* is property, and by extension during the Middle Ages this word frequently indicated serf.[48] Thus one might perhaps feel justified translating the address: "to all our Barcelonian serfs (or property —i.e., slaves?)." Considerably later in the Middle Ages some rulers— especially in the German Empire—used "unfree" *ministeriales* to carry out vital administrative functions. Because of their relation to the locus

118   Jewish Policy during the Dissolution

of power these officials eventually rose to noble status.[49] More to the point of the present study is the establishment, also later in the Middle Ages and only in some regions, of Jews as royal *servi*.[50] Obviously such a status for Jews that was popular more than three centuries after the letter under discussion was written is hardly helpful in interpreting ninth-century conditions.

Further, the use of the verb *tendo* and its derivatives in the phrases "in nostram fidelitatem semper omnimodis tenditis" and "in omnibus tendentes permaneatis" bears the connotation of engaging in military activity on a regular basis.[51] Thus my translation of the address may well call to mind the much later British military usage of referring to various regiments as the "king's own." It should be noted that such units were not comprised of royal serfs.[52]

The uses of *peculiaris* and *tendo* in the letter admittedly are disturbing because of their imprecision and the possibility of a variety of connotations.[53] The role played by Judah the Hebrew, Charles's *fidelis*,[54] in bringing to the king's attention the continuing loyalty and service of his "own Barcelonians" as well as the existence of important and thriving Jewish communities at Barcelona and in its environs seems to complicate the matter further. It seems fair to observe that the king's own Barcelonians are not to be identified with the Church hierarchy and its entourage nor does it seem that the addressees were royal officials or their followers. Yet, even if it is unlikely that the two most logical choices—the bishop and count—are to be identified with the king's own, to hypothesize on the basis of this letter alone that the addressees were the Jews of Barcelona would be mere guesswork.

An examination of the political situation in Carolingian Spain during the later 860s and 870s may perhaps cast some further light on the king's own Barcelonians. In ca. 868 Wilfrid the Hairy murdered Charles's governor in Carolingian Spain and gradually succeeded in usurping control of much of the region.[55] Wilfrid was opposed by the then bishop of Barcelona John.[56] The usurper, however, did have ecclesiastical support in some quarters and pursued a policy of trying to establish a church and bishop in the Jewish dominated town of Ausona. Quite naturally the Jews of Ausona may have failed to appreciate Wilfrid's policy in this regard, and they opposed his efforts successfully at least until the

Jewish Policy during the Dissolution 119

death of Charles the Bald.[57] It should be emphasized that the Jewish communities of Barcelona and Ausona were not only in close geographical proximity but had close relations and shared common interests.[58] It would seem that the Church of Barcelona—Bishop John and his successor Bishop Frodo—opposed Wilfrid and supported Charles. The Jews of Carolingian Spain would seem to have shared the interests of the Barcelona ecclesiastical hierarchy in this case. During this period, however, royal officials—dukes, counts, and viscounts—who had served Charles were replaced by Wilfrid's men.[59] A hypothesis which identifies the Jews of Barcelona as the king's own Barcelonians is given a modicum of circumstantial support by the above examination of the political situation in Carolingian Spain ca. 876. Firm conclusions on this point, however, are out of the question.

While Charles seems to have been consistent in pursuing a pro-Jewish policy,[60] men like Wilfrid the Hairy and Hincmar quite obviously did otherwise. Although Charles the Bald surely lacked the effectiveness of his grandfather and even of his father, he seems to have been able to sustain the traditional Carolingian Jewish policy. An episode that took place in the mid-860s illustrates this well. Bishop Rothadus of Soissons (833-869) pursued a pro-Jewish policy in accordance with Charles's aims but was charged by Hincmar with violation of both canon law and Carolingian Jewry law. Rothardus was accused of selling some silver crowns belonging to his church to the Jews. Hincmar acting in his capacity of archbishop deposed Rothardus. Charles, however, with papal support ordered the latter reinstated. The king prevailed.[61]

As compared with the Jewish policy of Charles we are less well informed about the Jewish policies pursued by his brothers Louis the German (d. 876) and Lothair (d. 855). The Middle Kingdom which fell to Lothair along with the imperial title lasted only twelve years. Two of his three sons, namely, Charles and Lothair II, inherited lands north of the Alps and lost their kingdoms to their uncles Charles and Louis. Lothair I's remaining son, Louis II, inherited the Italian segment of the Middle Kingdom and survived until 875. Thus one need be aware that treatment of Jewish policy in the Middle Kingdom during the period of

120   Jewish Policy during the Dissolution

the dissolution of the Carolingian empire is limited essentially to the reigns of Lothair I and Louis II.[62]

During the first decade after the Treaty of Verdun in 843 there is simply no explicit evidence indicating whether Lothair continued his father's pro-Jewish policy or reversed it. The absence of any radical change in the condition of the Jewish communities in his *regnum* would seem to suggest that he had done nothing negative. For example, the prelates who assembled at the Council of Pavia in 850 complained vigorously against the prevailing practice of Jews being used as judges in cases involving Christians.[63] In this context it is perhaps appropriate to remember that throughout the early Middle Ages the *lex Judaeorum* seems to have been exerting subtle influences upon the *lex Langobardorum*.[64] It might be suggested that the Jewish *judices* about whom the clerics complained played a role in this process.

At Pavia it was also complained that Jewish tax and toll collectors exercised power over Christians and should be driven from their governmental positions. Those who continued to permit Jews to exercise public functions contrary to both the canon and Roman laws were threatened by the assembled prelates with excommunication.[65] Lothair is not indicated as having approved the work of the assembly at Pavia, nor is there clear evidence that he rejected the Council's anti-Jewish policy as Charles the Bald had rejected the Paris program at Épernay four years earlier. It might be hazarded, however, that the need perceived by the prelates to act and the absence of any evidence for governmental approval of their legislation suggest that Lothair and his son Louis II were not pursuing a vigorous anti-Jewish policy.

Among the ecclesiastical magnates of the Middle Kingdom, the hierarchy at Lyons pursued a Jewish policy that was contrary to traditional Carolingian aims. We have seen how Agobard opposed Louis the Pious and how his successor Amulo played a role in support of the prelates of *Francia Occidentalis* who drew up the Paris program for the elimination of Jews in Charles the Bald's realm. In addition Amulo observed in the years 845-846 that he had initiated a policy of coercion against pro-Jewish Christians and in general preached anti-Jewish sermons in accordance with the program outlined by Agobard in his letter to Nibridius in 827.

The situation in the Lyonnais as gleaned from the writings of Agobard and Amulo indicates that there was close and substantial interaction between Jews and Christians not only in economic matters and on a social basis but in religious affairs as well. Most striking in this regard is not the prelates' knowledge of Hebrew theology and Jewish customs but the admitted preference shown by a worrisome number of Christians for Jewish sermons, holiday celebrations, and sabbath observances. In short, there seems to have been an open contest in this region between Jewish proselytizers whose sermons were very attractive to Christians and the ecclesiastical hierarchy who under Agobard and Amulo were fighting a losing battle. It should be observed, parenthetically, that the legislation enacted and enforced by Louis the Pious may have strengthened the Jewish position; but whether this gave the Jews an unfair advantage in this contest with the Church or whether imperial intervention simply insured that the struggle would be a fair one is a moot point.

With the accession of Archbishop Remigius at Lyons in 852, the archdiocese seems to have found a shepherd who was able not only to protect his won flock but to reverse the losing trend of the past three decades. In the apparently open and ongoing contest for souls in the archdiocese of Lyons and its subordinate dioceses of Mâcon and Châlons as well as in the archdiocese of Vienne, Remigius and his supporters preached to the Jews and won some converts among them — especially among the young.[66]

In a letter to Emperor Lothair, Remigius described his success in winning souls from Judaism for Christianity through preaching and through the influence exercised by converts on their former co-religionists. By implication Remigius also defended himself and his followers against any charges delating that force had been employed in this contest. Remigius's major problem, however, was that he saw the Jews, now that they were losing, as acting unfairly in the struggle. According to Remigius the Jews not only attempted to coerce their former co-religionists to reject their newfound road to salvation and return to Judaism but shipped a large number of Jewish children, i.e., potential converts to Christianity, from the cities of Lyons, Châlons, Mâcon, and Vienne to Arles where the ecclesiastical hierarchy was either unable or unwilling to pursue a policy of proselytism.[67]

Remigius's main purpose in writing this letter to the emperor, however, was not to brag about his methods and success nor was it to defend himself and his followers against complaints of illegal activity as Agobard had been forced to do twenty-five years earlier. Remigius's primary intention was to obtain the emperor's support so that the ecclesiastical hierarchy at Arles would be allowed and encouraged to pursue a policy similar to that which had won some initial success in Lyons and its subordinate dioceses.[68]

The complete absence of evidence concerning the nature of the Jewish policy at Arles in the wake of this letter should not be assumed to demonstrate that Lothair I ignored Remigius's plea.[69] Lothair, however, died within a year or two, at most, of Remigius's campaign, and the cities in question fell to his son Charles of Provence. The latter lost control of them in short order to the local magnates and to Charles the Bald.[70] Charles the Bald's consistently pro-Jewish policy, as discussed above, made it highly unlikely that Remigius and his followers won many more successes.

When Louis II assumed sole power in Italy upon his father's death in 855, some effort seems to have been made to have him pursue a vigorously anti-Jewish policy. A text survives that purports to include information from a document issued by Louis II that ordered the expulsion of all Jews from Carolingian Italy by the Kalends of October 855.[71] The turbulent nature of affairs in Italy at this time makes it impossible to ascertain which of the many parties contending for power prepared this expulsion edict in the hope that Louis would approve it—clearly it never became his official policy. It might be noted in this context, however, that the able Church reformer Pope Leo IV died in July of 855, the month of Louis's alleged anti-Jewish decree. Louis had supported Anastasius, Leo's opponent, and tried to have him made pope in 855. Thus Louis was solidly positioned against the reformers, and it is therefore even more unlikely that he would have reversed the traditional Carolingian pro-Jewish stance and embraced an ecclesiastical anti-Jewish policy. It is perhaps possible that the *desideratum* of expelling the Jews from northern Italy was a plank in the platform of the reformers. They may have hoped to have their policy approved in the bargaining over the choice of a new pope that followed Leo's death. We have already

Jewish Policy during the Dissolution 123

seen that in 850 the reform-minded Italian prelates who gathered at Pavia favored a strong anti-Jewish policy, and the desired decree of 855 may have been a continuation of this attack. It should be remembered that the Paris program of 846 also aimed at freeing the empire from Jews.[72]

In *Francia Orientalis* Louis the German seems to have pursued a policy of encouraging Jewish merchant activity and the establishment of permanent Jewish settlements. Jews and other merchants were guaranteed, whether they were from Louis's kingdom or from some other land, that they would be asked only to pay a "fair toll." This regulation concerned all of their goods, but special mention was made of slaves presumably to assure Jewish traders that they would not be subject to the harsher legislation of the increasingly moribund Jewry provisions of the Roman law. Thus in this case we see yet another enactment of Carolingian Jewry law which replaced the restrictions of the Roman law for the benefit of Jewish merchants.[73]

Louis's encouragement of Jewish settlement was strongly supported by Bishop Witgarius of Augsberg who was highly thought of by the Jewish community in his city.[74] Similarly Jewish settlements were built up at Regensburg and Salzburg with the aid of the ecclesiastical establishment.[75] St. Anskar (d. 865), the apostle of the North, who traveled widely in Germany and Scandinavia was very probably familiar with Jewish merchants.[76] At Constance, Bishop Salomon II seems to have had a favorable impression of Jews, and at the nearby monastery of Saint Gall the old monks who contributed stories to Notkar's collection of anecdotes spoke well of the Jews and gave particular attention to Jewish merchants.[77] Close relations between Christians and Jews were also indicated in a curious letter written by an anonymous cleric to King Louis. The cleric seemed worried that Jewish dietary habits were influencing Christians.[78]

Quite obviously Louis's pro-Jewish policy neither went so far as to encourage Christian observance of Jewish dietary laws nor was it particularly innovative. As early as Charlemagne's reign Arno, Archbishop of Salzburg, and other bishops with whom he worked indicated that they

124 Jewish Policy during the Dissolution

were interested in the support of an important learned Jew for their *Ostpolitik*.[79] The significance of Jewish-Christian cooperation is emphasized by the fact that Arno's letter discussing his high regard for this Jew was retained for inclusion in a formulary.[80] Thus it is hardly surprising to find, not long after Louis's death, that influential men who seem to have been Jews like Isaac and Solomon were serving the king of Bavaria in the important matter of renewing trade legislation that was favorable to the Jews.[81] Lest we be misled by a welter of detail it is important to insist that the continued flourishing of Jewish merchants and the ongoing development of Jewish settlements in *Francia Orientalis* were the result of Louis the German's continuation of traditional Carolingian Jewish policy. In this he was supported by his lay and ecclesiastical officials.

When we turn to the environs of the crumbling Carolingian empire, the picture of political fragmentation is no less vivid. By the mid-840s the Muslims were in control of Sicily, Bari, and Taranto. Raiding by Muslim land and sea forces was endemic in the south of Italy, and the north was certainly not immune from attack. So far as can be ascertained, however, the pro-Jewish policy established by the Byzantine emperor Michael II was not abandoned by his successors Theophilus (829-842) and Michael III (842-867).[82] When examining Byzantine Jewish policy in Italy during this period, it is perhaps more useful, in light of the political instability of the area, to focus upon local conditions rather than to assume that the imperial writ from Constantinople was rigorously enforced.

At Oria during this period the Jewish community was permitted by the Byzantine governor of the region to exercise its traditional rights and privileges. For example, Jewish courts operating under Jewish law and headed by Jewish judges had jurisdiction over Jews even in the most serious kinds of cases. Not only were law breakers ordered to be executed, for example, but such sentences were also carried out.[83] There flourished also at Oria several "well-established academies (*midrashot*)"; this may well be taken as an index of the wealth and well-being of the community as a whole.[84] The Byzantine governor seems to have relied upon Jews from Oria to perform certain official tasks of an administrative nature. Among the more elevated appointments was that of R. Shefatiah as ambassador to the Muslim ruler of Bari.[85]

Although we are best informed about the situation at Oria, Christian authorities elsewhere in Italy seem to have been no less interested in seeing the Jewish communities in their localities flourish. At Venosa, for example, the academy mentioned in chapter V continued to gain recognition; and when its revered dean, Nathan ben Ephraim, died in 846, his passing was commemorated with an elaborate and laudatory Hebrew inscription.[86] In this regard it should be noted that through the 840s and 850s the remarkable funerary inscriptions for which Venosa has justly received attention continue.[87]

Despite the fact that the Muslims had conquered substantial parts of Byzantine Italy, the Jews living in the Christian parts were permitted and perhaps even encouraged to maintain close relations not only with the Islamic East but with Jews throughout Italy. Noted scholars such as R. Aaron of Baghdad came from the Muslim East to Italy sometime between 850 and 860. He was welcomed by the Jewish community at the Christian-dominated port city of Gaeta.[88] This strongly suggests that Aaron was traveling on a Jewish ship since it is hardly likely that a Christian ship would have been found at the Muslim port from which he left, nor can we assume that a Muslim ship would have been well received at Gaeta. From Gaeta Aaron went on to Benevento and then to Oria. At Benevento he led religious services, and at Oria he served as a judge.[89] His ability to move freely is emphasized by later claims that he "served as a medium for the spread of Oriental mysticism to Northern Italy"[90] and by the fact that he was feted by Saudan the Muslim ruler of Bari in whose city the Jewish community flourished under Islamic rule as it had previously under Byzantine domination.[91] Perhaps it also should be noted that R. Aaron, after being permitted to travel throughout the peninsula, left for Baghdad from the port of Bari.[92]

As might be expected, the mobility enjoyed by Jews in Italy for cultural and religious purposes had an economic analogue. Trade was commonplace within Italy between Jews dwelling in areas dominated by the Byzantines, such as Oria, and those in cities that still were or had been part of the Carolingian empire such as Benevento.[93] Concerning long-distance trade, the Radanites, who have often been mentioned in the course of this study, continued during this period to flourish and to ply their trade in the Byzantine empire. It is clear that the government at Constantinople continued to favor these merchants since the capital city of the empire was one of their markets.[94]

In the Bulgar kingdom which was subject to both Carolingian and Byzantine influence Jewish traders were well received. The newly Christianized Bulgars were, in fact, in danger of Judaizing because their Jewish contacts apparently imbued them with a reverence for a literal interpretation of the Old Testament. Indeed Jews at court seem to have made sport of their amiable but ignorant barbarian hosts by baptizing them. In 866 the Bulgar prince, Michael Bogar, apparently became worried about what we must consider a hoax perpetrated by his Jewish familiars and wrote to Pope Nicholas requesting an opinion concerning the validity of a baptism performed by a Jew. Nicholas who was nothing if not politically astute warned the Bulgars to avoid Jewish or Judaizing practices and concluded for the benefit of the new converts that the baptisms performed by Jews were, indeed, valid.[95]

The favorable position enjoyed by Jews dwelling in the Byzantine environs of the Carolingian empire was attacked by the first of the Macedonian emperors, Basil I (867-886). Scholars do not agree about why Basil decided to pursue an anti-Jewish policy, nor are the sources clear concerning the policy's basic characteristics. Contemporaries and near contemporaries writing in Greek such as the continuator of Theophanes's chronicle described Basil's campaign in the following manner:

First he caught in his net for submission to Christ the . . . stubborn Jewish people. At the start he had them attend disputations . . . if they were persuaded that Christ stood higher than the Law and the Prophets, he ordered them . . . to be baptized. He offered to those who came high positions and promised them exemptions from the taxes with which they were burdened. He indicated that he would give official rank to men who lacked standing. Thus he freed many from their cloak of obstinacy and brought them to faith in Christ. After the emperor died, however, most of the Jews returned like dogs to their vomit.[96]

As described above by a supporter of the Macedonian dynasty, Basil's policy was one of pure and simple bribery. The emperor's contem-

Jewish Policy during the Dissolution 127

porary Christian critics attacked his Jewish policy of buying converts with gifts and promises. They not only condemned him for failing to ascertain whether a true conversion had taken place and for being hasty and immoral but pointed out that his actions were contrary to the canons.[97] It is implied in later Greek sources that whatever success Basil might have had with the Jews was due to his fondness for them.[98]

Although Basil's Greek supporters and his critics described his policy as one of nonviolent persuasion and bribery, later non-Greek sources indicate that the emperor became frustrated with his lack of early success and embarked upon a vigorous and violent empire-wide campaign of forced conversions. The basic evidence in support of the alleged second stage of Basil's policy is the mid-eleventh century Hebrew chronicle of the Ahimaaz family. According to this account the head of the family, Shefatiah, was called to Constantinople for a disputation. Shefatiah was well treated by Basil and even was provided with kosher food, but the Italian scholar remained convinced of the truth of Judaism. Then Basil became angry and decided upon a policy of forced conversion. His daughter, however, was ill, and the celebrated Shefatiah who was still at Constantinople effected a cure by exorcising the demon that possessed her. The grateful emperor then provided the Jews of Oria with an exemption from his order that all should be converted and presented Shefatiah with a diploma to that effect.[99]

The details of this encounter—Shefatiah's personal visit to Constantinople, his relations with the emperor, the cure of Basil's daughter, and the exemption granted to Oria—have the ring of a "pious legend." Nonetheless the course of events—attempted persuasion through disputation and kindness followed by failure and empire-wide persecution—have generally been accepted by scholars because of the apparent support found in tenth- and eleventh-century sources.[100] Two liturgical poems attributed by some scholars to Amittai, Shefatiah's son, and a penitential prayer attributed to their contemporary R. Silano of Venosa are often argued to lament Basil's persecution.[101] Yet even if it were assumed that these compositions referred to Basil's alleged persecution and were contemporary with it—and such a conclusion is in no way justified by the poetic evidence—[102] there are numerous contradictions between these works and the chronicle of Ahimaaz. For example, the chronicle indicates that R. Shefatiah's city of Oria was exempted from the persecution. Those scholars who interpret the poems attributed to Amittai and the prayer of R. Silano as referring to the persecution agree that these works show that the Jews of Oria suffered greatly. In fact, the attempt to identify these compositions with Basil's policy of forced conversions hinges in large part on the argument that the Jews of Oria were subject to vigorous persecution.[103]

It should be pointed out that in eleventh-century traditions as well as in later ones, Oria and often other Jewish communities were depicted as being exempted from the persecution because of Shefatiah's influence with Basil. These traditions, however, emphasized the cruelty of the persecution and the use of torture. In this context it became popular to depict the olive press as the primary instrument by which Jews were compelled to accept Christianity. Throughout the Hebrew sources that have even the most limited claim for consideration in the question of Basil's persecution we have seen two themes developed: the glory of the Ahimaaz family and the suffering of Jews.[104]

In the Hebrew sources there is not a single text that is incontrovertibly contemporary with Basil's alleged persecution. Not a single Greek text whether favorable to Basil or critical of him indicates that he ordered the forcible conversion of the Jews in the empire. A tenth-century Latin source does, however, indicate that the Emperor Basil "had many Jews baptized by force."[105] Basil's own official documents say nothing of forcing the Jews to convert. There is no decree or any reference to such a decree in any Greek source. In about 894 Leo VI, Basil's son and successor, issued a novel stating: "we desiring to supply that which our father did not, do hereby annul all the old laws enacted with reference to the Hebrews and command that they shall not dare to live in any other manner than in accordance with the pure and salutary Christian faith."[106]

Basil's laws issued and/or complied throughout the 870s and early 880s (the alleged period of persecution) in the *Procheiron*,[107] the *Epanagogē*[108] and the *Basilika Code*[109] did not go beyond the material in Justinian's *Code*. Although the last was certainly not pro-Jewish, it did include the following protections and rights which also were included in the *Basilika*:

Jewish Policy during the Dissolution 129

1. Christians must not disturb unoffending Jews. A Christian guilty of violence or theft is liable to a Jewish plaintiff for the object involved, plus double its value.[110]
2. Synagogues may not be used for the quartering of soldiers.[111]
3. If a civil case involves only Jewish litigants, they may have it decided by judges of their own choosing, the ruling to be upheld by the civil official.[112]
4. No non-Jew may be an overseer over Jews.[113]
5. Jews may not be required by law officers to desecrate their Sabbath or holidays.[114]
6. Violence to the persons of Jews, to their synagogues, or their homes is forbidden.[115]
7. Synagogues may be repaired.[116]
8. Jews may serve as guardians of non-Jews.[117]
9. It is permitted to the Jews to circumcise their own children.[118]

On the whole it seems doubtful that Basil ordered the forced conversion of the Jews of the empire. It is possible, however, that at some point in the later ninth century, perhaps during Basil's reign or perhaps during the reign of his son Leo VI (886-912), some Byzantine official may have made an inconsequential effort to advance an anti-Jewish policy. The traditional Jewish religio-historical view of such an effort — which Baron has aptly termed the lachrymose interpretation of history — mixed with pious legends, extolled in liturgical compositions, and linked to historical events during the Middle Ages ultimately found a place in the works of sympathetic modern scholars. These specialists have been willing to see the Jews of Byzantine Italy as having been crushed in the olive presses of Basil's fanatical persecution.[119]

On the Spanish frontier of the Carolingian empire the kingdom of Asturias continued to survive in an atmosphere of almost continual conflict. This warfare was waged not only by Christians against Muslims and vice versa but by a bewildering constellation of combinations of forces that paid little attention to religious affiliation. During this period when the Carolingian empire was in the process of dissolution, the Asturian rulers

Ordoño I (850-866) and Alfonso III (866-910) managed to expand their frontier as far south as the Duero River.[120] Sources with a clerical bias, especially later ones, have traditionally depicted even these early stages of the "Reconquest" as a holy war.[121] Some scholars, therefore, see the Asturian policy during this period as vigorously anti-Jewish. The Asturians are characterized as the "heirs of the Visigoths" and are said to have destroyed the synagogues they found, killed Jewish scholars, and burned their books.[122] Although it is possible and perhaps even probable that Jewish communities in enemy-held areas were subject to the same treatment that non-Jews received during and after a military campaign, there is simply no reason to believe that either Ramiro I (d. 850) or his successors Ordoño I and Alfonso III singled out the Jews in their own territories for harsh treatment.[123]

In fact when we begin to get a larger sample of documentary evidence toward the latter part of Alfonso's reign, a very different picture emerges. It is clear that these early successes in the "Reconquest" led to a vigorous pro-Jewish policy rather than to an anti-Jewish policy. The Asturian monarchs were in great need of people to settle the newly conquered areas, and they granted lands on favorable terms to both Christians and Jews.[124] The latter seems to have been settled in noteworthy numbers in the fertile valleys of the Torío and Bernesga rivers as well as in Galicia. In his conquests of Muslim-held towns like Coimbra where a Jewish community had been well established, Alfonso did not pursue an anti-Jewish policy of burning synagogues, murdering rabbis, and burning books.[125]

The period under discussion witnessed the dissolution of the Carolingian empire and the continued weakening of royal power to the advantage of the lay and ecclesiastical aristocracy. Despite this turmoil the Jewish policy that had been established by the early Carolingians and had been systematized by Louis the Pious was pursued by the latter's sons. The process of developing Carolingian Jewry law continued. This legislation tended toward treating Jews like the other peoples who lived under Carolingian rule, and this tendency was manifest in the elimina-

Jewish Policy during the Dissolution 131

tion of the restrictive Jewry provisions of the Roman law. Jewish merchant activity and immigration were also encouraged. This was especially evident in Carolingian Spain and seems to have been the case in *Francia Orientalis* as well. It is during this era that the Radanite traders based in southern Gaul seem to have flourished most vigorously.

The weakening of royal power made it possible for some elements within the "Church party" to have placed before the king an anti-Jewish program. These efforts such as the Paris Program in 846 and the attempts of the bishops at Pavia in 850 led to nothing. The former, indeed, was vigorously rejected in each and every point by Charles the Bald. The example of Agobard who had been humbled and humiliated by Louis the Pious may well have deterred other prelates who would otherwise have pursued illegal anti-Jewish policies. The unrewarded efforts undertaken by Archbishop Amulo and Archbishop Remigius illustrate the effectiveness of imperial policy and the difficulties placed in the path of Christian proselytism.

In the environs of the crumbling Carolingian empire, the Jewish communities of Byzantine Italy and Christian Spain not only flourished but in the latter area seem to have undergone substantial development. As King Alfonso III gained repeated successes in expanding his realm at the expense of the Muslims, he encouraged Jewish immigration with exceptionally attractive concessions. The oft-cited persecution attributed to Alfonso's contemporary, Basil I, the Byzantine emperor, turns out to have been much exaggerated and cannot be shown to have had a noteworthy effect in Italy where Jewish merchant activity and scholarly endeavor flourished.

CHAPTER VII

Conclusions

The division by scholars of medieval European history into three chronological periods: the early, high, and later Middle Ages, has led to the expectation that generalizations be formulated to characterize various aspects of these eras. In the present study, 400 years of Jewish policy have been examined and discussed for an area that includes most of Western Europe. During this period several hundred rulers from dozens of dynasties led scores of polities in the area under consideration. In light of the sheer number of persons involved in decision-making capacities and the varying circumstances in which each of them functioned, it seems hardly likely that many far-reaching generalizations concerning early medieval Jewish policy could emerge.

The Church, however, was one institution in which elements of common interest often overcame great diversity. The detailed examination of Church canons and of ecclesiastical pronouncements from the period discussed in this study makes clear that many important churchmen both individually and in council indicated that they feared the proselytizing carried on by Jews. These ecclesiastics were greatly worried by the attraction that various aspects of Judaism had for substantial numbers of both Christians and pagans. Therefore, it is not surprising that the thrust of conciliar legislation was aimed at protecting Christians from Jewish missionary activity and at eliminating Judaizing and Jewish customs followed by Christians.[1] On occasion stronger measures were

Conclusions 133

advocated, but there was no general consensus throughout the early Middle Ages in support of these efforts. For example, though some clerics advocated and even baptized Jews by force, this endeavor never received the support of the canons. Major clerical figures like Gregory the Great and Isidore of Seville condemned such acts and vigorously opposed them.

Much of the conciliar legislation during the early Middle Ages that concerned Jews was ignored because of the general political impotence of the Church. The efforts of the Church to influence those who exercised secular power to prevent Jews from owning Christian and pagan slaves, from holding governmental offices in which they exercised authority over Christians, from building new synagogues, and from carrying on missionary activity were on the whole unsuccessful. Thus throughout most of the period and in most of the regions under consideration the Jews flourished much to the distress of influential churchmen. The latter understood that Judaism posed a serious threat to the success of Christianity among the barbarians but could do little about the situation.

The Church often worked diligently to have secular rulers enact and pursue anti-Jewish policies that would result in the segregation of Jews from Christians as well as in the limitation of the economic and political activities of Jews. Few rulers, however, were so influenced during the four centuries discussed herein. In Italy, for example, none of the eight Ostrogothic rulers (493-554) pursued an anti-Jewish policy, and only one of the twenty-one Lombard kings (569-774) seems to have flirted with the idea of instituting such a program. Among the Visigoths who ruled part of Gaul and Spain, the twenty-eight monarchs from Euric (d. 484) to Roderic and Achila (ca. 711) were not, by and large, anti-Jewish. In fact, only six Visigothic kings can be shown to have formulated or pursued anti-Jewish policies. The Christian rulers of the tiny kingdoms in Spain that survived the Muslim conquest claimed to be successors of the Visigoths, and they pursued Jewish policies more like those of the majority of their putative predecessors than like those of the minority. In Merovingian Gaul, perhaps three of the eighteen kings who ruled from 481 to 639 pursued anti-Jewish policies. The thirteen *rois fainéants* (639-751), as might be expected, seem to have taken no anti-Jewish measures on their own. The mayors of the palace from the Carolingian house and the dukes of Aquitaine were manifestly pro-Jewish. The dukes, in fact, presumably dominated the part of Gaul that Julian of Toledo labeled a "brothel of blaspheming Jews." Of the thirty-one Byzantine emperors from Zeno to Basil I, three established anti-Jewish policies. It should be noted, however, that these policies were not enforced by imperial officials in Italy, the region with which we are concerned in this study. Therefore it seems reasonable to suggest that there was no real Byzantine anti-Jewish policy in Western Europe. The ten members of the Carolingian dynasty who ruled from 751 to 877 did not pursue anti-Jewish policies, and finally, the sixty-seven popes who served during the period covered in this work did not pursue a coordinated anti-Jewish policy although it might be argued, as noted above, that such a policy was formulated by the Church.[2] Thus, of the several hundred rulers of the various polities considered here perhaps twelve can be shown to have formulated and pursued anti-Jewish policies.

The value in terms of historical analysis of such a statistic is, however, dubious. For a substantial number of these rulers we have no positive evidence for any kind of Jewish policy; for others the evidence is circumstantial and hardly conclusive. It would seem, on the face of it, that we must withhold judgment concerning those rulers about whom the sources are silent.

Before abandoning the argument from silence, however, certain peculiarities concerning the nature of the surviving evidence should be examined. In general most of the Latin narrative sources from this period were written by clerics.[3] These authors, in distributing praise and blame, were wont to extol the virtues of rulers who served God and the Church and to condemn the vices of those who did not do so. In this context it was not regarded as good to be pro-Jewish. Individuals, however, who might be considered to have pursued anti-Jewish policies by bringing about the baptism of Jews or by refusing to rebuild synagogues were considered worthy of praise for these acts.[4] It should be noted, in addition, that a literary genre was developed in which a clerical writer who sought to praise his subject might well attribute to the ruler anti-Jewish policies whether or not he, in fact, had put forth any.[5]

Conclusions   135

In light of these literary predispositions it is not likely that very many anti-Jewish efforts went unnoticed in the Christian sources. Perhaps some such acts were falsely attributed to a would-be "hero" to enhance his image or serve as an *exemplum* for others.[6] Within the medieval Jewish historiographical and liturgical tradition there was a tendency to emphasize the suffering of the Jews in exile. Thus it was virtually obligatory to remember in detail each real or alleged case of victimization. Indeed it was not unusual for a modicum of exaggeration to surface in such situations. The lachrymose interpretation of history is not a malady confined to modern specialists.[7]

Conversely, in the Latin narrative sources information concerning an important individual who was pro-Jewish might be suppressed to "protect" his reputation. This clearly is the situation in the case of Emperor Louis who pursued a vigorous pro-Jewish policy as indicated by his official documents and contemporary letters. The three contemporary biographies devoted to praising him, however, completely ignore his Jewish policy; historians have given him the sobriquet "pious."[8]

It cannot and should not be argued from silence, however, that the absence of evidence for an anti-Jewish policy means that the individual in question pursued an overtly pro-Jewish policy. Paradoxically, if we were to rely on the narrative evidence alone, we would know nothing of Louis the Pious's pro-Jewish policy. It is safer, nevertheless, to conclude that someone pursued a pro-Jewish policy only if there are positive data or there is strong circumstantial evidence to that effect.

Among the several dozen important early medieval figures who have been shown to have pursued pro-Jewish policies, it is somewhat startling to realize that many of them were outstanding historical figures such as Theodoric the Great, Charles the Great, Gregory the Great, Reccared, Alfonso III, Pope Gelasius, and Brunhild. It is also remarkable that the Carolingians (the most successful dynasty in early medieval Europe) from Peppin I through Charlemagne, Louis the Pious, and Charles the Bald developed a vigorous and consistently pro-Jewish policy. The peculiar insights and talents that enabled these figures to leave such a substantial mark on the age in which they lived probably varied greatly from individual to individual. Clearly their pro-Jewish policies were not the source of their success. Yet could it be only coincidence that these impressive figures all pursued pro-Jewish policies?

Despite evidence for rare and invariably unsuccessful anti-Jewish policies, we should not lose sight of the major point that in terms of early medieval values and institutions most rulers were overwhelmingly pro-Jewish.[9] This observation rests upon the interpretation of several features of early medieval society that are very different from our own. From the point of view of the Church, given its *desiderata* in Jewish matters, any ruler who did not act forcefully to suppress close Jewish-Christian relations, keep Jews from prospering, and keep Judaism from flourishing may be considered to have been pro-Jewish. To ignore Jewish activity and neglect protecting Christians from Jews was in the eyes of many churchmen to be pro-Jewish. If a ruler did not work diligently to keep Jews in their proper place according to the canons, then he was guilty of giving them his tacit support.[10]

It must be remembered that the Church can be considered to have been at war with all those who obdurately refused to be orthodox Christians. Heretics were hunted down mercilessly, and pagans were tortured and terrorized until they accepted Christianity. Yet Judaism was given a protected legal status by the secular authority. If one compares, for example, Carolingian Jewish policy with Carolingian Saxon policy in religious matters, a great gulf is evident. The Saxons were required to become Christians and to abandon their pagan gods. Failure to convert was a capital offense, and apostasy was also subject to capital punishment. The vigor with which the Carolingians pursued their Saxon policy resulted in bloodletting of epic proportions, and although religion was not the only motivation in this campaign, it certainly held a prominent place.[11] In contrast, the Carolingian Jewish policy, like the Jewish policies of most early medieval rulers, permitted the Jews to pursue their religion freely—such tolerance was unique for any group when Christians dealt from a position of strength.

It may be suggested that the barbarian rulers who eagerly tried to deal the death blow to both heresy and paganism but generally guaranteed to the Jews religious tolerance were influenced to some degree

Conclusions   137

both by Roman law and by their Jewish subjects. The Roman codes protected the practice of Judaism as a religion and also recognized the Jews as a people with its own law. The barbarian monarchs who often ruled over diverse peoples with a plethora of tribal laws understood this principle of the personality of the law and therefore recognized the legitimacy of Jewish law just as they recognized Lombard, Saxon, or Salic law. In the case of the Jews, however, these barbarians grasped the essential characteristic that the Jewish law was (and remains) an inextricable part of Judaism as a religion, fundamental to the existence of the Jews as a people. By contrast, Charlemagne and Louis the Pious recognized the legitimacy of the Saxon law as the proper vehicle by which the Saxon people were to be judged but understood that their pagan religion could be divorced from their constitution without destroying their identity as a folk. They could retain their identity as a people and become Christians; this they did. The Jews, however, could not become Christians and retain their identity as a folk. That the barbarian rulers of Western Europe grasped this essential would seem evidence of close and friendly cooperation between the policy makers and learned Jews who were both articulate and influential.[12]

The barbarian rulers inherited a body of Roman Jewry law and a body of canon Jewry law that aimed at protecting Christians from Jews by limiting the activities of the latter not only in religious matters but in the economic and political arenas as well. The thrust of early medieval Jewish policy was the gradual elimination, both through overt legislation and through custom, of the limitations embodied in Roman and canon Jewry law. Early medieval Jewry law developed very slowly, and we see it most clearly in the official acts of the Carolingians. During the four centuries covered by this study, it is fair to conclude that barbarian Jewry law, as epitomized by Carolingian efforts, replaced the limitations of the restrictive Roman Jewry provisions and made Jews the legal equals of any other people in Western Europe. In religious affairs, the Jews enjoyed the unprecedented privilege of toleration. The position of the Jews in early medieval Europe is no better exemplified than in the confrontation of Lyons in which Louis the Pious imposed his pro-Jewish policy upon the recalcitrant Archbishop Agobard.

138   Conclusions

It is perhaps most difficult to develop convincing generalizations concerning why early medieval rulers pursued policies that intended to encourage and help the Jews when such policies led the monarchs to act contrary to the interest of Christianity as interpreted by many churchmen. Quite obviously, religion was not the rulers' most compelling motive. Even Louis the Pious who defended his pro-Jewish policy by maintaining that apostolic teaching "does not prohibit us from doing kindnesses also to all the rest [i.e., non-Christians], but exhorts, rather, that we pursue humbly the course of Divine mercy" hardly can be assumed to have established a vigorous religious warrant for his efforts in light of the ecclesiastical opposition that he faced.

Strong incentives must have been at work in early medieval Europe to encourage so many rulers, including men like Charlemagne, Theodoric the Great, and Gregory the Great, to pursue pro-Jewish policies. Perhaps these men realized that their efforts to rule would be enhanced by having the support of the well-organized Jewish communities that flourished in many of the *civitates* of Western Europe. Perhaps these men saw that the Jews were literate, learned in languages, and comparatively wealthy; that the Jewish communities had long-standing contacts with each other and with Jewish communities in the East; that Jewish merchants were useful to the economic development of their polities; that Jewish doctors were more advanced in their practice of medicine than their non-Jewish counterparts; that Jewish diplomats had advantages in dealing with non-Christian governments; and that Jewish fighting men served and fought well. In return for the support of the Jews, Christian rulers had only to protect Jewish religious freedom and legal autonomy.

The obvious advantage of having Jewish support very probably could be seen by even the less than great rulers in early medieval Western Europe. Thus it is not surprising that only a very few rulers chose to pursue anti-Jewish policies. Although these men generally received ecclesiastical approbation for their efforts, all the anti-Jewish policies launched during the early Middle Ages were failures. It has been shown throughout this study that secular figures who launched anti-Jewish campaigns were motivated in general by political and economic concerns rather than by religious ones. These anti-Jewish efforts follow a general pattern. The Jewish community committed its support to a particular faction or ruler. Then the opposition won and pursued an anti-Jewish policy to punish its enemies. In some cases, however, the victor did not seek revenge upon the Jews because they had opposed him. Thus, for example, the Visigoth, King Wamba, came to a rapprochement with the Jews after he defeated them and eliminated their candidate for the throne. Parenthetically it should be noted that the failure of secular anti-Jewish policies meant the failure of ecclesiastical efforts to have the restrictive Jewry provisions of the Roman and the canon law enforced.

It is important to emphasize the seriousness with which the Church regarded the Jewish threat. The ultimate victory of Christianity in Western Europe during the Middle Ages should not obscure the problems that the Church faced in winning that victory. If we understand that the canons were intended to deal with real problems the Church faced, it seems clear that ecclesiastics were not acting hysterically because of an insignificant Jewish threat. Rather, they saw Jews converting pagan and Christian slaves to Judaism; they saw Christians flocking to hear Jewish sermons; they encountered noteworthy numbers of Christians who Judaized by celebrating Jewish feasts, by resting on the Jewish sabbath, and by dining on Jewish-processed food. If, however, we do not understand the lamentation, legislation, and polemic that poured from ecclesiastical sources as evidence of real conditions, then we must postulate some sort of deeply seated collective religio-psychological fear that drove churchmen to attack a chimera. Although theories of a collective inferiority complex or institutional paranoia might appeal to social psychologists, it seems that historians are on safer ground if they see the behavior of churchmen in more mundane terms.[13] In short, the vigorous pro-Jewish policies pursued by many early medieval rulers and the abject failure suffered by the few who pursued anti-Jewish policies suggest that the churchmen of the early Middle Ages had fears based upon an accurate appraisal of events.[14] They were not flailing at fantasies but faced a serious and growing Jewish problem which they had no success in solving.

To conclude: early medieval rulers were fundamentally pro-Jewish in their policies as understood within the framework of contemporary val-

140 Conclusions

ues. Judaism was the only religion other than orthodox Christianity that was legally permitted. In light of the treatment by Christians of heretics, pagans, and Muslims the position accorded to Judaism is astounding. Throughout the early Middle Ages a general pattern of Jewish policy evolved that included the elimination of the restrictive Jewry provisions of the Roman law, the rejection of the anti-Jewish provisions of the canon law, and the cooperative development by secular rulers and their Jewish subjects of a Jewry law that gave Jews the same basic rights enjoyed by other national groups. Just as other peoples in early medieval society lived according to their national laws, so too the Jews were permitted also to live according to their own law. These pro-Jewish policies succeeded in general, and the Jewish population in Western Europe grew both by natural increase and by immigration from Muslim-controlled lands. Jewish communities flourished, Jewish scholarship advanced, and many new synagogues were built. Jewish merchants and landowners were encouraged by governmental protection. The efforts of various churchmen, individually and in council, to segregate Jews from Christians; to limit Jewish activities; and to restrict their social, economic, and religious endeavors failed as did the occasional secular anti-Jewish policy that was launched.

Notes and Bibliography

Abbreviations

AA SS: *Acta Sanctorum*, Brussels, 1643 ff.
AHR: *The American Historical Review*.
BEC: *Bibliothéque de l'Ecole des Chartes*.
BZ: *Byzantinische Zeitschrift*.
CJ: *Codex Justinianus*, ed. P. Krüger, II. Berlin, 1929.
CSHB: *Corpus Scriptorum Historiae Byzantinae*, ed. L. Dindorf, et al. Bonn, 1826-97, 48 vols.
EHR: *The English Historical Review*.
Hefele-Leclercq: Hefele, K. J. von, and Leclercq, H. *Histoire des conciles*. Paris, 1907-1913, 5 vols.
IRMA: *Ius Romanum Medii Aevi*.
Ius Graecoromanum, eds. J. and P. Zepos. Athens, 1931 and Darmstadt, 1962, 8 vols.
Jaffé-Wattenbach: *Regesta Pontificum Romanorum*, eds. P. Jaffé and G. Wattenbach. Leipzig, 1885.
JPOS: *Journal of the Palestine Oriental Society*.
JQR: *Jewish Quarterly Review*.
JRS: *Journal of Roman Studies*.
JSS: *Journal of Jewish Social Studies*.
Karl der Grosse: Lebenswerk und Nachleben, ed. W. Braunfels. Düsseldorf, 1965-1967, 4 vols.
LRE: Jones, A. H. M., *The Later Roman Empire*. Norman, Okla., 1962, 2 vols.
MA: *Le Moyen Âge*.
Mansi: *Sanctorum Conciliorum Nova et Amplissima Collectio*, ed. J. D. Mansi. Florence, 1759-1778, 53 vols.
MGH: *Monumenta Germaniae Historica*.
    AA: *Auctores Antiquissimi*.
    Cap: *Capitularia Regum Francorum*.
    Conc: *Concilia*.
    Dip. Kar: *Diplomata Karolinorum*.
    Epist: *Epistolae*.
    Form: *Formulae*.
    LL: *Leges*.
    SS: *Scriptores*.
    SRG: *Scriptores Rerum Germanicarum*.
    SRL: *Scriptores Rerum Langobardorum*.
    SRM: *Scriptores Rerum Merovingicarum*.
MGWJ: *Monatsschrift für Geschichte und Wissenschaft des Judentums*.
NA: *Neues Archiv der Gessellschaft für ältere deutsche Geschichtskunde*.
Nov: See *CJ*.

PAAJR: *Proceedings of the American Academy for Jewish Research*.
PL: *Patrologiae Cursus Completus: Series Latina*, ed. J. Migne. Paris, 1844-1864, 221 vols.
REJ: *Revue des études juives*.
RHD: *Revue historique de droit français et étranger*.
SRH: Baron, Salo, W., *A Social and Religious History of the Jews*. New York, 1952-1967, 2nd ed., vols. I-XI.
SSCI: *Settimane di Studio del Centro Italiano di Studi sull'alto Medioevo*.
WHJP: *The World History of the Jewish People*, second series, *Medieval Period — Dark Ages*, vol. II, ed. Cecil Roth, et al. London, 1966.

Notes

Preface

1. Yitzhak F. Baer, *Galut* (New York, 1947), trans. by Robert Warshow, p. 116.
2. Salo W. Baron, "The Jewish Factor in Medieval Civilization," *Ancient and Medieval Jewish History* (New Brunswick, N.J., 1972), p. 514, n. 55. The study is an expanded and annotated version of the presidential address delivered at the annual meeting of the American Academy for Jewish Research in 1941 and published in *PAAJR*, 12 (1942), 1-48. Baron first discussed the lachrymose conception in "Ghetto and Emancipation," *The Menorah Journal*, 14 (1928), 515-526, when he used the phrase "lachrymose theory" (p. 526). Since 1928 Baron has not abandoned his attack on "the eternal self-pity characteristic of Jewish historiography." For additional bibliography see "The Jewish Factor," p. 514, n. 55. In his review of the first edition of Baron's *SRH*, Yitzhak Baer, *Zion* (1937-1938), p. 291, vigorously assails the lachrymose characterization of Jewish historiography. He reinforces Baron's expectation that "it would not be readily accepted by the majority of Jewish scholars" ("The Jewish Factor," p. 513, n. 54) and attacks Baron for providing ammunition with which the anti-Semites can attack Jews. Although Baron's June 1928 attack on Jewish historiography has served as the basis for much recent rethinking on the subject, Cecil Roth, "Jewish History for Our Own Needs," *The Menorah Journal*, 14 (1928), 419-434, levied a far more fundamental and thoroughgoing attack along the same lines in the same journal only a month earlier. Baron and Roth's optimism about the future in the late 1920s, like that of many historians, was deeply affected by the emergence of Hitler and the Second World War. As will be seen *passim* neither Roth nor Baron fully overcame this nightmare in their writing of history. The Holocaust continues to reinforce the lachrymose conception. Bernard Weinryb, "Reappraisals in Jewish History," *Salo Wittmayer Baron Jubilee Volume* (Jerusalem, 1975), II, 939ff., provides a useful overview of many problems that bedevil the writing of Jewish history.

3. Baron, "The Jewish Factor," pp. 259, 265, vigorously opposes this tendency.
4. Baer, *Galut*, p. 16.
5. *The Jews in the Visigothic and Frankish Kingdoms of Spain and Gaul* (Cambridge, Mass., 1927), p. 11.
6. *Juifs et Chrétiens dans le monde occidental, 430-1096* (Paris, 1960), p. 105.
7. In general see the treatment of the historiography by Bernard S. Bachrach, "A Reassessment of Visigothic Jewish Policy, 589-711," *AHR*, 78 (1973), 11ff. See in addition, Jeremy Adams, "Ideology and the Requirements of 'Citizenship' in Visigothic Spain: The Case of the Judaei," *Societas*, 2 (1972), 317-332, and P. D. King, *Law and Society in the Visigothic Kingdom* (Cambridge, 1972), pp. 132ff.
8. See *SRH*, III, 47ff. on the Merovingians and p. 33 where Baron observes, "Perctarit's decree boded ill for the future of Jews"; and *SRH*, IV, 51ff. "Negatively too. The Carolingian legislation left a permanent imprint on Jewish life in Europe through Agobard s anti-Jewish outbursts, which it had provoked." Cf. Irving A. Agus, *The Heroic Age of Franco-German Jewry* (New York, 1969), and Arthur Zuckerman, *A Jewish Princedom in Feudal France, 768-900* (New York, 1972), who present dramatically exaggerated pictures of the power and influence of the Jews.
9. On the weakness of the Visigothic monarchy see Philip Grierson, "Election and Inheritance in Early Germanic Kingship," *Cambridge Historical Journal*, 7 (1941), 11-14, and R. D. Shaw, "The Fall of the Visigothic Power in Spain," *EHR*, 82 (1906), 212; and on the subjection of the Church Aloysius K. Ziegler, *Church and State in Visigothic Spain* (Washington, 1930), pp. 126-133, and J. N. Hillgarth, "Coins and Chronicles: Propaganda in Sixth Century Spain," *Historia*, 15 (1966), 500. On the *Regnum Francorum* see the works of C. de Clercq, *La législation réligieuse franque de Clovis à Charlemagne* (Louvain, 1936), and "La législation réligieuse franque depuis l'avènement de Louis le Pieux jusqu'aux Fausses Décrétales," *Revue du droit canonique*, 4 (1954), 371-404; 6 (1956), 144-162, 263-289, 340-372; 7 (1957), 15-48, Karl F. Morrison, *The Two Kingdoms, Ecclesiology in Carolingian Political Thought* (Princeton, 1964), and F. L. Ganshof, "L'Eglise et le pouvoir royal dans la monarchie franque sous Pépin III et Charlemagne," *SSCI*, 7 (1959), 95-141. On the strength of the Jewish communities and especially their wide distribution over much of the western part of the Roman empire see the toponymical evidence found in older works like G. Caro, *Sozial- und Wirtschaftsgeschichte der Juden im Mittelalter und der Neuzeit* (Leipzig, 1908),I; *Gallia Judaica. dictionnaire géographique de la France d'après les sources rabbiniques* (Paris, 1897), ed. H. Gross; and *Germania Judaica: von den ältesten Zeiten bis 1238*, 2nd ed. (Tübingen, 1963), eds. I. Elbogen et al. Bernhard Blumenkranz, "Les premières implantations de Juifs en France: du Ier au début du Ve siècle," *Comptes Rendus, Académie des Inscriptions et Belles-Lettres* (Paris, 1969), pp. 162-174, is very important not only for the information it presents but because of the method it suggests. Also for this period D. S. Blondheim, *Les parlers judéo-romans et la Vetus Latina* (Paris, 1925), is important. Fundamental from another point of view is W. G. Braude, *Jewish Proselyting* (Provi-

dence, R.I., 1940), pp. 24-25, who demonstrates that it was an active policy among Jews to convert others to their religion during the first five centuries of the Christian era, but cf. Cecil Roth, "Economic Life and Population Movements," *WHJP*, II, 390.

10. Lynn T. White, Jr., *Medieval Technology and Social Change* (Oxford, 1962), p. 2, observed: "The historian of Frankish institutions too often recalls to the wearied mind Eliza on the ice: hypothesis clutched to bosom, he leaps from suspect charter to ambiguous capitulary, the critics baying at his heels." This may be generalized to the early Middle Ages.

11. Gavin I. Langmuir, "Majority History and Post-Biblical Jews," *AHR*, 27 (1966), 362.

12. *Karl der Grosse: Lebenswerk und Nachleben*, ed. W. Braunfels (Düsseldorf, 1965-1967). An excellent discussion of this work and of Charlemagne historiography in general is Donald Bullough, *"Europae Pater*: Charlemagne and His Achievements in Light of Recent Scholarship," *EHR*, 65 (1970), 59-105.

13. Peter Classen, "Karl der Grosse, das Papsttum und Byzanz," pp. 537-608; Walthar Björkman, "Karl und der Islam," pp. 672-682; J. M. Wallace-Hadrill, "Charlemagne and England," pp. 683-698; and Josef Deér, "Karl der Grosse und der Untergang des Awarenreiches," pp. 719-791, all in volume I, of *Karl der Grosse*.

14. "Barbarians," "Childebert," "Chlotaire II," "Reccared," and "Sisebut," *Encyclopaedia Judaica* (Jerusalem, 1972), vol. 4, cols. 205-206; vol. 5, cols. 422-423, 616-617; vol. 13, cols. 1608-1609; and vol. 14, col. 621.

Chapter I

1. Katz, *Jews in Spain and Gaul*, p. 10; James Parkes, *The Conflict of the Church and the Synagogue* (London, 1934), pp. 351-353; Ziegler, *Church and State*, pp. 186-189, E. A. Thompson, *The Goths in Spain* (Oxford, 1969), pp. 52-54; King, *Law and Society*, p. 132, n. 3; Baron, *SRH*, III, 35-36; Jean Juster, "La condition légale des juifs sous les rois visigoths," *Études d'histoire juridique offertes à Paul Frédéric Girard*, II (Paris, 1913), 275ff. More generally on the Visigoths see Dietrich Claude, *Geschichte der Westgoten* (Stuttgart, 1970) and the older work by Felix Dahn, *Die Könige der Germanen* (Leipzig, 1885), IV.

2. Sidonius Apollinaris, *Epist.*, III, iv (p. 43); IV, v (p. 57); VI, xi (p. 100). Katz, *Jews in Spain and Gaul*, pp. 23, 127, 131; Bernhard Blumenkranz, *Les auteurs chrétiens latins du moyen âge sur les juifs et le judaïsme* (Paris, 1963), p. 43; Blumenkranz, *Juifs et Chrétiens*, pp. 44, 156; and Parkes, *Church and Synagogue*, p. 343.

3. Canon 40 (Mansi, VIII, cols. 331-332). Parkes, *Church and Synagogue*, pp. 319-320, and Katz, *Jews in Spain and Gaul*, p. 55.

4. Jean Juster, *Les Juifs dans l'empire romain* (Paris, 1914), I, 186, n. 11; II, 247-248; and Bachrach, "Visigothic Jewish Policy," p. 13.

5. *V. Caesar.*, chs. 29, 30 (pp. 467ff.). Cf. Katz, *Jews in Spain and Gaul*, p. 121.

6. Thompson, *The Goths*, p. 54.

7. Canon 34 (Mansi, VIII, col. 330). Cf. Baron, *SRH*, III, 245, n. 43.

8. *LRV*, 2.8.3; 2.1.10 with regard to legal and religious protections and 3.15; 3.72; 9.4.4; 16.4.1 and 2; are examples of laws meant to keep Jews from proselyting. This legislation will be discussed in detail in chapter III since its importance is basically for the *Regnum Francorum*.

9. *V. Caesar.*, ch. 32 (p. 469) on ransom. Cf. Blumenkranz, *Auteurs chrétiens*, p. 63, n. 6. For the Council of Orange see the discussion by Parkes, *Church and Synagogue*, p. 320.

10. Baron, *SRH*, III, 245, n. 42.

11. For a detailed review of the early literature on the subject see Katz, *Jews in Spain and Gaul*, pp. 171-178. More recent studies have not varied greatly from this basic approach. See Thompson, *The Goths*, pp. 315-316; Baron, *SRH*, III, 36ff., King, *Law and Society*, p. 132; and Adams, "Ideology," pp. 317-332. Cf. Bachrach, "Visigothic Jewish Policy," pp. 11-34, for an overall new interpretation and especially pp. 11-12 for a review of the literature.

12. III Tolet., canon 14. And *LV*, xii, 2.12. Blumenkranz, *Juifs et Chrétiens*, p. 106; Juster, "La condition légale," II, 319, and Thompson, *The Goths*, p. 111.

13. Thompson, *The Goths*, p. 111.

14. Gregory I, *Epist.*, IX, 228. This letter indicates that Pope Gregory believed that Reccared refused bribes from Jews. Whether Reccared did, in fact, refuse bribes we do not know. See Bachrach, "Visigothic Jewish Policy," pp. 14-16, and cf. Baron, *SRH*, III, 246, n. 44.

15. Braude, *Jewish Proselyting*, chap. 9. The framers of canon 14 at III Toledo demonstrate a fundamental lack of understanding of Jewish customs. The idea of "mixed" marriages so common today, i.e., a marriage of a Jew to a non-Jew, is inconceivable in early medieval Jewish law. Jews could marry converts to Judaism, though the latter were often discriminated against. Cf. Baron, *SRH*, III, 246.

16. The absence of *Responsa* literature from Visigothic Spain on these points makes any conclusion on the reaction of the Hispano-Jewish community to Reccared's law no more than conjecture. A study of a sample of more than 300 *Responsa* concerning Jews in pre-Crusade Europe indicates that the problems created by the offspring of the Jewish mistresses of Christian men were of no great significance. In short, they were not even mentioned. On these *Responsa* see Irving A. Agus, *Urban Civilization in Pre-Crusade Europe* (Leiden, 1965), 2 vols. The effect of the decisions by the *Geonim* of Sura and Pumpedita on the Jewish community in Visigothic Spain is yet to be explored. The controversial decision made by Natronai Gaon of Sura concerning the sons of Bustenai (fl. ca. 660) by his Persian "slave" Dara may be of interest in the present context. See Ben Zion Wacholder, "The Halakah and the Proselyting of Slaves during the Gaonic Era," *Historica Judaica*, 18 (1956), 99-101.

17. Thompson, *The Goths*, p. 111; cf. Juster, "Condition légale," p. 308.

18. Conc. Narbon., canons 4, 9, 14. Thompson, *The Goths*, p. 112; Katz, *Jews in Spain and Gaul*, pp. 59, 71, 76, 112; and Jean Régne, *Étude sur la condition des juifs de narbonne du ve au xive siécle* (Narbonne, 1912), pp. 6-8.

19. Gregory, I, *Epist.*, VII, 21.

20. IV Tolet., canon 58. The records of five provincial synods survive from

Reccared's reign (Seville 590, Saragossa 592, Toledo 597, Huesca 598, and Barcelona 599), and no anti-Jewish acts were passed at any of them. See Thompson, *The Goths*, p. 112.

21. Thompson, *The Goths*, p. 103; Cf. Franz Görres, "Könige Rekared und das Judentum (586-601)," *Zeitschrift für wissenschaftliche Theologie*, 49 (1891), 284-296.

22. IV Tolet., canon 58 and *LV*, xii, 2.13. Katz, *Jews in Spain and Gaul*, p. 11; Franz Görres, "Die Religionspolitik des Westgotenkönigs Witterich (reg. 603-610)," *Zeitschrift für wissenschaftliche Theologie*, 49 (1898), 102-105; and Thompson, *The Goths*, pp. 157-161.

23. *LV*, xiii, 2.13 and 14. Thompson, *The Goths*, pp. 165-167.

24. Katz, *Jews in Spain and Gaul*, pp. 12-13, 25, and Thompson, *The Goths*, pp. 166-168.

25. Hillgarth, "Coins and Chronicles," p. 500, n. 6; Ziegler, *Church and State*, p. 190; and Thompson, *The Goths*, p. 166, all argue against Byzantine influence on Sisebut's policy. Cf. Paul Goubert, "Administration de l'Espagne Byzantine," *Revue des Études Byzantines*, 4 (1946), 120. Baron, *SRH*, III, 37, declares that Sisebut's policy is "unexplained," but suggests (pp. 38, 246, n. 46) that he was influenced by the "Byzantine Jews' 'betrayal' to the Persians and worse their attacks on Christians." This is a reasonable hypothesis insofar as it helps to establish the ambience in which the new policy was formulated. Yet we may presume that Sisebut's Orthodox predecessors also knew of Jewish power, influence, and rough treatment of Christians in the East, and these monarchs did not pursue anti-Jewish policies.

26. Thompson, *The Goths*, p. 165, argues that "Sisebut's Christian piety" was the motivating force in the formulation of his anti-Jewish policy.

27. Ziegler, *Church and State*, p. 92.

28. Thompson, *The Goths*, p. 163, notes that Sisebut's "*Life* of St. Desiderius of Vienne is a competent work of hagiography and also of political propaganda." See also Bachrach, "Visigothic Jewish Policy," p. 17.

29. Sisebut, *Epist.*, 9. Wallace-Hadrill, *Early Germanic Kingship*, p. 30. Cf. Thompson, *The Goths*, p. 163.

30. Ziegler, *Church and State*, p. 190, for Isidore's opposition to the policy of forced conversions. Cf. Baron, *SRH*, III, 39, 247, n. 47.

31. Parkes, *Church and Synagogue*, pp. 370-371. Cf. Ziegler, *Church and State*, pp. 190, 198.

32. Thompson, *The Goths*, p. 166, and Ziegler, *Church and State*, p. 190.

33. Aurasius, *Epist.*, 20; *LV*, xii, 2.15. Parkes, *Church and Synagogue*, p. 355; Katz, *Jews in Spain and Gaul*, p. 34; and Blumenkranz, *Juifs et Chrétiens*, p. 61. Cf. Thompson, *The Goths*, p. 166.

34. IV Tolet., canons 57, 59, 65. Thompson, *The Goths*, p. 178; Katz, *Jews in Spain and Gaul*, pp. 13, 50, 75; Juster, "Condition légale," p. 280; and Franz Görres, "Die Religionspolitik des spanischen Westgotenkönigs Swinthila, des ersten katholiken 'Leovigild' (621-631)," *Zeitschrift für wissenschaftliche Theologie*, 49 (1908), 253-266. Cf. Ziegler, *Church and State*, p. 190. Cf. Baron, *SRH*, III, 40.

35. Cf. Thompson, *The Goths*, p. 168. This is only a conjecture, but Isidore,

Notes   149

who recounts Suinthila's accession, completed his history of the Goths while that king was still on the throne. For his account see Isidore, *Historia Gothorum*, chs. 61-65.

36. IV Tolet., canons 65, 66, 59, 63, 62, 64. Thompson, *The Goths*, pp. 178-179, and Katz, *Jews in Spain and Gaul*, pp. 13, 50, 118. Cf. Adams, "Ideology," p. 325.

37. Thompson, *The Goths*, pp. 178-179, and Katz, *Jews in Spain and Gaul*, p. 13.

38. IV Tolet., canon 58. See the discussion by Thompson, *The Goths*, p. 179.

39. Thompson, *The Goths*, pp. 181-182.

40. *Ibid.*

41. *Ibid.*, pp. 183-184.

42. The pope's letter has not survived, and we have only Bishop Braulio's answer to it (*Epist.* 21, cols. 667-670). See C. H. Lynch, *Saint Braulio, Bishop of Saragossa (631-651)* (Washington, D.C., 1938), pp. 55-56, 100-102, 131-132, 145-147; Dahn, *Die Könige*, VI, 641-650; and Thompson, *The Goths*, pp. 184-185. Cf. E. A. Synan, *The Popes and the Jews in the Middle Ages* (New York, 1965), pp. 57-58.

43. IV Tolet., canon 3, and *LV*, xii, 2.17; 3.14 and 15. For the text of the *Placitum*, see Dahn, *Die Könige*, VI, 650-653. Also see the discussion by Katz, *Jews in Spain and Gaul*, p. 14; Lynch, *Bishop Braulio*, p. 130; and Thompson, *The Goths*, p. 186.

44. Thompson, *The Goths*, pp. 196ff.

45. *Ibid.*, pp. 188-189.

46. *Ibid.*, pp. 190-199; Katz, *Jews in Spain and Gaul*, pp. 14-15; Parkes, *Church and Synagogue*, p. 358; and Juster, "Condition légale," p. 282. Also see *LV*, xii, 2.16.

47. *LV*, xii, 2.16. Thompson, *The Goths*, pp. 196-197: "His aim was to prevent proselytism." The Seventh Council of Toledo which Chindasuinth called in 646 took no action against the Jews and did not even reaffirm the anti-Jewish acts of the Fourth Council. See also Katz, *Jews in Spain and Gaul*, p. 14. Cf. Parkes, *Church and Synagogue*, p. 359.

48. Thompson, *The Goths*, pp. 199-217.

49. VIII Tolet., *Tomus* (ed. by Zeumer, *leg.* i), also canons 10, 12, and *LV*, xii, 2.2-11. Katz, *Jews in Spain and Gaul*, pp. 15-16; Parkes, *Church and Synagogue*, pp. 359-362; Blumenkranz, *Juifs et Chrétiens*, pp. 331-333; Ziegler, *Church and State*, p. 193; and Thompson, *The Goths*, pp. 206-207.

50. Parkes, *Church and Synagogue*, pp. 360-361.

51. IX Tolet., canon 17.

52. X Tolet., canon 7. Juster, "Condition légale," p. 291, recognizes that the wealth of the Jewish community, "la force de l'argent des persècutès," was a factor in their successful avoidance of the law. Yet Juster does not grasp the overall importance of the Jews as a faction on the political scene. See also Thompson, *The Goths*, pp. 208-209.

53. Thompson, *The Goths*, p. 208.

54. Katz, *Jews in Spain and Gaul*, p. 15.

55. *Isid. Contin. Hisp.*, 35: "licet flagitiosum, tamen bonimotum filium." Cf.

Thompson, *The Goths*, p. 199, who translates the above as "amiable and debauched."

56. Thompson, *The Goths*, pp. 200-201.
57. Braulio, *Epist.*, 37. Cf. Thompson, *The Goths*, p. 198.
58. Lynch, *Bishop Braulio*, pp. 131-135.
59. *Ibid.*, pp. 135-140; Thompson, *The Goths*, p. 201. Braulio, *Epist.*, 38, 39, 40.
60. Eugenius, *Carm.*, XXV. See Thompson, *The Goths*, p. 199, who forcefully rejects the suggestion that "the poet wrote this scurrilous epitaph at the King's own request and that it is nothing more than a monument of the old sinner's repentance." See also Lynch, *Bishop Braulio*, p. 137.
61. Thompson, *The Goths*, pp. 199-200.
62. *Ibid.*, p. 208.
63. Julian, *Historia.*, chs. 5-13. 15, 26, 28; Julian, *Insultatio*, ch. 5; Julian, *Iudicium*, chs. 2-4; Lucas of Tuy, *Liber de historia*, ch. 6 (col. 767). On this last text see Katz, *Jews in Spain and Gaul*, pp. 16-17, n. 8, and also in a more general vein, Thompson, *The Goths*, pp. 219-231.
64. Julian, *Insultatio*, chs. 1-2; *Historia*, ch. 5. See Katz, *Jews in Spain and Gaul*, p. 17, and Thompson, *The Goths*, p. 228.
65. Thompson, *The Goths*, p. 220. On the general topic of capitals in the early Middle Ages see E. Ewig, "Résidence et capitale pendant le haut moyen âge," *Revue historique*, 230 (1963), 25-72.
66. Katz, *Jews in Spain and Gaul*, pp. 148-151; Thompson, *The Goths*, p. 248; and Régné, *Juifs de Narbonne*, pp. 10ff. Cf. Ziegler, *Church and State*, p. 194.
67. *LV*, xii, 3.1-3.28. Parkes, *Church and Synagogue*, pp. 362-365, and Thompson, *The Goths*, pp. 234-237.
68. *LV*, xii, 3.10, 17, 19, 21, 24, and 25. Thompson, *The Goths*, pp. 236-237, and Parkes, *Church and Synagogue*, pp. 365-366.
69. *LV*, xii, 3.28. Cf. King, *Law and Society*, pp. 133ff.
70. XVII Tolet., canon 8, Thompson, *The Goths*, pp. 247-248.
71. Ziegler, *Church and State*, p. 114, and F. X. Murphy, "Julian of Toledo and the Fall of the Visigothic Kingdom in Spain," *Speculum*, 27 (1952), 1.
72. Thompson, *The Goths*, pp. 230-231, and Murphy, "Julian of Toledo," pp. 1-2. XII Tolet., *Tomus*.
73. Paul à Wengen, *Julianus, Erzbischof von Toledo* (St. Gall, 1891), pp. 31-39; Katz, *Jews in Spain and Gaul*, p. 17; and A. Helfferich, *Entstehung und Geschichte des Westgothen-Rechts* (Berlin, 1858), p. 192. Cf. Murphy, "Julian of Toledo," pp. 2-7, 13-14.
74. See Thompson, *The Goths*, pp. 228-229; Ziegler, *Church and State*, pp. 116-117, and the older works cited by Murphy, "Julian of Toledo," p. 2. Cf. Murphy's own conclusions, pp. 17-19.
75. Thompson, *The Goths*, p. 231; cf. Murphy, "Julian of Toledo," pp. 3-4, 17-19.
76. Ziegler, *Church and State*, pp. 114-117, and the works discussed there. Cf. Murphy, "Julian of Toledo," pp. 12-13.
77. XII Tolet., canons 1,2.

78. *Ibid.*, canon 9. See Ziegler, *Church and State*, p. 117.
79. Thompson, *The Goths*, pp. 242-245.
80. XVI Tolet., *Tomus*, and canon 1; *LV*, xii, 2.18. Ziegler, *Church and State*, p. 195, and Baron, *SRH*, III, 45. Cf. King, *Law and Society*, p. 199.
81. Thompson, *The Goths*, pp. 247-248; Katz, *Jews in Spain and Gaul*, pp. 148-151; and Ziegler, *Church and State*, pp. 198-199, who concludes concerning the entire Visigothic anti-Jewish effort: "Tragic as the whole policy was, it was ridiculously ineffective."
82. Thompson, *The Goths*, p. 245, and Ziegler, *Church and State*, pp. 126, 128.
83. XVII Tolet., *Tomus*, and canon 8. Thompson, *The Goths*, pp. 247-248. Egica exempted the Jews of Septimania from the decree of enslavement. It seems that he knew that he could not enforce his anti-Jewish policy there and simply refrained from trying. Cf. Katz, *Jews in Spain and Gaul*, p. 21, n. 5.
84. Thompson, *The Goths*, pp. 247, 315-316. Cf. Katz, *Jews in Spain and Gaul*, p. 21; Parkes, *Church and Synagogue*, pp. 368-369; Rafael Altamira, "Spain under the Visigoths," in *The Cambridge Mediaeval History*, ed. H. M. Gwatkin, et al. (Cambridge, 1926), II, 181.
85. *Isid. Contin. Hisp.*, 53: "his Gothos acerva morte persequitur." Thompson, *The Goths*, p. 243.
86. This tradition is quite old; see, for example, Solomon ibn Verga, *Shebet Yehudah*, pp. 56-59. This fifteenth-century Jewish historian portrays the Jewish reaction to Sisebut's anti-Jewish policy as one of lamentation. He contends that a group of Jews, crying and moaning, begged for an audience with the king and tried to debate the theological validity of the royal policy. Jules Tailhan, "La ruine de l'Espagne gothique," *Revue des questions historiques*, 31 (1882), 384-386, provides a variation on this theme in arguing that the Jews were naturally too timid to be involved in a conspiracy to overthrow the Visigothic kingdom.
87. Altamira, "Spain under the Visigoths," p. 182; Luis G. de Valdeavellano, *Historia de España* (Madrid, 1952), I. 1, 359-361; and Thompson, *The Goths*, pp. 248-249.
88. Lucas of Tuy, *Chron.*, bk. III, era DCCXXIII (IV, 69-70).
89. Heinrich Graetz, "Die westgothische Gesetzgebung in Betreff der Juden," *Jahresbericht des judisch-theologischen Seminars: Fraenckelscher Stiftung* (Breslau, 1858), p. 19, but see his later work, *Geschichte der Juden von den ältesten Zeiten bis auf die Gegenwart* (4th ed.; Leipzig, 1909), V, 156.
90. Dahn, *Die Könige*, V, 231-242; VI, 421.
91. Katz, *Jews in Spain and Gaul*, p. 22; Ziegler, *Church and State*, p. 196; and J. E. Scherer, *Die Rechtsverhältnisse der Juden in den deutsch-österreichischen Ländern* (Leipzig, 1901), p. 26.
92. Lucas's work is in need of a new critical edition and further study. See the brief bibliographical note in Valdeavellano, *Historia de España*, I. 1, 54-55.
93. Altamira, "Spain under the Visigoths," p. 182, notes Witiza's connection with Tuy and also places a great deal of faith in Lucas's chronicle.
94. Gonzalo Martinez Díez, *La colección canónica Hispana* (Madrid, Barcelona, 1966), I, 166ff. Ziegler, *Church and State*, pp. 121-122; and Thompson, *The*

152 Notes

Goths, p. 249. Cf. the extreme position taken by Franz Görres, "Das Judentum im westgotischen Spanien von König Sisebut bis Roderich (612-711)," *Zeitschrift für wissenschaftliche Theologie*, 48 (1905), 361: "Die Acten des letzten (18) Toletanums, das unter dem viel verleumdeten König Witiza (701-710) stattfand, sind verloren gegangen, wahrscheinlich durch klerikale Fanatiker beseitigt." For a fuller presentation of this position, see Franz Görres, "Charakter und Religionspolitik des vorletzten spanischen Westgotenkönigs Witiza," *Zeitschrift für wissenschaftliche Theologie*, 48 (1905), 96-111.

95. Altamira, "Spain under the Visigoths," pp. 182-183; Valdeavellano, *Historia de España*, I. 1, 361-363; Shaw, "Visigothic Power in Spain," pp. 215-216; and Thompson, *The Goths*, pp. 215-216.

96. *Isid. Contin. Hisp.*, 74.

97. E. de Saavedra, *Estudio sobre la invasión de los árabes en España* (Madrid, 1892), provides the generally accepted view of the events of the conquest. See also Valdeavellano, *Historia de España*, I. 1, 361-363; Altamira, "Spain under the Visigoths," pp. 183ff., Thompson, *The Goths*, pp. 249-251; Shaw, "Visigothic Power in Spain," pp. 223-228; and Juster, "Condition légale," p. 298, n. 1. On the numismatic evidence, see George C. Miles, *The Coinage of the Visigoths of Spain: Leovigild to Achila II* (New York, 1952), pp. 40ff., 444ff.

98. The generally accepted reconstruction of the events of the conquest established by Saavedra (n. 97, above) is summarized by Altamira, "Spain under the Visigoths," pp. 183ff. Concerning the alliance of Christians and Muslims he writes (p. 184): "This connexion between the Muslims and the sons of Witiza is confirmed by all the chroniclers, and forms a trustworthy starting-point for the history of the invasion."

99. See, for example, Américo Castro, *España en su Historia: cristianos, moros y judiós* (Buenos Aires 1948).

100. Katz, *Jews in Spain and Gaul*, pp. 32-41, reviews the anti-Jewish literature.

101. Thompson, *The Goths*, p. 316.

Chapter II

1. See below note 49.

2. Gelasius, *Epist.*, col. 146. For the date see Jaffé-Wattenbach, *Regesta*, I, no. 654.

3. Gelasius, *Epist.*, cols. 146-147. For the date see Jaffé-Wattenbach, *Regesta*, I, no. 742. For further material on Jewish ownership of Christian slaves in Theodoric's kingdom and in Rome see Cassiodorus, *Varia.*, IV, 43.

4. Note the list of legislation in the *Theodosian Code* concerning Jews in Parkes, *Church and Synagogue*, pp. 379-381, and *CTh.*, III, 1.5; VIII, 16.24; XII, 1.99; XVI, 8.1.2; XVI, 9.1 and 2; *Const. Sirm.*, 6; and *Th. Nov.*, 3, for the laws dealing with Jewish ownership of slaves, proselytism, and rank.

5. On Telesinus's relationship with Pope Gelasius see Katz, *Jews in Spain and Gaul*, pp. 120, 138, and Blumenkranz, *Juifs et Chrétiens*, p. 44. On the question of Telesinus's status see the discussion by Baron, *SRH*, III, 27, 241-242, and the works cited there. Although it is certainly rash to generalize about Jews of high

Notes 153

rank from the example of Telesinus, it is statistically improbable that evidence of his existence would have survived if he were the only one of high rank. Further, if Jews of the senatorial class were very rare, one might expect Gelasius to have treated the matter in some way to have illuminated this situation.

6. On Theodoric's legislation in general see Wilhelm Ensslin, *Theoderich der Grosse* (Munich, 1947), pp. 227-243; A. H. M. Jones, "The Constitutional Position of Odoacer and Theodoric," *JRS*, 51 (1961), 126-130; and Jones, *LRE*, I, 254. Since 1953 some have argued that this edict was not issued under the auspices of Theodoric the Great. By the early 1960s a small group of revisionists agreed that the Visigothic ruler Theodoric was responsible for it ca. 460. The case for this position is made fully by its most ardent protagonist Giulio Vismara, "Edictum Theoderici," *IRMA*, part I, 2b aa a (Milan, 1967) with a full review of the literature. It should be emphasized, however, that even Vismara admits in his conclusion (p. 190) that the solution he proposes does not establish the revisionists' position as a certainty. Rather he notes that the entire problem is a question of probabilities. Georges Chevrier and Georges Pieri, "La roi romaine des burgondes," *IRMA*, part I, ab aa d (Milan, 1969), p. 5, n. 1, do not seem to be convinced by the arguments put forth by Vismara; and J. Gaudemet, "Le Bréviaire d'Alaric et les epitomes," *IRMA*, part I, 2b aa b (Milan, 1965), p. 7, appears to reserve judgment. A long list of those who vigorously oppose the revisionist position as well as the shorter list of those who support it can be found in the works cited above.

7. Theodoric, *Edict*, 143. Baron, *SRH*, III, 26, notes that Theodoric and Cassiodorus strengthened Jewish judicial autonomy by omitting the restrictions of previous legislation but concludes that Theodoric and still more his chancellor Cassiodorus gave the Jews this additional power by accident. To conclude that both Cassiodorus and Theodoric were ignorant of the true meaning and significance of edict 143 is unreasonable.

8. The nature and intent of Theodoric's legislation are crucial to the discussion of his Jewish policy. Theodoric's stated intention of leaving the old law in force (see note 5 above) is contradicted by the specific substance of several sections of the new promulgations. In general it is agreed that the ability of imperial officials to enforce the provisions of the *Theodosian Code* with regard to the limitations placed upon Jews was curtailed. See Juster, *Les Juifs dans l'empire romain*, II, 250, 263ff., and Baron, *SRH*, III, 142. Cf. Ensslin, *Theoderich der Grosse*, pp. 327, 390, n. 3 for example.

9. *Anon. Vales.*, II, xvi, 94. Blumenkranz, *Juifs et Chrétiens*, pp. 41, 181, 390, and Baron, *SRH*, III, 141. Cf. Ensslin, *Theoderich der Grosse*, p. 390, n. 3.

10. Cassiodorus, *Varia*, II, 27. Cf. Vismara, "Edictum Theoderici," p. 42, attempts to show that this letter contradicts the *Edictum*, no. 143 by arguing that Theodoric abridged, in part, the Jews' privilege to live according to their own law by making them subject to the will of the king. Not only does this argument miss the main point of Cassiodorus's letter, but it is a very weak reed, indeed, in building an argument against Ostrogothic sponsorship of the *Edictum Theoderici*. It is perhaps more revealing that Vismara ignores the other letters of Cassiodorus concerning the Jews (see below) that clearly are consistent with the *Edictum* no. 143.

11. *CTh.*, XVI, 8.22, 25, 27 and *Th. Nov.*, 3.3 and 5.
12. See Katz, *Jews in Spain and Gaul*, p. 74, and Andrew Sharf, *Byzantine Jewry from Justinian to the Fourth Crusade* (London, 1971), p. 22.
13. *Anon. Vales.*, II, xiv, 80, line ff.; Procopius, *BG.*, I, x, 24ff. On the prohibitions see *CTh.*, XVI, 8.16.
14. Cassiodorus, *Varia*, IV, 33.
15. Katz, *Jews in Spain and Gaul*, pp. 73-76, gathers all the data on such violence and confounds it in drawing a generally bleak picture. Parkes, *Church and Synagogue*, p. 207, treats Theodoric in his historical context and provides a more reasonable view of events.
16. Cassiodorus, *Varia.*, IV, 43.
17. *Anon. Vales.*, II, xiv, lines 80ff. There has been much discussion of the sentence "Quare Judaei baptizatos nolentes, dum ludent frequenter oblatam aquam in aquam fluminis iactaverunt." See Parkes, *Church and Synagogue*, p. 207, n. 2, and compare Baron, *SRH*, III, 241. The latter's translation of "dum ludent" as "while playing" misses the nuance intended by the author and should be understood as "while mocking." Cf. G. B. Picotti, "Osservationi su alcuni punti della politica religiosa di Teoderico," *SSCI*, 3 (1955), 201ff.
18. Cassiodorus, *Varia.*, V, 37.
19. *Anon. Vales.*, II, xiv, lines 80ff.
20. Cassiodorus, *Varia*, II, 27.
21. Sharf, *Byzantine Jewry*, pp. 44-45.
22. *Ibid.*, pp. 44ff.
23. See, for example, Baron, *SRH*, III, 241; Parkes, *Church and Synagogue*, p. 207, fails to grasp fully Theodoric's bias in favor of the Jews.
24. A good and easily available account of Justinian's wars is to be found in Jones, *LRE*, I, 269-278, 287-294 (the Gothic wars are treated *passim*).
25. Procopius, *BG*, I, ix, 3-6.
26. *Ibid.*, I, ix, x, *passim*. Procopius's lack of surprise at Jews engaging in military operation would seem to strengthen the notion that situations similar to that at Naples were not uncommon. E. A. Thompson, "The Barbarian Kingdoms in Gaul and Spain," *Nottingham Medieval Studies*, 7 (1963), 28-29.
27. Sharf, *Byzantine Jewry*, p. 34.
28. See, in general, Baron, *SRH*, III, 8-15; Parkes, *Church and Synagogue*, pp. 246ff.; P. Browe, "Die Judengestzgebung Justiniens," *Analecta Gregoriana*, 8 (1935), 101-146; and Sharf, *Byzantine Jewry*, pp. 21-26.
29. *CJ.*, I, 9.15, limits the rights of Jews given in *CTh.*, II, 1.10. *CTh.*, XVI, 8.8 is omitted from *CJ*.
30. *CTh.*, XVI, 9.3 is another important example of an omission in *CJ*.
31. *CJ.*, I, 9.10, 16, and 18; I, 10.1 and 2.
32. *Ibid.*, I, 9.18.
33. *Ibid.*, I, 5.21 and *Nov.*, 45.
34. *CJ.*, I, 5.12; I, 19.18; X, 32.49; and *Nov.*, 45.
35. *Nov.*, 146. See the discussion by Baron, *SRH*, III, 233 and the literature cited there.
36. *Nov.*, 146.

Notes   155

37. Precopius, *Hist. Arcana*, chs. 28-29. See the discussion by Sharf, *Byzantine Jewry*, p. 23.

38. Procopius, *BG.*, V, x, *passim*, provides considerable detail on the events at Naples following the fall of the city and notes that the populace vented its frustrations on the priest Asclepiodatus. The Byzantines tried to develop amicable relations with the Neapolitans. Not a word is said about the Jews of Naples having been ill-treated either by the Christian inhabitants or by the conquerors.

39. Gregory, *Epist.*, XIII, 15, shows that the Jewish community and synagogue were flourishing in the post-invasion period.

40. *Ibid.*, VI, 29; IX, 104.

41. In the post-invasion period it is clear the the Byzantines took no official action aginst the synagogues at Cagliari, Palermo, Terracina, or at Naples. See Gregory, *Epist.*, IX, 195; VIII, 25; IX, 38; I, 34; II, 6 and XIII, 15, respectively. There is no positive evidence that would indicate official action by the Byzantine government against synagogues in Italy during this period.

42. Gregory, *Epist.*, XIII, 15.

43. On Jewish slave holding in Italy see Gregory, *Epist.*, II, 38; III, 37; IV, 9, 21; VI, 29, 30; VIII, 21; IX, 104. On the laws violated see notes 29-30 above. Cf. Blumenkranz, *Auteurs chrétiens*, p. 76, n. 19.

44. Gregory, *Epist.*, IV, 21.

45. *Ibid.*, IV, 9, 21, for the bishops of Cagliari and of Luna, respectively.

46. *Ibid.*, IX, 40, and I, 42, for merchants and a probable moneylender, respectively.

47. *Ibid.*, I, 66.

48. Scholars generally concede that on an empire-wide basis Justinian's anti-Jewish policy was a failure. This position is expressed cogently by Sharf, *Byzantine Jewry*, pp. 35-36.

49. There is as yet no first-class modern monograph dealing with this important era in Italian history. Thomas Hodgkin, *Italy and Her Invaders*, V, chs. 1-7, is still serviceable, and Peter Llewellyn, *Rome in the Dark Ages* (New York, 1970), chs. 2-3, can be useful on occasion.

50. The best general study of Gregory remains F. H. Dudden, *Gregory the Great* (London, 1905), 2 vols.

51. For example, Dudden, *Gregory*, II, 153ff.; Solomon Katz, "Pope Gregory the Great and the Jews," *JQR*, 24 (1933), 113ff.; and Baron, *SRH*, III, 28ff.

52. Gregory, *Epist.*, VIII, 25. See, for example, Katz, "Pope Gregory," pp. 120-121, and Baron, *SRH*, III, 32.

53. Katz, "Pope Gregory," p. 114.

54. Parkes, *Church and Synagogue*, p. 213. Cf. Solomon Grayzel, "The Jews and Roman Law," *JQR*, 59 (1968), 93-117.

55. In *CJ.*, I, 9.15, 18, and *Nov.*, 131, Justinian modified *CTh.*, XVI, 8.25 and *Th. Nov.*, 3.3 and 5, in such a manner as to make the "repair" of a synagogue subject to interpretation by the ecclesiastical authorities. The new process could easily have permitted the confiscation of the building. Justinian also gave great flexibility to those who would harass Jews by permitting the Church to con-

fiscate any synagogue that could be shown to occupy property belonging to an ecclesiastical institution of any kind. Gregory, *Epist.*, I, 34; II, 6; VII, 25; IX, 38, and IX, 195, illustrate the pope's protection of Jewish interests from bishops and their followers who using the flexible approach made possible by Justinian's legislation sought to take control of synagogues or otherwise harass Jews at worship. Cf. Katz, "Pope Gregory," pp. 121-124.

56. Gregory, *Epist.*, II, 6; XIII, 15.

57. Baron, *SRH*, III, 30, observes that Gregory followed imperial prohibitions concerning Jewish ownership and control of Christian and would-be Christian slaves. After making this observation, Baron discusses Gregory's decisions that frequently subverted not only the harsher law of Justinian but also on occasion the more lenient legislation of the *Theodosian Code*. Baron apparently fails to see Gregory's casuistry. See also Katz, "Pope Gregory," pp. 121-131, but cf. Blumenkranz, *Juifs et Chrétiens*, p. 262, who notes Gregory's flexibility.

58. There is simply no legal means by which Gregory's position, for example, in *Epist.*, IV, 29, can be reconciled with the laws promulgated by Justinian (see notes 31, 32 above). Cf. Katz, "Pope Gregory," p. 131.

59. *CTh.*, XVI, 9.3, and the discussion by Parkes, *Church and Synagogue*, p. 215.

60. Gregory, *Epist.*, IV, 21. Baron, *SRH*, III, 31, suggests that Gregory went along with Jewish domination of Christian *coloni* for economic reasons. Katz, "Pope Gregory," p. 130, misunderstands the text and believes that Gregory changed the conditions concerning the position of a *colonus*.

61. Gregory, *Epist.*, IV, 9. Scholars have much exaggerated Gregory's willingness to enforce the law when Jews would be disadvantaged by such action. See above notes 57-59.

62. Gregory, *Epist.*, IX, 40.

63. *Ibid.*, I, 42.

64. *Ibid.*, IX, 104. Gregory's casuistry in this letter is certainly remarkable. It also should be pointed out that some Jews underwent baptism to facilitate their slave-trading activities (*Epist.*, IX, 104) and that Gregory made no effort to condemn such practice. In fact he went along with it. See Blumenkranz, *Juifs et Chrétiens*, p. 328, and cf. Parkes, *Church and Synagogue*, pp. 216-217.

65. Gregory, *Epist.*, II, 38; IV, 31; V, 7; VIII, 23.

66. Parkes, *Church and Synagogue*, pp. 213-214.

67. *Ibid.*, p. 219. This is the general view. See Baron, *SRH*, III, 31-32, but cf. Katz, "Pope Gregory," p. 119-120, who does not believe that Gregory's theological attitude represented his personal attitude. Katz seems to believe that Gregory's putative legalism represented his personal beliefs. Grayzel, "Jews and Roman Law," pp. 106-107, adds nothing new.

68. Parkes, *Church and Synagogue*, pp. 220-221. Cf. Dudden, *Gregory*, II, 153, who is at a loss to understand the pope's Jewish policy.

69. Among the more important situations that were widely known were Jewish raiders in Palestine; the Jewish king of the Himyarites, Dhū Nuwās, who massacred the Christian population of Najrān; the imperial war with the autonomous Jewish island polity of Yotabē (Tirān) at the entrance to the Gulf of Aquaba; the

military adventures of Jewish fighting men from Na'rān (near Jericho) and Beit Ramlá; the riots at Constantinople in 578; and the violence at Antioch in 592. J. Starr, "Byzantine Jewry on the Eve of the Arab Conquest," *JPOS*, 15 (1935), 280-293; Baron, *SRH*, III, 66-70; and Sharf, *Byzantine Jewry*, pp. 30-33, 43-47, with the extensive bibliography they provide.

70. See chapter III.
71. Bernard S. Bachrach, *Merovingian Military Organization, 481-751* (Minneapolis, 1972), pp. 39-41, 60-61, and Hodgkin, *Italy and Her Invaders*, V, ch. 5.
72. Bachrach, "Visigothic Jewish Policy," pp. 14-16.
73. Sharf, *Byzantine Jewry*, p. 34.
74. In 593 a Jew in Sicily named Nasas proclaimed that he was the prophet Elijah who, it is traditionally believed, will appear before the coming of the Messiah. Gregory (*Epist.*, III, 37) observed that this Nasas seduced Christians into worshiping at his synagogue and that he acquired Christian slaves and used them in his service. The prefect of Sicily, however, took no action against Nasas. When a new prefect replaced the old one, Gregory exhorted him to take action. This episode which scholars have generally discussed in religious terms provides a capsule view of governmental impotence and connivance as well as of Jewish influence. See Sharf, *Byzantine Jewry*, p. 65 and cf. L. I. Newman, *Jewish Influence on Christian Reform Movements* (New York, 1925), pp. 410ff., and cf. Katz, "Pope Gregory," p. 127, n. 67.
75. Gregory, *Epist.*, XIII, 3.
76. Sharf, *Byzantine Jewry*, pp. 42-60, provides a good account of this policy and its aftermath. Baron, *SRH*, 15-25, 234-240, is also useful (see esp. p. 23). Andrew Sharf, "Jews in Byzantium," *WHJP*, II, 53-55, summarizes the position which he originally elaborated in "Byzantine Jewry in the Seventh Century," *BZ*, 48 (1955), 103-115. Cf. Starr, "Byzantine Jewry," pp. 280-293.
77. Sharf, "Jews in Byzantium," p. 55.
78. *V. Zos.*, p. 839. See the discussion by J. Starr, *Jews in the Byzantine Empire 641-1204* (Athens, 1939), pp. 86-87.
79. See note 74 above.
80. Sharf, "Jews in Byzantium," p. 55ff., and Cecil Roth, "Italy," *WHJP*, II, 102-108. A special tax may have been imposed on Jews. For a discussion of this and the extensive literature on the subject see Sharf, *Byzantine Jewry*, pp. 189ff.
81. Our best guide to the history of Italy during this period remains Paul the Deacon, *Historia Langobardorum*, Bks. III-V. André Guillou, *Régionalisme et Indépendance dans l'empire byzantin au VIIe siècle: l'example de l'exarchat et de la Pentapole d'Italie* (Rome, 1969), shows the local autonomy enjoyed by the Byzantine enclaves in seventh-century Italy. There is no reason to believe that the power of Constantinople increased during the next century.
82. *Lex Rom. Cur.*, 2, 1.8; 3, 1.5; 3, 7.2, respectively. See Parkes, *Church and Synagogue*, pp. 199, 209.
83. Canon 27 (Mansi, XII, col. 294).
84. *MGH, Conc.*, II, 1, 16 (Canon 10).
85. J. J. Rabinowitz, "Jewish and Lombard Law," *JSS*, 12 (1950), 301-310 (Reprinted in *Jewish Law: Its Influences on the Development of Legal Institu-*

tions (New York, 1955), pp. 182ff.), provides a convincing case in regard to Jewish influence on Lombard marriages. Rabinowitz's position in general, however, is weakened by a manifest anti-Germanist bias (pp. 299-300) and an overall propensity to exaggerate the importance and pervasiveness of Jewish influences. Thus even when Rabinowitz has a strong case as he does on the Lombard marriage law, the reader may tend to be hypercritical. See, for example, the overcautious reaction of Baron, *SRH*, III, 244.

86. For the increase in polygamy see Paul the Deacon, *Hist. Lang.*, Bk. V, ch. 33. On Grimoald's divorce cf. Baron, *SRH*, IV, 20.

87. Sharf, *Byzantine Jewry*, p. 56.

88. *Ibid.*

89. Canon 27 (Mansi, XII, col. 294).

90. *MGH, Conc.*, II, 1, 16, canon 10.

91. Sharf, "Jews in Byzantium," pp. 55-57.

92. *Carmen de Syn. Tinic.*, 190.

93. Bk. IV, ch. 51, and bk. V, chs. 33-37. In ch. 37, Paul notes that Perctarit was mild and gentle in all things.

94. During the mid-eighth century there were practicing Jews in the Lombard capital of Pavia. See Blumenkranz, *Juifs et Chrétiens*, pp. 70 and 162ff., and Roth, "Italy," p. 113.

95. Hodgkin, *Italy and Her Invaders*, V, 239ff. and esp. 303.

96. Roth, "Italy," p. 113, sets the date of Perctarit's alleged persecution as 661, the first year of the monarch's reign. While Roth provides neither a source nor an argument of support, this date is not an unreasonable one. In fact, if Perctarit did initiate an anti-Jewish policy upon ascending the throne, then his ten-year exile would account for the failure of that policy. If this line of reasoning is followed, then it is highly likely that the Jews of the Lombard kingdom supported Grimoald, under whom the Jewish (and pagan) custom of polygamy seems to have increased. All things considered, Roth's date for Perctarit's edict may well be better than the traditional date. On the traditional date see Blumenkranz, *Juifs et Chrétiens*, p. 134. Blumenkranz's assumption that Aripert also carried on an anti-Jewish policy cannot be sustained. The *Carmen de Syn. Tinic.*, 190, clearly indicates that Perctarit followed his father in becoming a Christian but says nothing about Aripert's Jewish policy.

Chapter III

1. Bernard S. Bachrach, "Procopius and the Chronology of Clovis's Reign," *Viator*, 1 (1970), 21-31.

2. J. M. Wallace-Hadrill, *The Long-Haired Kings* (London, 1962), pp. 169ff., and Bachrach, *Merovingian Military Organization*, pp. 8ff.

3. Katz, *Jews in Spain and Gaul*, p. 127, and Blumenkranz, *Auteurs chrétiens*, p. 43. Sidonius Apollinaris, *Epist.*, VI, 11, and Eleutherius, *Oratio*, col. 102.

4. *V. Caesarii*, Bk. I, chs. 28-31. Cf. Katz, *Jews in Spain and Gaul*, pp. 114-115, and the works cited there.

5. Wallace-Hadrill, *The Long-Haired Kings*, pp. 177ff.

6. Scholars have long debated the "civic status" of Jews in Merovingian Gaul.

The majority of historians seem to agree that Jews were subject to the Roman law (see the discussion by Katz, *Jews in Spain and Gaul*, pp. 83-84). Katz, himself (p. 84), disagrees and believes that the acceptance of Orthodox Christianity by the Franks led to the result that "the Roman law . . . lost its significance and force." Katz sees this as an apparently long-term effect, but he underestimates the continuing impact of Roman law throughout medieval Europe. See, for example, Eric John, *Land Tenure in Early England* (Leicester, 1960), who has demonstrated that Roman law had an impact of consequence even in such an unlikely place as Anglo-Saxon England. Of interest also in this context is the less controversial work by Ernst Levy, *West Roman Vulgar Law* (Philadelphia, 1951). Parkes, *Church and Synagogue*, ch. 9, *passim*, takes a not unreasonable view of Jewish "civic status."

7. Most of the Jews in Gaul during Clovis's reign were subject to the *Lex Romana Visigothorum*. Of the hundreds of laws included in the *LRV* there are only seventeen in which Jews are singled out and distinguished from non-Jews. Those Jews who were not subject to the *LRV* were subject to the *Lex Romana Burgundionum* (*LRB*); this will be discussed below.

8. *LRV*, 2.8.3.

9. *Ibid.*, 2.1.10.

10. See Braude, *Jewish Proselyting*, pp. 24-25, who demonstrates that it was an active policy among Jews to convert others to their religion during the first five centuries of the Christian era. The Roman laws discussed below that were embodied in the *LRV* may be viewed as a response to this policy.

11. *LRV*, 3.1.5, 16.4.1, and the most important of the lot, 16.4.2.

12. *Ibid.*, 3.7.2 and 9.4.4.

13. *Ibid.*, 16.3.1.

14. *Ibid.*, 16.2.1.

15. *Ibid.*, *Nov.*, 3.

16. Wallace-Hadrill, *The Long-Haired Kings*, p. 177. In general see de Clercq, *Le législation réligieuse franque de Clovis à Charlemagne*, pp. 8-13, and cf. L. Duchesne, *L'Église au VIe siècle* (Paris, 1925), 501-502, who seems to imply that the focus of the legislation concerned bishops rather than simple clergy.

17. The *acta* of the council are found in *MGH, Conc.*, I, 2-14.

18. See Wallace-Hadrill, *The Long-Haired Kings*, pp. 185ff.

19. Hefele-Leclercq, *Hist. des conciles*, II, 2, 1016-1017, 1053-1054, 1125-1129.

20. *MGH, Conc.*, I, 64.

21. Cf. the interpretations of Katz, *Jews in Spain and Gaul*, pp. 88ff., and Parkes, *Church and Synagogue*, p. 324. On the impact of excommunication see F. E. Hyland, *Excommunication, Its Nature, Historical Developments and Effects* (Washington, 1928), pp. 14-38. Cf. Baron, *SRH*, III, 50, 252, n. 63.

22. For the idea of "national councils" as applied to the Merovingians see Hefele-Leclercq, *Hist. des conciles*, II, 2, 1132, and de Clercq, *Le législation réligieuse franque de Clovis à Charlemagne*, p. 9.

23. Braude, *Jewish Proselyting*, pp. 24-25.

24. Auguste Longnon, *Géographie de la Gaulle au VIe siècle* (Paris, 1878), plates II, III.

25. See note 3 above, but cf. Blumenkranz, *Auteurs chrétiens*, p. 51.

26. The antiquity of this community is the subject of ongoing debate. See, for example, Katz, *Jews in Spain and Gaul*, pp. 9, 22, 24. It is clear, however, that in the later fifth century when Sidonius Apollinaris was Bishop of Clermont, a substantial Jewish community was there (*Epist.*, III, 4; IV, 5; VI, 11; VIII, 13). Sidonius, as these letters indicate, enjoyed good relations with the Jews of his city. On Sidonius, in general, see C. E. Stevens, *Sidonius Apollinaris and His Age* (Oxford, 1933).

27. Gregory, *VP*, 6.7. Gallus was bishop from 527-551.

28. *MGH, Conc.*, 66-71.

29. *Ibid.*, p. 67. See Katz, *Jews in Spain and Gaul*, p. 90, and Parkes, *Church and Synagogue*, pp. 324-325.

30. *MGH, Conc.*, I, 67. For the definition of *judex* see Niermeyer, *Mediae Latinitatis Lexicon Minus*, p. 561. Cf. Katz, *Jews in Spain and Gaul*, p. 119; Parkes, *Church and Synagogue*, p. 325; and Blumenkranz, *Juifs et Chrétiens*, p. 342, who all limit their interpretation of the term *judex* to judge.

31. See the discussion by Parkes, *Church and Synagogue*, p. 325.

32. See note 15 above.

33. Bachrach, *Merovingian Military Organization*, p. 72, and Bachrach, "Charles Martel, Mounted Shock Combat, the Stirrup, and Feudalism," *Studies in Medieval and Renaissance History*, 7 (1970), 70-71.

34. See above note 24.

35. See above Preface, note 9, for a guide to Jewish communities.

36. *LRB*, XIX, 4.

37. *LB*, V, 1-6.

38. *Ibid.*, CII, 1-3. See Baron, *SRH*, III, 50.

39. Hefele-Leclercq, *Hist. des conciles*, II, 2, 1017-1022, 1025, 1031-1046, indicates that at least four councils were held in the Burgundian kingdom before it was conquered by the Merovingians.

40. *MGH, Conc.*, I, 22.

41. Parkes, *Church and Synagogue*, p., 322, and Katz, *Jews in Spain and Gaul*, p. 113.

42. *MGH, Conc.*, I, 64.

43. *Ibid.*, I, 67.

44. *Ibid.*, I, 14, 28, 33.

45. The prohibition concerning socializing between Jews and Christians during Holy Week emphasizes this anxiety on the part of the clergy. King Childebert may have attempted to enforce this canon ca. 538 because the drunkenness, license, and generally immoral behavior common among Christians during this holiday throughout the early Middle Ages could well have given Jews the opportunity to ridicule Christianity. On the repeated conciliar prohibitions of Holy Week socializing see *MGH, Conc.*, I, 83, 158, and *MGH, Cap.*, I, 417. See the discussion by Parkes, *Church and Synagogue*, pp. 327, 332, and Katz, *Jews in Spain and Gaul*, p. 60.

46. Blumenkranz, *Juifs et Chrétiens*, pp. 175ff.

47. Parkes, *Church and Synagogue*, pp. 320-321.

Notes   161

48. *MGH, Conc.*, I, 94. Katz, *Jews in Spain and Gaul*, p. 100.
49. *MGH, Conc.*, I, 94, canon 31. Cf. note 11 above.
50. Gregory, *VP*, 6, 7. Gallus did not sign the minutes of the councils at Orleans in 533 and 538 which enacted anti-Jewish measures (*MGH, Conc.*, I, 65, 84-86).
51. Gregory (*Hist.*, Bk. IV, chs. 7, 11, 12, 15, 16) provides much information on the strife at Clermont and the close relation between Cautinus and the Jews of the city. Fortunatus, *Opera Poetica, Carm.*, 5.5, writing about events that took place about two decades later noted that factional strife at Clermont was serious. Poetic license, however, permitted Fortunatus to depict the factionalism as composed strictly of Jews on one side and Christians on the other side. See the discussion by Blumenkranz, *Auteurs chrétiens*, pp. 64-66, and cf. Baron, *SRH*, III, 51-52, who fails to see the dynamics of factional conflict at Clermont.
52. *Vita Ferreoli*, p. 101.
53. *Ibid.* The term Saracen in this text is a manifest anachronism owing to either an interpolation or a copyist's error. On this see Baron, *SRH*, III, 253, n. 67, who seems unaware, however, of the relation of the succession, the duration of Childebert I's reign, and the overall political situation.
54. Bachrach, *Merovingian Military Organization*, pp. 29-30.
55. *MGH, Conc.*, I, 99-161.
56. *Ibid.*, p. 158, canon 13. On *tellonarii* see King, *Law and Society*, p. 198.
57. *MGH, Conc.*, I, 156, 159, canons 2 and 16, respectively.
58. See note 15 above.
59. *MGH, Conc.*, I, 158, canon 14.
60. *Ibid.*, p. 159, canon 16.
61. *Ibid.*, pp. 158-159, canons 14 and 15, respectively.
62. Gregory, *Hist.*, Bk. IV, ch. 35. Cf. Parkes, *Church and Synagogue*, p. 340, who believes that Euphrasius bought the valuables from the Jews, and also Katz, *Jews in Spain and Gaul*, p. 127.
63. Gregory, *Hist.*, Bk. V, ch. 11. See also Fortunatus, *Carm.*, 5.5. On the chaos in Sigibert's erstwhile kingdom after his murder see Bachrach, *Merovingian Military Organization*, pp. 43ff. On the question of numbers see Blumenkranz, *Juifs et Chrétiens*, p. 34. Cf. Baron, *SRH*, III, 253, n. 67.
64. Gregory, *Hist.*, Bk. VIII, ch. 1.
65. *Ibid.*, Bk. VI, ch. 17. On Chilperic's personality and temperament see Wallace-Hadrill, *The Long-Haired Kings*, pp. 195-199.
66. Gregory, *Hist.*, Bk. VI, ch. 17. See also the detailed discussion in Katz, *Jews in Spain and Gaul*, pp. 25, 37, 57, 62, 74, 112, 122-123, 132, 165; Parkes, *Church and Synagogue*, pp. 334, 340; and Blumenkranz, *Juifs et Chrétiens*, pp. 12, 41, 53, 70, 73, 150, 222, 224, 256, 266, 379. *V. S. Germani*, ch. 64, provides an earlier example of such violence. In a text written ca. 568 Germanus is depicted as visiting Civray-sur-Cher where he learned about the case of a certain Amantius. The latter who had been a Jew sought to become a Christian and was baptized. The Jews of the town, however, imprisoned him. According to Fortunatus, Germanus's hagiographer, the bishop freed the imprisoned convert through a miracle.

67. On the general background of the Gundovald affair see Walter Goffart, "Byzantine Policy in the West under Tiberius II and Maurice: The Pretenders Hermenegild and Gundovald (579-585)," *Traditio*, 13 (1957), 73-118. In note 1 Goffart provides extensive bibliographic references. On the military aspects see Bachrach, *Merovingian Military Organization*, pp. 54-55, 57-60.

68. On the Jewish community of Marseilles see Katz, *Jews in Spain and Gaul*, pp. 24, 25, 28, 125, 132, 144. On the émigrés from Clermont who went to Marseilles see note 63 above.

69. Gregory, *Epist.*, I, 45.

70. Goffart, "Byzantine Policy," p. 94, n. 88, pp. 103-104.

71. On the Jewish community at Bordeaux see Katz, *Jews in Spain and Gaul*, pp. 6, 25, 117, 155-156, and for Gundovald's reception at Bordeaux see Gregory, *Hist.*, Bk. VII, ch. 31.

72. For Gundovald's island haven see Gregory, *Hist.*, Bk. VI, ch. 24, and on Jewish ships in the area see Gregory, *GC*, ch. 95.

73. Goffart, "Byzantine Policy," pp. 96ff.

74. L. Herzfeld, *Handelsgeschichte der Juden des Alterthums* (2nd ed.; Brunswick, 1894), pp. 259-278, tends to exaggerate somewhat. R. Anchel, *Les Juifs de France* (Paris, 1946), p. 20, is on the right track when he points out the strategic location of Jewish settlements in relation to trade. V. Parvan, *Die Nationalität der Kaufleute in römischen Kaiserreiche* (Breslau, 1909), pp. 120-121, overreacts to Herzfeld and does not appreciate the nature of the evidence sufficiently. Katz, *Jews in Spain and Gaul*, pp. 125-126, seems also to be reacting to Herzfeld's exaggerations but in pp. 127ff. provides a generally sound treatment of the evidence. See also the more recent handling of the subject by Roth, "Economic Life," pp. 13-48, which though general is very useful.

75. Sharf, *Byzantine Jewry*, pp. 44-45, discusses an important episode in the reign of Tiberius II that makes clear the emperor's pro-Jewish policy. Underlying Byzantine Jewish policy at this time was the realistic appreciation of Jewish influence as seen, for example, in the circus factions and other military and paramilitary activities. On this see above ch. II, notes 22 and 69.

76. Gregory, *Hist.*, Bk. VI, ch. 5. Parkes, *Church and Synagogue*, pp. 334, 340, characterizes Priscus, the Jewish mintmaster and merchant, with whom Chilperic found it interesting to dispute, as an intimate of the monarch. See note 66 above.

77. Gregory, *Hist.*, Bk. VIII, ch. 1.

78. *Ibid.*, Bk. VII, ch. 23.

79. *MGH, Conc.*, I, 155-185.

80. Gregory, *Epist.*, 9, 213; 9, 215.

81. See, for example, *V. Columbani*, Bk. I, chs. 19-20; *V. S. Desiderii*, chs. 1-10, 16, 19, 20; and Fredegarius, Bk. IV, ch. 36.

82. Fredegarius Bk. IV, ch. 20.

83. The process by which Chlotar II came to power over the entire *regnum Francorum* has been the subject of many interpretations. For example, Heinrich Mitteis, *Der Staat des hohen Mittelalters* (Weimar, 1962), p. 52, considers the Edict of Paris "die Magna Carta des fränkischen Adels." By contrast, Wallace-

Hadrill, *The Long-Haired Kings*, p. 214, does not consider it "as a royal surrender to the new power of the landed aristocracy, to which the king owed his victory over Brunechildis." Yet Wallace-Hadrill does admit that "Nobody would deny that magnates, lay and ecclesiastical, were gainers by some of these provisions." While the relative power exercised by Chlotar and the magnates is a question of importance as is the question of the king's power in relation to previous Merovingian rulers, it seems important to realize that the conclave at Paris was intended, in part at least, to arrange the basis for Chlotar's take over of the newly obtained territory.

84. *MGH, Cap.*, I, no. 9, ch. 10, and *MGH, Conc.* I, 190, canon, 17.
85. Katz, *Jews in Spain and Gaul*, p. 12.
86. See note 80 above.
87. *MGH, Conc.*, I, 199, 204.
88. *V. Sulpicii Biturgi*, ch. 4.
89. Fredegarius, Bk. IV, ch. 65.
90. Blumenkranz, *Juifs et Chrétiens*, p. 100, considers the tale pure invention or perhaps an embellishment of the activities of Sulpicius of Bourges (see above n. 88). S. Schwarzfuchs, "France and Germany under the Carolingians," *WHJP*, II, p. 125, characterizes this evidence as a pious legend. Starr, "Byzantine Jewry," p. 288, n. 1, is less certain that it is a legend. He is followed by Sharf, "Jews in Byzantium," p. 53-54. Wallace-Hadrill, *The Long-Haired Kings*, p. 211, n. 2, is less skeptical than the specialists in Jewish history. Baron, *SRH*, III, 47, 53, 54, 250, does not doubt Dagobert's attempted suppression of the Jews.
91. On the Merovingian expansion eastward and subsequent economic developments see Wallace-Hadrill, *The Long-Haired Kings*, pp. 210ff., and cf. A. Bergengruen, *Adel und Grundherrschaft im Merowingerreich* (Wiesbaden, 1958), who emphasizes the development of the nobility; Renée Doehaerd, *Le haut moyen âge occidental, economies et sociétés* (Paris, 1971), 248-249 on trade. See, for example, Gregory, *Epist.*, IX, 104, which concerns a Jew who dealt in pagan slaves and who acquired some Christian slaves in the course of his trading in Gaul.
92. See above note 90, and add Blumenkranz, *Auteurs chrétiens*, p. 102, and Roth, "Economic Life," p. 16. Blumenkranz, *Juifs et Chrétiens*, p. 100, n. 142, lists the sources that follow Fredegar on this point. Cf. Wallace-Hadrill, *The Long-Haired Kings*, p. 211, n. 2, who thinks that the *Gesta Dagoberti* may be independent of Fredegar.
93. Bachrach, "Visigothic Jewish Policy," p. 17, on Sisebut's feelings toward Brunhild. For Suinthila's position on the Jews see Thompson, *The Goths*, p. 178; Katz, *Jews in Spain and Gaul*, pp. 13, 50, 75; Görres, "Die Religionspolitik des spanischen Westgotenkonigs Swinthila," pp. 253-266; and Ziegler, *Church and State*, p. 190. On Sisenand's relations with Dagobert see Bachrach, *Merovingian Military Organization*, p. 86.
94. Thompson, *The Goths*, p. 196.
95. On the fragmentation of power during the last century of Merovingian history see Bachrach, *Merovingian Military Organization*, ch. V.
96. *MGH, Conc.*, I, 210.
97. Fredegarius, Bk. II, ch. 37.

98. Bachrach, "Visigothic Jewish Policy," pp. 26-27.
99. Julian, *Historia*, 5 and *Insultatio*, 1, 2.
100. The inscription is published in the *CIJ*, I, *Europe*, no. 671, and also by Katz, *Jews in Spain and Gaul*, pp. 152ff. with an English translation. A good recent photograph is found in Bernhard Blumenkranz, "Les origines et le moyen âge," *Histoire des Juifs en France* (Toulouse, 1972), plate 2. For further discussion and bibliography see Baron, *SRH*, III, 251, n. 59.
101. The basic study of these minters is Ponton d'Amecourt, "Description raisonée des monnaies mérovingiennes de Châlons-sur-Sâone," *Annuaire de la société française de numismatique et d'archéologie*, IV (1873), 128-131, and *Essai sur la numismatique mérovingienne comparée à la géographie de Grégoire de Tours* (Paris, 1864), pp. 51, 68, 69, 83, 112, 184, 189. This topic is treated effectively by Katz, *Jews in Spain and Gaul*, pp. 122-123. For additional evidence of continued Jewish influence during the era of the "do-nothing" kings see *V. Audoini*, ch. 9, for example.
102. Aegidius, *Epitome*, pp. 34, 74, 178, 248, 250, 258.

Chapter IV

1. *MGH, Cap.*, I, no. 18, ch. 10.
2. Jews lived under the Roman law and were considered *Romani*; see, for example, above ch. III, n. 6.
3. The original documents no longer exist, but mention of them is found in a contemporary letter of Pope Stephen III, "Ad Aribertum Narbonnensem Archiepiscopum" (Stephen, *Epist.*, col. 857). The *praecepta* issued by Peppin and his sons seem to be edicts confirming property rights. This is the view of Régné, *Juifs de Narbonne*, pp. 27ff.; Israel Levi, "Le roi juif de Narbonne et le Philoméne," *REJ*, 48 (1904), 206-207; Katz, *Jews in Spain and Gaul*, pp. 94-95, 162; Aryeh Graboïs, "Un principaute juive dans la France du midi à l'epoque carolingienne?" *Annales du Midi*, 85 (1973), 198, n. 40. Cf. Zuckerman, *A Jewish Princedom*, pp. 50ff., who contends that Pope Stephen is referring to a vast Jewish state including much of southern Gaul and northeastern Spain and ruled by a descendant of King David sent to the West by the Caliph of Baghdad. It seems reasonable that if even a fraction of what Zuckerman imagines were true then Archbishop Aribert or Pope Stephen would have known some of these facts and have mentioned them in his letters. Thus, for example, the alleged marriage of Peppin's sister Alda to the Jewish king (Zuckerman, p. 122) and her necessary conversion to Judaism would surely have attracted ecclesiastical attention. On this last point, among many, see Graboïs, "Un principaute," p. 196, n. 31 and p. 199.
4. Cf. above, ch. II, notes 60, 64.
5. Bernard S. Bachrach, "Military Organization in Aquitaine under the Early Carolingians," *Speculum*, 49 (1974), 14.
6. Pope Stephen's answer to Aribert's letter (above n. 3) makes it clear that Charlemagne did not withdraw the *praecepta* despite the archbishop's complaint.
7. See note 3 above and the discussion in Bernard S. Bachrach, "Some Observations on the Role of the Jews in the Establishment of the Spanish March, 768-814," *Hispanica Judaica* (forthcoming). Cf. Synan, *Popes and Jews*, pp. 62-63.

Notes 165

8. Stephen, *Epist.* col. 857.
9. Bachrach, "Military Organization in Aquitaine," pp. 15-17. The various collections of Roman law drawn up in the barbarian kingdoms—Alaric's *Breviary*, the *Lex Romana Burgundionum*, and the Roman law of Chur—all omit the part of the *Const. Sirm.*, VI which was added to *CTh.* and which was meant to prohibit Jews from performing military service. See Bachrach, "Jews in the Spanish March," n. 16. For the obligations of free alodial landholders in the Carolingian realms to do military service and the institutional demands of that service see Bachrach, "Military Organization in Aquitaine," pp. 28-31 (p. 1, n. 1 provides an extensive bibliography on the subject).
10. Alcuin, *Epist.*, IV, p. 32. It is unlikely that Alcuin is correct when he says that the Carolingians gained control of 300 miles of coastal territory; this would mean that Valencia, not to mention Tortosa, Tarragona, and Barcelona, would have been taken from the Muslims. Cf. Zuckerman, *Jewish Princedom*, pp. 137ff., who not only accepts Alcuin's exaggeration at face value but credits the Jewish king with securing these gains through diplomatic efforts. See on Gerona, Bachrach, "Jews in the Spanish March," n. 17.
11. Bachrach, "Military Organization in Aquitaine," pp. 18-21.
12. *Ibid.*, pp. 24-28.
13. *V. Hlud.*, ch. 8, p. 611.
14. *Concilium Barcinonense* (Mansi, vol. 18, cols. 253-254). See Ramon d'Abadal i de Vinyals, *Catalunya carolingia* (Barcelona, 1926-1952) II, 1, pp. 291-292, and Zuckerman, *A Jewish Princedom*, pp. 135-136, 319.
15. *Concilium Narbonense supurium* (*MGH, Conc.*, II, 11, 829). Much of the material in the text of this council points toward the conclusion drawn by the editor, Werminghoff, that the text is spurious. Elie Griffe, *Histoire réligieuse des anciens pays de l'Aude* (Paris, 1933), pp. 246-250, attempts to ascertain when and under what conditions various elements in the text were placed there. He demonstrates that the material concerning Ausona was included ca. 906. This is accepted by Zuckerman, *A Jewish Princedom*, p. 176 who, however, believes the text as a whole is not spurious.
16. *Ḳebhutsat Ḥakhamin*, I, 110-111 (trans. II, 23-24). *Teshubhot geoné mizraḥ u-ma'arabh*, no. 26, p. 9a. Zuckerman, *A Jewish Princedom*, pp. 318-319, treats these *responsa* in a reasonable manner.
17. See note 9 above.
18. Bachrach, "Military Organization in Aquitaine," pp. 25-26. Zuckerman, *A Jewish Princedom*, pp. 194-195, believes that Hermoldus Nigellus's account of the siege is based upon a Jewish account and follows the Jewish calendar. It is clear that Hermoldus dates some events according to lunar reckoning. It should be pointed out, however, that Christians also used a lunar calendar to calculate some of their holy days.
19. See above notes 9 and 11.
20. On Jewish landholders in the Lyonaise see Alfred Coville, *Recherches sur l'histoire de Lyon du Vme siècle au IXme siècle (450-800)* (Paris, 1928), pp. 523-527, 536, 540-542. Arthur Zuckerman, "The Political Uses of Theology: The Conflict of Bishop Agobard and the Jews of Lyons," *Medieval Studies*, 3 (1970), 37, n. 50 follows Coville.

166 Notes

21. *V. Hlud.*, ch. 14, p. 613.
22. Roth, "Economic Life," p. 35, and Schwarzfuchs, "France and Germany under the Carolingians," p. 128, concerning Kalonymus. The monk of Saint Gall, Notker (*Gesta Karoli Magni Imperatoris, MGH, SSRG*, new series ed. H. Haefele (Berlin, 1959), Bk. I, ch. 16), recounts an anecdote illustrating Charlemagne's close relations with a Jewish merchant. Another more stylized story is to be found in the writings of Agnellus of Ravenna (*Lib. Pont. eccl. Ravenn.*, ch. 143). Such materials as these have led scholars to agree on the importance of Jewish merchants in the Carolingian empire. It is generally believed that a Jewish quarter was established at Aachen during Charles's reign, but only further archaeological work can provide firm conclusions. By 820, however, we have written evidence for the Jews at Aachen, and the text would seem to indicate that they were not newly arrived since their warehouses and other installations were well established. See Blumenkranz, *Juifs et Chrétiens*, p. 17; Katz, *Jews in Spain and Gaul*, p. 129; Roth, "Economic Life," p. 35; and Walter Kaemmerer, "Die Aachener Pfalz Karls des Grossen in Anlage und Überlieferung," *Karl der Grosse*, I, 345ff.
23. Although Charlemagne's dedication to intellectual activities has been exaggerated, there is general consensus that he did "collect" scholars for his palace school. On Jewish books hostile to Christianity see Katz, *Jews in Spain and Gaul*, p. 68.
24. *MGH, Form.*, p. 448. See Blumenkranz, *Juifs et Chrétiens*, pp. 21-22, and R. Kestenberg-Gladstein, "The Early Jewish Settlement in Central and Eastern Europe: Bohemia," *WHJP*, II, 309 and the bibliography cited p. 440, n. 1.
25. Roth, "Economic Life," pp. 32-35. and cf. Katz, *Jews in Spain and Gaul*, p. 130, who objects to the notion that the terms Jew and merchant were virtually interchangeable and notes that the documents "regularly mention Jews and other merchants." Katz's conclusion that "The Jews had no monopoly of trade in Carolingian Gaul" is certainly accurate but misses the point. What is striking is the frequency (as both Katz and Roth agree) with which the word Jew appears in merchant contexts. On the important place of Jews in long-distance trade see below. James Parkes, *The Jew in the Medieval Community* (London, 1938), p. 44, treats the topic well. So does Charles Verlinden, "A propos de la place des Juifs dans l'economie de l'Europe occidentale aux IXe et Xe siècles," *Storiographia e storia in onore Eugenio Duprè Theseider* (Rome, 1974), I, 21-37, but cf. Blumenkranz, *Juifs et Chrétiens*, pp. 13-32.
26. *MGH, Cap.*, I, no. 46, ch. 4. See also no. 131, ch. 1.
27. This is not the palce to debate the Pirenne thesis with its immense bibliography. See, however, the recent volume by Bryce D. Lyon, *Henri Pirenne* (New York, 1974). The question of the continued importance of Syrian merchants in the West after the Muslim conquests has often been discussed. See for example, Roth, "Economic Life," pp. 20ff., and the bibliography he cites.
28. L. Rabinowitz, *Jewish Merchant Adventurers: A Study of the Radanites* (London, 1948), with its extensive bibliography should be read with the caution advised by Roth, "Economic Life," pp. 23ff.
29. Adapted and translated from Ibn Kurradadhbah, *Le Livre des routes et des royaumes*, ed. and trans. by M. J. de Goeje (Leiden, 1889), pp. 114ff. Ibn

Kurradadhbah was the director of the police and the postal service in the province of Jibal and Media under the Caliph al-Mu'tamid, and the account of the Radanites may well be based upon contact with them. Some of his material derives from earlier sources as well. The account of the Radanites makes it clear that they were not a new phenomenon in the ninth century but a well-established fact of economic and commercial life. Their significance was very probably increased by the Islamic conquests which made life more difficult for Christian merchants, especially for those from the West who would want to trade in Muslim countries. See Starr, *Jews in the Byzantine Empire*, pp. 111-112, and Roth, "Economic Life," p. 24 as well as the material cited in note 28 above.

30. See F. W. Buckler, *Harunu'l Rashid and Charles the Great* (Cambridge, Mass., 1931) for a general treatment. More important, however, is Björkman, "Karl und Islam," pp. 672-682.

31. F. M. Stenton, *Anglo-Saxon England* (2nd ed.; Oxford, 1947), pp. 219-220. For a more recent treatment see Wallace-Hadrill, "Charlemagne and England," pp. 683-698.

32. Katz, *Jews in Spain and Gaul*, pp. 63, 133; Blumenkranz, *Juifs et Chrétiens*, pp. 14, 41, 182-183; Baron, *SRH*, IV, 45, 174, 257, 322; Buckler, *Harunu'l Rashid*, p. 21, and Björkman, "Karl und Islam," p. 677.

33. *ARF, ann.* 801-802. Charlemagne ordered that a fleet be prepared to transport Isaac and his party. This suggests that a rather large group formed the embassy. The author of the *ARF* consistently mentions only Isaac in connection with the embassy after the death of Sigimund and Lantfrid; it seems reasonable to conclude that after the death of the Christians, the Jew was in charge of the mission. See also *Ann. Fuld., an.* 802.

34. See note 29 above.

35. *ARF, ann.* 801-803.

36. Notker, *Gesta Karoli*, Bk. II, ch. 14.

37. On trade with Britain see above note 31.

38. *MGH, Cap.*, I, no. 131, ch. 3: "Ut nemo Judeus monetam in domo sua habeat." See the discussion by Parkes, *Church and Synagogue*, p. 338, and Katz, *Jews in Spain and Gaul*, p. 123. On the Merovingians see above ch. III, n. 101.

39. On Charles's attempts to regulate and control coinage see Philip Grierson, "Money and Coinage under Charlemagne," *Karl der Grosse*, I, 501-536, and pp. 527ff., for the relation of coinage to Charles's reforms in metrology which had significance also in the markets of the empire.

40. *MGH, Cap.*, no. 131, ch. 2.

41. On Charlemagne's concern about free men sinking into serfdom and their loss to the army see Bachrach, "Military Organization in Aquitaine," pp. 29ff. From the point of view of clerics it was dangerous for a Christian to fall into the hands of a Jew because it was assumed, and probably with good reason, that an effort would be made to convert the unfortunate to Judaism.

42. *MGH, Cap.*, I, no. 63, ch. 13; no. 177, ch. 8; and *Coll. Anseg.*, no. 75. The repetition of these prohibitions and their inclusion in the collection made by Ansegius may well suggest that they were regarded as important. See Katz, *Jews in Spain and Gaul*, pp. 53-54. The problem of Christians celebrating the sabbath on

Saturday rather than on Sunday was a difficult one and went far beyond cases where Jews forced Jewish practices upon their Christian dependents. (See, for example, Alcuin, *Epist.*, 144, who discussed some of these problems in a letter to Charlemagne.) The close relations between Jews and Christians discussed in earlier chapters seem to have continued to encourage the latter in Jewish practices despite ongoing Church prohibitions. In quasi-religious matters such as artistic representations of religious subjects Jewish influence can also be detected. See the discussion by Peter Bloch, "Das Apsismosaik von Germingny-des-Pres: Karl der Grosse und der alte Bund," *Karl der Grosse*, III, 245ff. and also the older and more general C. Roth, "Jewish Antecedents of Christian Art," *Journal of the Warburg and Courtauld Institutes*, 16 (1953), 28ff.

43. See note 26 above.

44. Kenneth Cahn, "The Roman and Frankish Roots of the Just Price of Medieval Canon Law," *Studies in Medieval and Renaissance History*, 6 (1969), 36ff., discusses Charlemagne's legislation on these points in relation to his policies.

45. *MGH, Cap.*, I, no. 131, ch. 3. It is important to note here that Charles took these cases so seriously that he had them handled in the royal court in his presence. See Parkes, *Church and Synagogue*, p. 338.

46. See note 39 above, and F. L. Ganshof, "Charlemagne et les institutions de la monarchie franque," *Karl der Grosse*, I, 379-383, and Wolfgang Metz, "Die Agrarwirtschaft im karolingischen Reiche," *Karl der Grosse*, I, 497-500.

47. On the possibility that Charles had Jews among his legal advisors see below note 54. According to *Exemplar epistole Iohannis patriarche*, ed. by G. Rauschen, *Die Legende Karls des Grossen* (Leipzig, 1890), p. 48, two Jews named Isaac and Samuel brought an official letter from the Byzantine emperor, Constantine V, to Charlemagne along with a number of exceptional gifts. Isaac is said to have had outstanding expertise and ability in Jewish law, and Samuel was a rabbi who knew both Latin and Greek. Scholars have tended to make two assumptions about this episode: Isaac and Samuel are considered to have been Byzantines acting for or under the orders of Constantine V, and the story, in the form we have it, is assumed to have many legendary aspects which make all of the information suspect. See, for example, M. Schwab, "Sur une lettre d'un empereur byzantin," *Journal asiatique*, 8 (1896), 498-509; Julius Aronius, *Resgesten zur Geschichte der Juden in fränkischen und deutschen Reiche bis zum Jahre 1273 (Berlin, 1887-1902)*, no. 68; and Starr, *Jews in the Byzantine Empire*, p. 95. Simply because Isaac and Samuel brought gifts and a letter from Constantine to Charles does not mean that they were initially the envoys of Constantine. As noted above, Charlemagne's envoy Isaac brought gifts from the caliph to the emperor, but he was not Harun al Rashid's ambassador in the first instance. If Charlemagne sent a Jewish envoy named Isaac to the caliph, he certainly could have sent the same man to the Byzantine court. In this context it may be pointed out that Constantine V had married a Khazar princess named Chichek who was baptized and received the name Eirene. Also at this time an elite corps of Khazar guards served the emperor at Constantinople. On this see D. M. Dunlop, "The Khazars," *WHJP*, II, 328, and Classen, "Karl und Byzanz," p. 555. Concerning Carolingian knowledge and dis-

cussion of the conversion of the Khazar aristocracy to Judaism see Chrétien de Stavelot, *Exp. in Matt.*, col. 1456A. The foregoing note has been developed simply to show that Charlemagne had available to him learned Jews.

48. F. L. Ganshof, "Charlemagne's Programme of Imperial Government," *The Carolingians and the Frankish Monarchy* (London, 1971), 69, and F. L. Ganshof, "Les traits generaux du systeme d'institutions de la monarchie franque," *SSCI*, 9 (1961), 104. See also Rudolf Buchner, *Deutschlands Geschichtsquellen im Mittelalter* (Weimar, 1953), pp. 15-29, 29-49, and F. L. Ganshof, *Recherches sur les capitulaires* (Paris, 1958), pp. 14-16, 74-89, with regard to the capitularies and the *capitula legibus addenda* in particular.

49. *MGH. Cap.*, I, no. 63, ch. 13. It is probably reasonable to see *Capitula de Iudaeis* (*MGH, Cap.* I, no. 131, chs. 1-4) and ch. 13 of *Cap.* I, no. 63 as *capitula legibus addenda*. On the debate over the authenticity of the *Capitula de Iudaeis* see Katz, *Jews in Spain and Gaul*, pp. 92, n. 7, 111, 113, who seems to follow A. Helfferich, "Zum Capitulare Karoli M. de Judaeis," *Zeitschrift für Rechtsgeschichte*, II (1863), 417-420, in accepting the first five chapters as authentic, although the fifth is later than Charles's reign. The sixth is regarded as false. See also Blumenkranz, *Juifs et Chrétiens*, pp. 358-362, who seems to follow this pattern but less explicitly. Parkes, *Church and Synagogue*, pp. 337-338, seems to take this position but misses the point about the ordeal. See on this F. L. Ganshof, "Charlemagne et l'administration de la justice dans la monarchie franque," *Karl der Grosse*, I, 411: "L'usage de la même ordalie fut prescrit, au moins comme moyen de preuve subsidiaire, au Chrétien accusé par un Juif." In n. 127, Ganshof accepts the authenticity of ch. 6, but notes "si ce capitulaire n'est pas de Louis le Pieux." B. Simson, *Jahrbücher des fränkischen Reiches unter Ludwig dem Frommen* (Leipzig, 1874), I, 6, n. 2, believes the entire *Capitula de Judaeis* to be a later collection of materials coming from the reigns of both Louis and Charlemagne. Boretius (*MGH, Cap.*, I, 258) doubts the authenticity of the entire text and believes that all six chapters were written after Charlemagne's reign.

50. *MGH, Cap.*, I, no. 131, ch. 4. Schwarzfuchs, "France and Germany under the Carolingians," pp. 126-127, argues that the Jews of the Carolingian Empire were forced into a kind of second class status after 802 because they found the oath of fealty required of all Charlemagne's subjects by the emperor to be unsuitable. This position is also taken by Guido Kisch, *Jews in Medieval Germany* (Chicago, 1949), p. 137. On the oath in general see F. L. Ganshof, "Charlemagne et le serment," *Mélanges d'histoire du Moyen Age dédiés à la mémoire de Louis Halphen* (Paris, 1951), pp. 259-270. Kisch and those who follow him concerning the oath fail to grasp the flexibility of the Carolingian position. The oath or more accurately the affirmation translated above illustrates clearly the pragmatism of Charlemagne and his willingness to accommodate the Jews. Since it was possible to develop a Jewish oath for judicial processes, there is no reason why a Jewish oath of fealty could not have been developed. As is shown below in numerous cases the Carolingian monarchs referred to various of their Jewish subjects as *fideles*. One could not have been a *fidelis* without first taking an oath of faithfulness.

51. *MGH. Cap.*, I, no. 131, ch. 4. It should be pointed out that although the

instructions refer to an oath the formula has no mention of swearing. Cf. Baron, *SRH*, IV, 49, who translates the affirmation but adds in brackets the words "[I swear that] " which are not part of the text.

52. Blumenkranz, *Juif et Chrétien*, p. 364, admits the existence of Jewish influence and usage here but argues that the oath was more Christian than Jewish because of the clause mentioning Dathan and Abiron which was common in Christian charters. He is correct in noting that Christian charters did include this curse but only those from a much later period. For example, the collection of Carolingian charters dating from Peppin, Carloman, and Charlemagne, i.e., the period under consideration in this chapter (*MGH, Dip.* I), does not include a single legitimate document that uses the Dathan and Abiron curse. Curiously, several spurious charters in the collection that were forged considerably later do include the curse (nos. 239 and 240). It is not impossible that Christian usage followed Jewish usage in this. See also Kisch, *Jews in Medieval Germany*, pp. 275ff., for a discussion of the influence of Jewish law on Jewry law. On learned Jews available to Charlemagne for consultation and service see note 47 above.

53. These epitomes are published in Haenal's edition of *LRV* and are discussed in the introduction to the edition, pp. xxvi ff., and Gaudemet, *Le Bréviaire d'Alaric et les epitomes*, pp. 41ff.

54. See, for example, Cahn, "The Roman and Frankish Roots of the Just Price," pp. 3-52 and esp. pp. 9-11.

55. *Scintilla*, p. 35; *Epit. Guelf.*, p. 35; *Monk's Brev.*, p. 35; and *Epit. S. Gall.*, p. 35. Cf. Katz, *Jews in Spain and Gaul*, pp. 85-87, 108-109.

56. *Monk's Brev.*, p. 35; *Scintilla*, p. 35; *Epit. Guelf.*, p. 35; and *Epit. S. Gall.*, p. 35. On the religious legislation see *Scintilla*, p. 35; *Epit. Guelf.*, p. 35; and *Monk's Brev.*, p. 35.

57. *Scintila*, pp. 75, 178, 248, 250, 258; *Epit. Guelf.*, pp. 75, 83, 179, 249, 251, 259; *Monk's Brev.*, pp. 75, 83, 249, 251, 259; *Lyons' Epit.*, pp. 179, 249, 251, 259; and *Epit. S. Gall.*, pp. 75, 83, 179, 251, 259.

58. *LRV*, XVI, iii, 2.

59. *Epit. Guelf.*, p. 251; *Lyons' Epit.*, p. 251; *Monk's Brev.*, p. 251; and *Epit. S. Gall.*, p. 251.

60. In general, I tend to follow the description of Charlemagne's position as described by Louis Halphen, *Charlemagne et l'empire carolingien* (Paris, 1947), pp. 120ff., "Charlemagne arbitre de l'occident."

61. In addition to the works cited in note 31 above see Cecil Roth, *History of the Jews in England* (Oxford, 1941), pp. 269ff.

62. F. Cantera Burgos, "Christian Spain," *WHJP*, II, 357-358.

63. On the relations between Charles and Alfonso see Einhard, *Vita Karoli*, ch. 16. The *ARF*, an. 798 and the *An. q.d. Einhardi*, an. 798, simply indicate that Alfonso sent gifts to Charles.

64. Hadrian, *Epist.*, LXXXIII, and the discussion by Blumenkranz, *Auteurs chrétien*, pp. 143-144. It has often been argued that the Adoptionists in Spain developed their ideas or at least some of their ideas under Jewish influence. Such influence even if slight would tend to suggest the existence of close relations between Christians and Jews. The entire question has recently been reexamined by

Wilhelm Heil, "Der Adoptianismus, Alkuin und Spanien," *Karl der Grosse*, II, 95-155 and pp. 99, 112, 116, 124, 129, 133 for the Jewish element. See also Blumenkranz, *Juif et Chrétien*, pp. 60, 64.

65. Cf. Cantera Burgos, "Christian Spain," p. 358, who argues that Hadrian's reproaches to Christians were intended for those in the southern or Muslim parts of Spain. Hadrian (*Epist.*, LXXXIII), however, addressed his letter "Episcopis per universam Spaniam."

66. Bernhard Blumenkranz, "The Roman Church and the Jews," *WHJP*, II, 69-73, and Baron, *SRH*, IV, 5.

67. Blumenkranz, *Auteurs chrétiens*, pp. 142-144, and Roth, "Italy," p. 118.

68. Blumenkranz, "The Roman Church and the Jews," pp. 73, 75.

69. Sharf, *Byzantine Jewry*, pp. 67ff.

70. Canon 8 (Mansi, XIII, cols. 427, 430).

71. See the discussion of these texts in Starr, *Jews in the Byzantine Empire*, pp. 97-98, and cf. Sharf, *Byzantine Jewry*, p. 67. On the nature of the *Ecloga* see A. A. Vasiliev, *History of the Byzantine Empire* (Madison, 1961), I, 241ff., and E. H. Freshfield, *Roman Law in the Later Roman Empire* (Cambridge, 1932), pp. 35ff.

72. Starr, *Jews in the Byzantine Empire*, pp. 97-98; *Ekloga* (appendix), IV, 6, 16, 24; VI, 26-28, 30.

73. George Ostrogorsky, *History of the Byzantine State* (New Brunswick, N.J., 1957), pp. 160ff., and Vasiliev, *The Byzantine Empire*, I, 238-240, 267-268.

74. The Venetian situation is described in detail by Hodgkin, *Italy and Her Invaders*, VIII, 231ff. A more recent overview is provided for the entire Italian situation by Classen, "Karl der Grosse und Byzanz," pp. 536-608.

75. H. J. Zimmels, "Scholars and Scholarship in Byzantium and Italy," *WHJP*, II, 179, and Shlomo Simonsohn, "The Hebrew Revival among Early Medieval European Jews," *Salo Wittmayer Baron Jubilee Volume* (Jerusalem, 1975), II, 832-858. Starr, *Jews in the Byzantine Empire*, pp. 99ff., for the inscriptions and pp. 102-103, on Nicephoros; F. Schirmann, "The Beginning of Hebrew Poetry in Italy and Northern Europe," *WHJP*, II, 250-251. In Sicily there was a strange occurrence concerning a man named Heliodorus who was either a Jew or had a close Jewish advisor. This Heliodorus may well have been some kind of leader in opposition to the Byzantines. The story is obscure and bears a superficial resemblance to the movement that took place in Sicily during the pontificate of Gregory I (see below ch. II, n. 74). On Heliodorus cf. Starr, *Jews in the Byzantine Empire*, pp. 95-96. Donald Bullough, "Social and Economic Structure and Topography in the Early Medieval City," *SSCI*, XXI, 1 (1974), 381, n. 39, points out that Venosa was on the side of the frontier that belonged to Lombard Benevento rather than to Byzantium in the "early medieval" period. Cf. Starr, *Jews in the Byzantine Empire*, pp. 100-103. Thus there may be some question as to whether the flourishing community at Venosa is illustrative of a Lombard pro-Jewish policy or a Byzantine pro-Jewish policy. It might be noted here that R. Silano of Venosa is said to have felt the rigors of Basil's alleged anti-Jewish policy. On this see ch. VI, n. 102.

76. Rabinowitz, *Jewish Law*, pp. 182-219, traces the continuing impact of

Jewish law on Lombard law during the early Middle Ages. Rabinowitz does, however, exaggerate, and his statements must be used with care. Close relations between Jews and Christians in the more northernly parts of Italy are not disputed. See, for example, the writings of Claudius of Turin and the discussion by Blumenkranz, *Auteurs Chrétiens*, pp. 150-151.

Chapter V

1. In general on Louis's administrative talents see F. L. Ganshof, "Louis the Pious Reconsidered," *History*, 42 (1957), 171-180, and Theodor Schieffer, "Die Krise des karolingischen Imperium," *Aus Mittelalter und Neuzeit, Festschrift zum 70. Geburtstag von Gerhard Kallen* (Bonn, 1957), 1-16. For brief discussions of Louis's Jewish policy see Blumenkranz, *Juifs et Chrétiens*, pp. 301-302; Zuckerman, "Agobard," p. 50; and Parkes, *The Medieval Community*, pp. 51-53. As will be seen below most scholars have concentrated their attention on the anti-Jewish activities of Archbishop Agobard of Lyons and largely ignored or drastically underemphasized the imperial policy during this period.

2. See, for example, Ganshof, "Louis the Pious," pp. 179-180.

3. Agobard, *Epist.*, 4 (p. 165); 6 (p. 181); 7 (pp. 182-183).

4. Schwarzfuchs, "France and Germany," p. 128; Blumenkranz, *Juifs et Chrétiens*, p. 40; and Zuckerman, *Jewish Princedom*, pp. 250-251, for opinions that the religion of the *magister Judaeorum* cannot be determined, that he was non-Jewish, and that he was Jewish, respectively.

5. See note 3 above. Cf. Zuckerman, *Jewish Princedom*, pp. 250ff.

6. See note 3 above. Zuckerman, "Agobard," pp. 27ff.

7. Louis's economic policies with regard to Jews are discussed below. Concerning the Roman law prohibiting the building of synagogues see ch. III, n. 15.

8. Agobard, *Epist.*, 7 (p. 184): "dum eis contra legem permittitur novas synagogas extruere." Agobard seems to entertain the idea, at least for the purpose of his argument, that all previous anti-Jewish legislation is in effect immutable. Thus he claims that although the Jews are permitted to build new synagogues, it is "against the law." In the early Middle Ages it is more realistic to see as legal that which the king or emperor permitted regardless of the laws that had been promulgated by earlier authorities.

9. Katz, *Jews in Spain and Gaul*, pp. 94-95, 125.

10. Agobard, *Epist.*, 7 (p. 183). These rights are confirmed in more specific circumstances in several of Louis's special charters for particular Jews. See below.

11. See *Imp. Form.*, no. 30 (pp. 309-310), discussed below. It is even possible that Louis permitted Jews to possess and deal in Christian slaves. Agobard, *Epist.*, 7 (p. 183) complained that he preached to Christians to encourage them to stop selling Christian slaves to Jews. He did not note that those who did so were breaking the law although it is clear that under both canon law and under the Roman law, before Louis may have amended it, such practices were illegal. On Louis's and Agobard's positions see Zuckerman, "Agobard," pp. 32-33.

12. Simchah Assaf, "Slaves and the Slave Trade among Jews in the Middle Ages," *Zion*, 4 (1938-1939), 91-92, provides a fine summary in Hebrew of Jewish law concerning slaves. Zuckerman, "Agobard," p. 25, n. 6, summarizes Asaf's

Notes   173

findings. More useful, however, is Wacholder, "The Halakah and the Proselyting of Slaves during the Gaonic Era," pp. 89-106.
    13. See ch. III, n. 11.
    14. Zuckerman, "Agobard," pp. 24ff., examines the evidence in detail. He emphasizes, however, the tangential issue of Agobard's attempts to baptize Jewish-owned slaves who were still pagan as well as those who had been already converted to Judaism and shows that Louis crushed the archbishop's efforts. Zuckerman fails to recognize the significance of Louis's actions.
    15. *Ibid*. Friedrich Wiegand, "Agobard von Lyon und die Judenfrage," *Festschrift seiner königlichen Hoheit dem Prinzregenten Luitpold von Bayern zum achtzigsten Geburtstage dargebracht von der Universität Erlangen*, I, *Theologische Fakultät* (Leipzig, 1901), 232-233, notes correctly that the Synod of Gangra (340-341) in canon 3 (Mansi, II, col. 1106) condemned anyone who would teach a slave to attack his owner, flee his authority, or fail to serve him as a slave should serve under the pretext of doing so for religious reasons. Zuckerman, "Agobard," pp. 23ff., emphasizes Wiegand's argument that it was the normal canonical position in the ninth century to respect the formulation of the Council of Gangra on this issue. Wiegand and Zuckerman argue that since Louis's position was consistent with the actions of the Council of Gangra, therefore it was the orthodox position. By contrast it should be noted that the council of Mâcon in 583, Pope Gregory I, and the Twelfth Council of Toledo in 681 all held that slaves belonging to Jews would be freed upon attaining baptism. As seen in previous chapters this tradition was often slighted in practice. In sum, it seems that canons and papal authority could be found to support either Louis's or Agobard's position. One cannot assume, however, that either Louis or Agobard or neither of them arrived at his position because of the respective canons. Neither can one assume that either man took a political position and then found the canons to support it.
    16. Amulo, *Liber contra Judaeos*, ch. 42, attacks the long-standing abuse by which Jews who held the office of toll collector used their power to bully Christians into becoming Jews. In 845-846 shortly after the end of the civil wars that followed Louis's death, the clergy of Charles the Bald's realm gathered at Meaux and Paris, and there they promulgated a long list of canons. Among these canons were enactments that aimed at restoring legal limitations upon Jews, limitations that Louis had apparently abrogated. See *MGH. Cap. II*, no. 293, ch. 73, pp. 416-417, notes 37-54, *passim*.
    17. The enactment cited in note 16 had a foundation in Roman law and also validity as Church canons.
    18. Agobard complains about what is being permitted. See for example, *Epist.*, 7 (pp. 183-184).
    19. Katz, *Jews in Spain and Gaul*, pp. 65-68, and Zuckerman, "Agobard," p. 35.
    20. *Form. Imp.*, no. 31 (pp. 310-311), and Agobard, *Epist.*, (p. 183) refer to *capitula* issued by Louis concerning Jewish matters. These *capitula* are not extant.
    21. This will be discussed below in relation to the problems and confusions that have arisen from studies of Louis's charters concerning Jewish matters.

22. Agobard, *Epist.*, 7 (p 184): "permittitur novas synagogas extruere" and the discussion above in note 8.

23. *Form. Imp.*, no. 31 (p. 310) and no. 30 (p. 309). The exact nature of these rights will be discussed below in relation to Louis's charters.

24. The rights of Jews to keep slaves and the right of Jews to live according to the *lex Judaeorum* suggest this. In addition the frequent remarks of Agobard concerning the unfettered missionary activity of the Jews suggests that the government made no attempt to stop the Jews from making converts. See above note 14.

25. See note 14 above.

26. *Form. Imp.*, no. 31 (p. 310): "Nemo fidelium nostrorum praesumat eorum mancipia peregrina sine eorum consensu ac voluntate baptisare." For a discussion of the relation of this element of the charter to the capitularies see below.

27. *Form. Imp.*, no. 30 (p. 309); no. 31 (p. 310) and no. 52 (p. 325).

28. Agobard., *Epist.*, 7 (p. 184). By ordering that the market should not be held on Saturday, Louis was simply adhering to the stipulation of the Roman law that guaranteed that no public business would be held on Jewish days of worship if the Jews were hurt by such an action. This also makes clear that control of the markets was an important element of Carolingian economic policy. See above ch. IV, n. 56.

29. Ganshof, *Recherches sur les capitulaires*, pp. 18ff.

30. On Bodo see Katz, *Jews in Spain and Gaul*, pp. 45-46, and Allen Cabaniss, "Bodo-Eleazar: A Famous Jewish Convert," *JQR*, 43 (1953), 313-318.

31. On Amalarius see Blumenkranz, *Auteurs chrétiens*, pp. 155, 172-173, and A. Wilmart, "Un lecteur ennemi d'Amalaire," *Revue Bénédictine*, 36 (1924), 323, 329. Cf. Allen Cabaniss, *Amalarius of Metz* (Amsterdam, 1954), who fails to grasp that their respective Jewish policies may have been a basic point of disagreement between Agobard and Amalarius.

32. Katz, *Jews in Spain and Gaul*, pp. 69-70, discusses this matter with extensive bibliography.

33. Blumenkranz, *Juifs et Chrétiens*, p. 11, and Blumenkranz, "The Roman Church and the Jews," p. 98.

34. Agobard, *Epist.*, 7 (p. 183) speaks of the "fautores" of the Jews at the court.

35. This episode is discussed in detail by Zuckerman, "Agobard," pp. 23ff.

36. Agobard, *Epist.*, 7 (p. 184). Zuckerman, "Agobard," p. 34, n. 38, wants to connect the patriarchs mentioned by Agobard with the putative *Nesi'im* of Narbonne. On the latter see Zuckerman's study, *Jewish Princedom*, which in its broad thesis is untenable.

37. Agobard, *Epist.*, 7 (p. 184).

38. Bouquet, VI, 624, no. CCXXXII. Cf. the freer translation by Parkes, *The Medieval Community*, p. 53. It is unfortunate that scholars specializing in Jewish history have not given sufficient attention to these sentiments although they have tended to treat the substance of the charter itself. See, for example, *Zuckerman*, "Agobard," p. 40.

39. See Zuckerman, "Agobard," p. 28-29.

40. Blumenkranz, *Juifs et Chrétiens*, p. 364, sees the formula of Louis's period as more influenced by Jews than the formula of Charles's time. But he does not make the distinction that the former probably originated from Charles's government and the latter from Louis's government. See ch. IV, n. 52.

41. *MGH, Cap.*, I, no. 131, ch. 5. Cf. ch. IV, n. 52.

42. F. L. Ganshof, "Charlemagne et l'usage de l'ecrit en matiére administrative," *MA*, 57 (1951), 1-25, points out the growing use of writing in Carolingian administration under Charlemagne and its increased emphasis under Louis the Pious. In note 20, Ganshof reminds us that the collection known as the *Formulae Imperiales* dates from the reign of Louis the Pious and that it was compiled in his chancery.

43. *Form. Imp.*, no. 39 (pp. 309-310); no. 31 (pp. 310-311); and no. 52 (p. 325).

44. *Form. Imp.*, no. 30 (p. 309) for the quoted passage, and nos. 31 and 52 (pp. 310 and 325, respectively).

45. *Form. Imp.*, no. 37 (pp. 314-315); and in no. 32 (p. 311).

46. *Form. Imp.*, no. 37 (p. 315). In the *Praeceptum* included in the *Form. Imp.*, 32 (p. 315), we find the phrase "sicut ipsi Iudei." M. Tangl, "Zum Judenschutzrecht unter den Karolingern," *NA*, 33 (1907), 197-200, argues that the *notae* which Zeumer interpreted as "sicut Judeis" and "sicut ipsi Judei" in his edition of the *Form. Imp.*, cited herein, should be read "sicut diximus" and "sicut iam diximus." On paleographic and diplomatic grounds Tangl's conjectures are far from compelling though they are not impossible. From the historical evidence we have seen in the previous chapter that the Carolingians frequently bracketed Jewish and non-Jewish merchants in the same formula. The similarity of the protections for Jewish and for non-Jewish merchants makes Zeumer's interpretation the more plausible one. Most scholars have followed Zeumer's interpretation. See, for example, Katz, *Jews in Spain and Gaul*, p. 86, n. 8; and Baron, *SRH*, IV, 260, n. 62. Cf. Kisch, *Jews in Medieval Germany*, pp. 136-137, 424-425 and esp. n. 20, who accepts Tangl's emendations and argues that they are of great importance because they illustrate in the negative, at least, that (p. 136) "no typical law of Jewry protection existed in the Frankish realm." Kisch is correct in the latter assertion, but this has nothing to do with the phrase "sicut Judeis" which means in this context just like the exemptions enjoyed by Jewish merchants. The entire frame of reference within which Kisch argues his case on this point and the previous literature on the subject cited in his notes illustrate how seriously the narrow emphasis of legal history can distort the historical reality. Kisch, n. 20, is incorrect in arguing that specialists in Jewish history have ignored Tangl's arguments. Tangl's arguments have not been ignored; they have been rejected. See Roth, "Economic Life," p. 386, notes 31-32. More important, however, are the studies by H. Laurent, "Marchands du palais et marchands d'abbayes," *Revue Historique*, 180 (1938), 281-297, and F. L. Ganshof, "Note sur 'Praeceptum Negotiatorum,' de Louis le Pieux," *Studi in onore di Armando Sapori* (Milan, 1957) I, 103-112.

47. The following description of the protection, peace, and complaint clauses is traditional. See Berthold Altmann, "Studies in Medieval German Jewish His-

tory," *PAAJR*, 10 (1940), 79ff.; Kisch, *Jews in Medieval Germany*, p. 136; and the works cited in their notes.

48. *Form. Imp.*, no. 30 (p. 309): "notum sit, quia istos Hebreos . . . sub nostra defensione suscepimus ac retinemus."; no. 31 (p. 310): "notum sit, quia praesentes Hebreos . . . sub nostra defensione suscepimus ac retinemus."; and no. 52 (p. 325): "notum sit, quia iste Hebreus . . . ad nostram veniens praesentiam, in manibus nostris se commendavit, et eum sub sermone tuitionis nostre recepimus ac retinemus." This last formula, unlike those cited above, was for a Jewish merchant from outside the empire. It was necessary for such a merchant to commend himself into the emperor's hands. He had to do so because he had not taken the oath of faithfulness to the emperor that all of the latter's subjects had taken. On the oath in the reign of Charlemagne see F. L. Ganshof, "Charlemagne et le serment," pp. 259-270 and above ch. IV, n. 50.

49. *Form. Imp.*, no. 30 (p. 309). Nos. 31 and 52 (pp. 310 and 325, respectively) are almost word for word copies of the above.

50. *Ibid.*, no. 31 (p. 310). See also nos. 30 and 52 (pp. 309-310 and 325, respectively). The stipulation that Jews be dealt with according to their own law refers in theory to the Roman law; but since under the latter Jews had the right to live under the *lex Judaeorum*, the actual process would be carried out under Jewish law.

51. See *Form. Imp.*, nos. 32 and 37 (pp. 311 and 314-315, respectively).

52. See above ch. III, n. 15.

53. *Form. Imp.*, no. 30 (p. 309). See also nos. 31 and 52 (pp. 310 and 325, respectively) in which the wording is exactly the same as in no. 30.

54. *Ibid.*, no. 30 (p. 309). See also nos. 31 and 52 (pp. 310 and 352, respectively) which have the same wording.

55. *Ibid.* no. 30 (p. 300) and no. 31 (pp. 310-311). The *capitula* mentioned in no. 31 concerning Jewish rights to receive punishment according to Jewish law are now lost. It is clear, however, that such rights were not necessarily enjoyed only by Jewish merchants. The same is clear for the procedure for bringing witnesses cited in notes 52 and 53 above. On the question of punishment see Baron, *SRH*, IV, 261, n. 63, who suggests that the *capitula* denoting flogging were consistent with and followed Jewish law "as communicated . . . by his Jewish advisors" to the emperor.

56. See note 50 above.

57. *Form. Imp.*, no. 30 (p. 309). See also nos. 31 and 52 (pp. 310 and 325, respectively) which note the same right.

58. *Ibid.*, no. 30 (p. 309).

59. *Ibid*.

60. *Ibid*.

61. Zuckerman, "Agobard," pp. 26-27.

62. See above note 14.

63. *Form. Imp.*, no. 31 (p. 310).

64. See note 28 above.

65. Agobard, *Epist.*, 7 (p. 184). Katz, *Jews in Spain and Gaul*, p. 129.

66. On early Carolingian policy see above ch. IV. On Louis see Bouquet, VI,

624, where the emperor sees to it that Jewish landholders in the south of France have their lands restored to them after a grasping official tried to usurp them.

67. See for example the problems encountered by David Herlihy, "Church Property on the European Continent, 701-1200," *Speculum*, 36 (1961), 81-105.

68. *MGH, Cap.*, I, no. 146, ch. 2. See also the discussion and works cited in ch. IV, note 22, above.

69. See note 44 above.

70. See the discussion by Roth, "Economic Life," pp. 33-34, and Schwarzfuchs, "France and Germany under the Carolingians," p. 129, but cf. Parkes, *The Medieval Community*, pp. 40ff. Verlinden, "Juifs dans l'economie," p. 28.

71. Georges Duby, *Rural Economy and Country Life in the Medieval West* (London, 1968), pp. 37ff., and Verlinden, "Juifs dans l'economie," pp. 22ff.

72. Agobard, *Epist.*, 7 (p. 183).

73. See the discussion by Zuckerman, "Agobard," p. 35, n. 42, who seems to doubt that Jews were involved in this activity because of the Jewish law that forbids such activity. Cf. Roth, "Economic Life," p. 27.

74. Agobard, *Epist.*, 7 (p. 185). It is likely that Agobard could have produced the two escaped slaves in this case since he was involved in litigation at the time. As to whether the business was as widespread as Agobard would have his readers believe cannot be documented. It should be noted that this activity dated from as early as Charlemagne's reign as indicated by the youth who had been kidnapped twenty-four years earlier in ca. 802 or 803. See Verlinden, "Juifs dans l'economie," pp. 24-25.

75. See note 16 above.

76. See Allen Cabaniss, *Agobard of Lyons, Churchman and Critic* (Syracuse, 1953), pp. 62-71.

77. See above ch. IV, n. 29.

78. *Form. Imp.*, no. 52 (p. 325). On the Jewish community at Saragossa see Roth, "Economic Life," pp. 34, 41; Blumenkranz, "The Roman Church and the Jews," p. 87; and Katz, *Jews in Spain and Gaul*, pp. 45-46.

79. See Katz, *Jews in Spain and Gaul*, pp. 54-55, and Parkes, *The Medieval Community*, pp. 54-55.

80. See above notes 30-33.

81. For a bibliography of works on Agobard see Cabaniss, *Agobard*, pp. 111-113, and the notes in Blumenkranz, *Auteurs chrétiens*, pp. 152ff.

82. Agobard, *Epist.*, 7 (p. 185).

83. *Ibid., Epist.*, 4 (p. 165), and 6 (p. 181). Cf. the discussions by Cabaniss, *Agobard*, p. 31, and Zuckerman, "Agobard," p. 24.

84. See, for example, the discussion by Blumenkranz, *Juifs et Chrétiens*, pp. 337-338.

85. See the discussion by Katz, *Jews in Spain and Gaul*, pp. 101-102.

86. Agobard, *Epist.*, 7 (p. 183), for example, discusses Jewish slaughtering practices. See Adrien Bressolles, *Doctrine et action politique d'Agobard* (Paris, 1949), p. 111, for Agobard's efforts to have Christians boycott Jewish processed wine and meat. That Bressolles who was a priest might not be aware of the ritual significance for Jews of processing these products is reasonable. Zuckerman, a rab-

bi, should have understood the religious basis for Agobard's position ("Agobard," p. 35). The presence of so lowly a functionary as the *mashgi'ah* would have been sufficient to convince Agobard of the religious elements in food processing.

87. See Agobard, *Epist.*, 7 (pp. 183-184), 9 (pp. 199-200).

88. See above note 83 for his position on slaves, and on the canon law see Agobard, *Epist.*, 6 (p. 182) and 4 (p. 165) that make it clear that Agobard believed he was resting his case on canon 16 of the Council of Mâcon that took place in Gaul in 583 (*MGH, Conc.*, I, p. 159). In addition there was a long tradition in the Western church that encouraged such activity. On this see Wiegand, "Agobard von Lyon," pp. 235, 237, 248. The argument by Zuckerman, "Agobard," pp. 24ff., that Agobard did not rely upon canon law for his right to baptize Jewish-owned slaves illustrates the situation well. The imperial court claimed that the owner's permission was necessary according to the action taken at the Council of Gangra, but Agobard focused on the health of the slave's soul and not the owner's legal rights. Zuckerman misleads his readers when he suggests that Agobard did not argue on the basis of canon law. The prelate did, but he was wrong. In his later discussion and in quoting Bressolles (*Agobard*, p. 106), Zuckerman (p. 29) seems to ignore the implication of his own note 4, p. 24. The fact that Agobard did not cite a specific reference to canon law in his letter "Consultatio et supplicatio de baptismo Judaeorum mancipiorum" (*Epist.*, 4, pp. 164-166) is irrelevant since on p. 165 he alluded to canon 16 of the Council of Mâcon, as noted above. Agobard quite clearly felt that he had canonical grounds for his position as evidenced by *Epist.*, 7 cited above. See also Egon Boshof, *Erzbischof Agobard von Lyon: Leben und Werk* (Cologne, 1969), pp. 102ff.

89. Cf. Zuckerman, "Agobard," p. 34, n. 36 and pp. 35ff., who sees this as one of Agobard's main aims.

90. *Ibid.*, p. 26. For a discussion of the extent of Agobard's putative efforts to convert Jews cf. B. Blumenkranz, "Deux compilations canoniques de Florus de Lyon et l'action antijuive d'Agobard," *RHD*, ser. 4, 33 (1955), 227-254 and 560-582. For further discussion see below ch. VI, n. 67.

91. Agobard, *Epist.*, 6 (pp. 179-180).

92. *Ibid.*, *Epist.*, 4 (p. 165): "Quod utique necesse non esset, si ille, qui magister est Judaeorum, ita adtenderet, ut vos ei faciendum dixistis. Nam si secundum vestram iussionem ille consideraret fideliter ministerium nostrum, sicut nos ei honorem exhibere volumus in ministerio suo, nulla esset necessitas iniuriam facere interrogando, nisi propter augmentum doctrinae. Caeterum de causis Judaeorum non esset ulla contentio aut discordia, si ille rationabiliter agere voluisset." The passage quoted above condenses several phases of the incident. The first phase ended with his loss of the case before the *magister*. The next phase resulted in the suits brought by the Jews. Since the latter won the first round, they would have had no reason to bring suit unless Agobard had seized the slave. The prelate as much as admitted that he did this (*Epist.*, 6, p. 182). By and large I agree with the chronology developed by Zuckerman, "Agobard," pp. 26-30, up to this point but with one serious reservation concerning his description of the process. On pp. 26-27 Zuckerman implies that the right of Jews who had special imperial charters of protection and privilege to appeal to the palace court is of relevance to the case at

this point. There is no ground for such a position. In the first phase Agobard was the plaintiff, and the court sent the *magister Judaeorum* to deal with the case. In the second phase the Jews went to court, but it is unclear if the case was pressed by the *magister* or by the wronged slave owner. If the former were the plaintiff, then this would be of importance in ascertaining the nature of the duties and the powers of the *magister*. If, however, the slave owner were the plaintiff, then he would simply be exercising his rights as an imperial subject (see Altman, "Studies," p. 82).

93. Agobard, *Epist.*, 4 (p. 164), should be read with the interrogation cited above in note 92 and with his constant complaining about Jewish influence, supporters, and patrons at court mentioned in *Epist.*, 7 (pp. 183-184).

94. Agobard, *Epist.*, 6 (p. 180); "Quoddam preceptum Judaei circumferunt, quod sibi datum ab imperatore gloriantur, in quo continetur, ut mancipium Iudaicum absque voluntate domini sui nemo baptizet."; and on the imperial seal see *Epist.*, 7 (p. 184): "dum ostendunt precepta ex nomine vestro, aureis sigillis signata." H. Breslau, "Zur Lehre von den Siegeln der Karolinger und Ottonen," *Archiv für Urkundenforschung*, 1 (1908), 363, 364, n. 4, concludes that the documents mentioned by Agobard are the same ones that are preserved in copies in the *Imperial Formulary* nos. 30 and 31 (pp. 309-311). There is no basis for such a conclusion. No. 30 alludes to men who are baptizing Jewish-owned slaves without the owners' permission but makes no mention of Lyons or of Agobard, and no. 31 grants to Jews mentioned in the charter who happen to be from Lyons the right to refuse permission to have their slaves baptized, but no mention at all is made of a controversy. Zuckerman, "Agobard," pp. 29-30, n. 22, follows Breslau in his conjecture.

95. There is no reason to assume that the charter issued to Domatus and Samuel (*Imp. Form.*, no. 30, p. 309) by Louis embodies this complaint as Zuckerman, "Agobard," p. 32 does. This charter in no specific way connects the beneficiaries to events at Lyons and Agobard's actions.

96. Agobard, *Epist.*, 7 (p. 183).
97. *Ibid.*
98. *Ibid.* Cf. Zuckerman, "Agobard," p. 33, n. 34 and the works cited there.
99. In addition to the material in notes 97, 98, 99, above see Agobard, *Epist.*, 7 (pp. 183-184), 9 (pp. 199-200).
100. *Ibid.*, 7 (p. 183).
101. *Ibid.*, 8 (pp. 185-199).
102. *Ibid.*, 9 (pp. 199-201). See the discussion by Blumenkranz, *Auteurs chrétiens*, pp. 167-168.
103. See the discussion by Katz, *Jews in Spain and Gaul*, pp. 55-56.
104. Cf. Cabaniss, *Agobard*, pp. 84ff.
105. See above note 31.
106. See, for example, Cabaniss, *Agobard*, pp. 69-70, who sees Agobard as motivated by an effort to stop the emperor from having secular law supercede canon law, to uphold the universality of Christianity against those who would stop baptism, and to sustain the doctrine of brotherhood against those who would deny slaves the right to be baptized. Zuckerman, "Agobard," pp. 36ff., by con-

trast, sees the prelate motivated by a desire to drive Jews from the lands that they possessed so that the Church could take them over. Wiegand, "Agobard von Lyon," pp. 242-244, sees Agobard as lacking good judgment because he escalated an insignificant matter into a question of principle.

107. Cabaniss, *Agobard*, pp. 1, 6, 27.
108. See above ch. I, n. 64.
109. Cf. Cantera Burgos, "Christian Spain," pp. 357-358.
110. *Theophanis contin.*, p. 48. See, for example, the discussions by A. Andreades, "Les Juifs et le fisc dans l'empire byzantin," *Mélanges Charles Diehl*, 1 (Paris, 1930), 7-29; F. Dölger, "Die Frage der Judensteuer in Byzanz," *Vierteljahrschrift für Sozial- und Wirtschaftsgeschichte*, 26 (1933), 1-24; Starr, *Jews in the Byzantine Empire*, p. 105; Sharf, *Byzantine Jewry*, pp. 189-200 and esp. p. 193; and Baron, *SRH*, III, 191, and 320-321 for a review of the literature. The notion that Michael himself was a Jew cannot be taken seriously. See on this Sharf, *Byzantine Jewry*, p. 81, n. 81.
111. Roth, "Italy," pp. 103-104.
112. See above ch. IV, n. 28.
113. H. J. Zimmels, "Scholars and Scholarship in Byzantium and Italy," *WHJP*, II, p. 179. On Jewish scholarly activity at Rome during this period see p. 177. See above n. 75, ch. IV.
114. Starr, *Jews in the Byzantine Empire*, pp. 104ff.
115. *Ibid.*
116. Roth, "Italy," pp. 100-121 and 402ff. *passim.*
117. Starr, *Jews in the Byzantine Empire*, pp. 99-100.
118. Roth, "Italy," pp. 101, 102-104, 106-108.

Chapter VI

1. The division of the Carolingian empire and the Treaty of Verdun have been subjects of great interest to historians, and this is reflected by a large bibliography. A useful guide to this material is in F. L. Ganshof, "Zur Entstehungsgeschichte und Bedeutung des Vertrages von Verdun (843)," *Deutsches Archiv für Erforschung des Mittelalters*, 12 (1956), 313-330. I tend to follow Ganshof's interpretation.

2. This material is treated in detail by F. Lot and Louis Haphen, *Le régne de Charles de Chauve* (Paris, 1909), pp. 141-148, and 162ff. Zuckerman, *Jewish Princedom*, pp. 295ff., goes over the same material with an emphasis on the Jewish question. In his earlier study "Agobard," pp. 36ff., Zuckerman had already put forward the idea that the anti-Jewish policy of the Church was intimately connected with its aim of getting back Church lands. Although it is certainly true that Jews were landholders and landowners and that some of these Jews almost surely were in possession of Church lands, it is even more evident that Christian magnates were in possession of the vast majority of the lands that the Church wanted returned.

3. *MGH, Cap.*, II, no. 293, canon 75 (p. 419). It is clear that this canon is based upon canon 59 of the Fourth Council of Toledo. Scholars have debated the accuracy of the text of the Toledo canon, but the intent of the framers of the

Notes   181

Paris canon is clear. On the scholarly controversy involving the earlier legislation see Thompson, *The Goths*, p. 178. It is significant that previous scholars have not grasped that the basic intention of the clerical party at Paris was to eliminate the Jews in the long term. For example, Zuckerman, *Jewish Princedom*, pp. 299-300, gives this canon little prominence and summarizes its intent as simply to "suppress Judaism." Katz, *Jews in Spain and Gaul*, p. 50, n. 3, relegates the problem to a footnote. Baron, *SRH*, IV, 18, virtually ignores Meaux-Paris, and Blumenkranz, *Juifs et Chrétiens*, p. 150, n. 316, confuses the canons as does Katz, *Jews in Spain and Gaul*.
    4. *MGH, Cap.*, II, no. 293, canon 73 (p. 416).
    5. *Ibid.*, pp. 416-417.
    6. *Ibid.*
    7. *Ibid.*, pp. 416-418, and canon 74 (419). Parkes, *The Medieval Community*, pp. 27ff., treats this legislation on segregation well but misses the main point that these measures were intended only for the short term. Parkes is particularly effective in characterizing the apprehensions of the clergy.
    8. *MGH, Cap.*, II, canon 73 (pp. 416-418).
    9. *Ibid.*
    10. *Ibid.*
    11. *Liber contra Judaeos*, ch. 42 (cols. 170-171).
    12. *Ibid.*, ch. 41 (col. 170).
    13. *Ibid.*, ch. 40 (col. 169).
    14. Parkes, *The Medieval Community*, pp. 53ff., treats this matter very well. Cf. Blumenkranz, *Juifs et Chrétiens*, pp. 75-76.
    15. *Liber contra Judaeos*, chs. 41 (cols. 170-171) and 59 (col. 184).
    16. *Ibid.*, ch. 43 (cols. 171-172).
    17. See above ch. V, note 102. It should be noted that the diocese of Lyons was not a part of Charles's kingdom and that Amulo served the clerical party at Paris essentially as an *amicus curiae* who submitted a brief in favor of one party although technically he was not a member of it. Amulo's work and policies will be discussed below in relation to Lothair's kingdom in which Lyons was located.
    18. *MGH, Cap.*, II, no. 257 (p. 261). For a general discussion of the meeting at Épernay see Lot and Halphen, *Charles le Chauve*, pp. 162ff.
    19. *Annales de Saint-Bertin*, an. 877 (p. 216) for Sedechias, and *Actes de Charles II*, no. 417 (p. 432) for Judah. The general tenor of Amulo's view concerning the growth of Jewish influence is exposed in the *Liber contra Judaeos* as illustrated in the discussion above, and see particularly ch. I, col. 142, which would seem to suggest that the situation had deteriorated, from the ecclesiastical point of view, since Agobard's time.
    It is not clear what role, if any, the Jews of Charles's realm played in helping him make the decision at Épernay. A contemporary observation (*MGH, Cap.*, II, no. 257, p. 261) makes it clear that Charles was supported by his magnates. A much debated and recently reinterpreted Hebrew source of considerably later date provides the following genealogy: "R Nathan son of Makhir son of Menahem of Ancona son of Samuel of Makhir of the County of Auvergne son of Solomon, he who broke in pieces the horn of the scoffer in the province of Rheims

by the name [of Hincmarus], son of Anatom son of Tsadok the Punctuator."
Zuckerman, *Jewish Princedom*, pp. 306ff., provides this reading and an extensive bibliography on the subject as well as identifying Solomon as having been a key figure in thwarting Hincmar and the anti-Jewish party at Épernay. If Zuckerman's reading is accepted, then it certainly is not impossible that Solomon was thought of by his descendants as having played a role in thwarting Hincmar's anti-Jewish efforts, perhaps at Épernay. Although these unsupported conjectures are not unreasonable, Zuckerman's fantasies about Solomon's Christian identity and career (pp. 308 and 325) lack even hypothetical credibility.

20. *MGH, Cap.*, II, no. 273, ch. 23 (p. 320). See the discussion by Katz, *Jews in Spain and Gaul*, p. 86.

21. As we have seen thus far—especially during the Carolingian era—Jewry law like the *addenda* to other national laws was a cooperative venture intended to aid in creating a legal *modus vivendi* for the various peoples, each with their own law, who were living in the Carolingian empire. Cf. Kisch, *Jews in Medieval Germany*, pp. 7ff.

22. In addition to the text cited in note 20 above see ch. III, n. 101, and ch. IV, n. 45.

23. See above ch. III, n. 56, and ch. V, n. 16.

24. See Amulo, *Liber contra Judaeos*, chs. 44 and 59 (cols. 172 and 184, respectively).

25. Dhuoda, *Liber manualis*, ch. 71.

26. *Ibid.*, and the discussion by Baron, *SRH*, IV, 202, and Blumenkranz, *Auteurs chrétiens*, p. 173.

27. *MGH, Cap.*, II, no. 281, ch. 31 (p. 361). See Katz, *Jews in Spain and Gaul*, p. 130.

28. See above ch. IV, n. 29.

29. Zuckerman, *Jewish Princedom*, p. 318. It may be observed that Zuckerman's treatment of Hebrew sources and the Jewish milieu is far better than his treatment of the Latin sources and the Christian milieu.

30. For example, Tsadok, Gaon of Sura (d. 823), his son Naḥshon (d. 882), and many others corresponded with the Jewish communities of Carolingian Spain. For the text see A. Cowley, "Bodleian Genizah Fragments," *JQR*, 18, old series (1906), 401. For further discussion and interpretation of this text see Jacob Mann, "The Responsa of the Babylonian Geonim as a Source of Jewish History," *JQR*, 7, new series (1916-1917), 486. This article with the same pagination is reprinted in Jacob Mann, *The Responsa of the Babylonian Geonim as a Source of Jewish History* (New York, 1973). Zuckerman, *Jewish Princedom*, p. 317-318, follows Mann as does Baron, *SRH*, VI, 332, n. 28.

31. *Teshubhot haGeonim*, ed. Musafiah, nos. 56-57. See also the brief mention by Baron, *SRH*, V, 19-20, and for a fuller discussion with substantial bibliography see Zuckerman, *Jewish Princedom*, 321-322.

32. See above ch. IV, notes 13-16. On Meir ben Joseph see Simon Epperstein, "Beiträge zur Geschichte und Literatur im gaonäischen Zeitalter," *MGWJ*, 56 (1912), 85, 88. Epperstein's conclusions are accepted by Zuckerman, *Jewish Princedom*, p. 321, n. 12.

33. See ch. IV, n. 16.
34. On Bodo in general see Allen Cabaniss, "Bodo-Eleazar," pp. 313-328, and "Paulus Albarus of Muslim Cordova," *Church History*, 22 (1953), 99-112. On Bodo's overt hostility see *Annales de Saint Bertin*, an. 847 (pp. 53-54). For Bodo's presence and apparent residence in the Jewish dominated town of Ausona see Zuckerman, *Jewish Princedom*, pp. 320-321, n. 11, with full bibliography.
35. *Annales de Saint Bertin*, an. 848 (p. 55). For the capture of William see *Chron. Fontanell.*, an. 848 (p. 302).
36. *Annales de Saint Bertin*, an. 852.
37. *Ibid.*, an. 877 (p. 216).
38. On the authorship see *Annales de Saint Bertin*, eds. F. Grat et al., introduction pp. vff.
39. See for example, Lot and Halphen, *Charles le Chauve*, p. 190,̀ n. 2, "Est-il besoin d'advertir que la 'trahison des juifs' est une plaisante invention de Prudence qui, comme presque tous ses collègues en épiscopat, exércrait les juifs. En 852 encore, il leur attribuera la prise de Barcelone par les Musulmans." In the wake of the defeat of the clerical party at Épernay, a group of scholars produced two important collections of forged documents: the *False Decretals* and the *False Capitularies*. Both of these collections embodied a substantial amount of anti-Jewish material. For the former see Blumenkranz, *Juifs et Chrétiens*, p. 303, n. 28, and for the latter *Benedicti Capitularia*, Bk. II, chs. 122 (p. 79), 195 (p. 83), 205 (p. 83), 423 (p. 97); Bk. III, chs. 276 (p. 120), 286 (p. 121), Add., II, ch. 11 (p. 134); and Add. IV, ch. 2 (p. 146). Cf. Blumenkranz, *Juifs et Chrétiens*, p. 303.
40. On Bordeaux see the material cited by Lot and Halphen, *Charles le Chauve*, p. 190, n. 2, but without reference to Jews. On Barcelona see Ibn el-Athir, *Chron.*, an. H. 236 (A.D. 850-851).
41. See Lot and Halphen, *Charles le Chauve*, pp. 99ff. and 112ff.
42. *Ibid.*, pp. 188-190. Lot and Halphen note that "Bordeaux n'était pas demeuré sous l'authorité immédiate de Charles" (p. 188). On p. 190, however, they identify William as "duc des Gascons" rather than as William, son of Bernard. What prompted their conclusion is not explicit, but it is thus clearly implied that the Duke of Gascony was Peppin's ally. There is, however, no sound evidence for such a conclusion, but there is overwhelming proof that William, son of Bernard, was Peppin's ally. Most scholars see the William who held Bordeaux as Bernard's son. See, for example, *Annales de Saint Bertin*, p. 56, n. 1.
43. Einar Joranson, *The Danegeld in France* (Rock Island, Ill., 1923), discusses Charles's extensive contact with the Vikings during the year 845 (pp. 26ff.), notes earlier contacts of the Vikings with Charles's men (p. 185), and discusses the stipendiary Danegeld (p. 49) by which "Charles engaged one group of Vikings as his mercenaries."
44. Lot and Halphen, *Charles le Chauve*, pp. 190-191, 204ff.
45. *Ibid.*, pp. 209-210.
46. *Recueil des actes de Charles II le Chauve*, ed. Tessier, II, no. 417 (p. 432): "In nomine sanctae et individuae Trinitatis. Karolus ejusdem Dei omnipotentis misericordia imperator augustus, omnibus Barchinonensibus peculiaribus nostris salutem. Sciatis quoniam superno munere congrua prosperitate valemus. Apud vos

quoque ut et idipsum maneat valde desideramus. Plurimas autem vobis grates referimus eo quod in nostram fidelitatem semper omnimodis tenditis. Venit denique Judas Hebreus fidelis noster ad nos et de vestra fidelitate multa nobis designavit. Unde vestrae fidelitate condignam remunerationem et decens proemium referre parati sumus. De nostrae igitur fidelitatis assiduitate nullo modo retardetis, sed in ea, prout melius scitis et potestis, in omnibus tendentes permaneatis, sicuti hactenus factum habetis. Valete. Et sciatis vos quia per fidelem meum Judacot dirigo ad Frodoynum episcopum libtas X de argento ad suam ecclesiam repare."

47. See the discussion between J. Calmette, "Une lettre close originale de Charles le Chauve," École française de Rome, Mélanges d'archéoolgie et d'histoire, 22 (1902), 135-139 (plates IV, V after p. 145 have a photograph of the letter under discussion), and Ph. Lauer, "Lettre close de Charles le Chauve pour les 'Barcelonais,'" BEC, 62 (1902), 696-699; (also J. Calmette, "Sur la lettre close de Charles le Chauve aux Barcelonais," BEC, 64 (1903), 329-334). Zuckerman, Jewish Princedom, p. 345, goes far beyond the evidence and either Calmette or Lauer when he concludes, "The letter is clearly addressed to townspeople of Barcelona organized not alone as a community but as a self-directing political entity."

48. Mediae Latinitatis Lexicon Minus, ed. Niermeyer, pp. 779ff.

49. On ministeriales see, for example, K. Bosl, Die Reichministerialität der Salier und Staufer (Munich, 1950-51).

50. Curiously, Zuckerman, Jewish Princedom, p. 346, discusses this peculiar relationship of some Jews to the imperial "chamber" but fails to grasp that the analogy if followed to its logical conclusion would destroy his argument.

51. Classically tendo is often associated with bending the bow, hurling the spear, and aiming a weapon, and its derivatives stretch into the area of marching, contending forcefully, and setting up tents in a military encampment (C. Lewis and C. Short, Latin Dictionary, (Oxford, 1879), pp. 1852-1853).

52. C. Barnett, Britain and Her Army, 1509-1970 (London, 1970), p. 114.

53. In dealing with this letter Zuckerman, Jewish Princedom, p. 343, n. 66, indicates that he is following Tessier's edition but introduces several changes without warning. For example, he puts commas around "peculiaribus nostris" thus placing it in apposition to "omnibus Barchinonensibus." Zuckerman also places a period after "augustus," capitalizes "omnibus," and begins "Barchinonensibus" with a small letter. (Other differences of less significance between Zuckerman's reading of the text and Tessier's reading include the former's failure to capitalize "Trinitatis," "Karolus," and "Dei," the inclusion of the words "in ecclesia" instead of "misericordia," and the failure to place a period after "Trinitatis." All these differences as well as those noted above concerning the address appear in the first two lines.). More to the point, however, is Zuckerman's translation (p. 342) of the address as he idiosyncratically punctuates it: "To all Barcelonians, our own special [subjects]." The word peculiaris permits the translation "own" or "special" but not both at the same time. In addition, the appositional punctuation demands a substantive that Zuckerman feels free to include in brackets.

54. Scholars have expended considerable energy in deciding whether "Judas Hebreus fidelis noster" is the same person as "fidelem meum Judacot." On this see I. Loeb, "Notes sur l'histoire des Juifs VIII – Juda, Juif catalan du IXe siècle,"

REJ, 10 (1885), 248, who follows Fidel Fita, "Hebreos de Barcelona en el siglo IX," *Boletín de la Real Academia de la Historia*, 4 (1884), 70, in concluding that the above phrases refer to the same person. See also Lauer, *Lettre close*, p. 697, who views "-cot" as a diminutive. For a fuller discussion see Zuckerman, *Jewish Princedom*, p. 343, n. 66.

55. This is reviewed by A. Lewis, *The Development of Southern France and Catalan Society, 718-1050* (Austin, 1965), pp. 109ff., and with a different emphasis by Zuckerman, *Jewish Princedom*, pp. 332ff. Their notes provide a detailed guide to the relevant literature.

56. *MGH, Cap.*, II, no. 303 (pp. 458-460).

57. See above ch. IV, notes 14, 15.

58. See above notes 30-32.

59. See the works cited in note 55 above.

60. Sedulius Scottus, *Carm.*, II, xxviii (p. 194), indicates that Jewish poets celebrated the reign of Charles the Bald during the king's own lifetime.

61. Flodoard, *Hist. Eccl. Rem.*, Bk. III, ch. 3, demonstrates a bias in favor of Hincmar.

62. René Poupardin, *Le royaume de Provence sous les Carolingiens* (Paris, 1901), provides a good account of the dissolution of royal power in the central part of Lothair's realm.

63. *MGH, Cap.*, II, no. 228 (p. 122).

64. See Rabinowitz, *Jewish Law*, pp. 182ff., with the reservations indicated above in ch. II, n. 85.

65. *MGH, Cap.*, II, no. 228 (p. 122).

66. *MGH, Epist.*, V, p. 239, where the letter is attributed to either Agobard or Amulo. See Blumenkranz, "Deux compilations," pp. 574-575, for a critical edition of the text and 243ff., for his attempts to attribute the letter to Agobard. For those who see Remigius as the author see K. Werner, *Alcuin und sien Jahrhundert* (Paderborn, 1870), p. 332; Gross, *Gallia Judaica*, pp. 76, 340; and Parkes, *The Medieval Community*, pp. 35-36, and cf. n. 3, p. 36, where Parkes admits that the authorship is uncertain. For further bibliography on the point see Katz, *Jews in Spain and Gaul*, p. 27, n. 3; Blumenkranz, "Deux compilations," p. 244; and Baron, *SRH*, IV, 262-263. There is no complete treatment of the secondary literature on this problem of authorship.

67. *MGH, Epist.*, V, p. 239. Blumenkranz, "Deux compilations," p. 244ff., in his attempts to identify Agobard as the author bases his case on one crucial point, i.e., only Louis the Pious could have been the addressee of the letter because only he ruled all the cities in question and Agobard is the only archbishop of Lyons who pursued an anti-Jewish policy during Louis's reign. As Baron, *SRH*, IV, 263, notes, however, the addressee need only have exercised authority at Arles as did Lothair. This weakens Blumenkranz's case substantially, especially in light of the conflict between Louis the Pious and Agobard as elaborated in chapter V above. If Lothair is the only likely prospect as addressee, then Agobard cannot have been the author (he died in 840); and either Amulo or Remigius must have carried out the above-mentioned policy. As late as 846, more than half a decade after taking office, Amulo could make no claim to having won any successes against the Jews

(see note 16 above). The letter in question (*MGH, Epist.*, V, p. 239) seems to imply that the author was successful shortly after attaining office "postquam . . . vestrae pietatis patrocinio . . . coepimus laborare." This would place the date in 852 or 853 if Remigius was, in fact, the author because of the implication that he began to work after receiving the bishopric from the man to whom he is writing. Incidentally, it should be noted that the hierarchy at Lyons throughout the generation under discussion was the beneficiary of the work and ideas of Deacon Florus. This point is made effectively by Baron, *SRH*, IV, 263.

68. *MGH, Epist.*, V, p. 239. In discussing Remigius's policy, specialists in Jewish history often judge the prelate to have coerced the Jews. Parkes, *The Medieval Community*, pp. 36ff., attacks this point of view. In light of previous Jewish successes during the generation of Agobard and Amulo, it seems likely that there was an ongoing battle between the rabbis and the priests for audiences to hear their respective sermons. The laments by Agobard and Amulo discussed above to the effect that Christians preferred Jewish sermons should perhaps be seen as a part of this contest.

69. Quite obviously the authorities at Arles in the period before the letter was written were manifestly pro-Jewish. The city was certainly regarded as "safe" by those Jewish communities that sent their children there. In attempting to assess Lothair's Jewish policy it is perhaps of marginal value to note that his wife, the Empress Irmengarde, was looked upon favorably by the Jews of his kingdom and that she was celebrated by Jewish poets. One must ask the rhetorical question — would the Jews have praised the empress if her husband had been active in pursuing an anti-Jewish policy? Unfortunately these poems by Jewish poets have not survived, and we have no way of knowing whether they selected as their theme the *Book of Esther*. For the reference to these Jewish poets see Sedulius Scottus, *Carm.*, II, xx (p. 186). Concerning Lothair, himself, it should be mentioned that he trusted Jewish merchants with the very important task of supplying his army. *MGH, Cap.* II, no. 228, ch. 24.

70. For the complex and confused history of this region see Poupardin, *Provence sous les carolingiens*, ch. 1.

71. *MGH, Cap.* II, no. 219, ch. 2. Cf. Baron, *SRH*, IV, 25-26, who argues persuasively that the document is not authentic but later (p. 61) uses it as though it were authentic.

72. On the confused state of affairs in Italy at this time see Llewellyn, *Rome in the Dark Ages*, pp. 269ff. Baron, *SRH*, IV, 245, confuses Lothair's wife who was the subject of praise by Jewish poets with Louis II's wife. See note 69 above.

73. *MGH, Cap.* II, no. 253, ch. 9 (p. 252). This text in its present form comes from an early tenth-century (903-906) confirmation of previous practices "qualiter temporibus Hludwici et Karlomanni ceterorumque regum iustissime exolvebatur" (p. 250).

74. *MGH, Form.*, 410. It is important to note with Blumenkranz, *Juifs et Chrétiens*, p. 45, n. 173, that Bishop Salomon II's letter indicating Witgarius's close relations with Jews was placed in a formulary and is therefore of greater importance than a simple letter.

75. See generally, Schwarzfuchs, "France and Germany under the Early Caro-

lingians," pp. 132ff.; Roth, "Economic Life," pp. 45-46; and Kestenberg-Gladstein, "Central and Eastern Europe: Bohemia," pp. 309-310.
76. V. Anscharii, ch. 4 (p. 693).
77. See above note 74, and Gesta Karoli, Bk. I, chs. 10, 16, and Bk. II, ch. 14.
78. MGH, Epist., V, 633-635. See the discussion by Blumenkranz, Auteurs chrétiens, p. 179.
79. See above ch. IV, n. 24.
80. Blumenkranz, Juifs et Chrétiens, p. 45, n. 273.
81. Among those in the entourage of Count Arbo who were knowledgeable about the levies in question are listed forty-one men. Three were *vicarii*, and the rest had no titles. Of these thirty-eight men one was named "Ysac," and he was followed on the list by "Salaman." The expertise that these men possessed—they swore as to the nature of the customs involved—suggests that they might have been *telonarii*. Roth, "Economic Life," p. 35, lists the names as "Isaac and Jacob" and considers them "noble."
82. See the brief summary of political conditions in Italy by Roth, "Italy," pp. 106ff. There are no specific data on the Jewish policies of either Theophilus or Michael. The former did cooperate with the Khazars (Dunlop, "Khazars," p. 347). Basil I, who is discussed below, however, is depicted as having taken a new course when he attempted to convert Jews to Christianity. This may well be the *tendenz* of the so-called Macedonian school of historiography. By way of support for Michael's harsh line toward the Church we have the evidence that he "demoted the strictly observant patriarch Ignatius, putting in his place Photius, a sophisticated layman and a scholar of note, who was raised through the necessary ecclesiastical degrees in a few days, some said in a few hours." In the well-known *Vision of Daniel* it is said of Michael, "He will make mock priests and will anger the Most High by his deeds. And God will destroy him . . . for the evil of his doings." For both the quotation and translation see Sharf, *Byzantine Jewry*, pp. 85 and 202. It should be noted that being regarded as "anti-Church" is hardly the same as being pro-Jewish although the two are often connected or confused.
83. *Chronicle of Ahimaaz*, p. 114 (pp. 66ff.); Starr, *Jews in the Byzantine Empire*, pp. 117-118; and cf. Roth, "Italy," p. 402, n. 6.
84. Zimmels, "Scholars," p. 179, and Starr, *Jews in the Byzantine Empire*, p. 117, based on the *Chronicle of Ahimaaz*, p. 114 (p. 67).
85. *Chronicle of Ahimaaz*, p. 118 (pp. 74-76), and Starr, *Jews in the Byzantine Empire*, pp. 122-123.
86. For the text Ascoli, "Iscrizioni," pp. 303ff. (no. 26). For a translation with bibliography see Starr, *Jews in the Byzantine Empire*, p. 111. Zimmels, "Scholars," p. 179.
87. Starr, *Jews in the Byzantine Empire*, pp. 111ff., published a useful sample in translation with bibliography.
88. *Chronicle of Ahimaaz*, pp. 112ff. (pp. 65ff.). Starr, *Jews in the Byzantine Empire*, pp. 115ff.
89. Starr, *Jews in the Byzantine Empire*, pp. 115ff.
90. Roth, "Italy," p. 104.
91. For Jewish feelings about life in Bari in the period after the Muslim con-

quest see the materials brought together and discussed by Starr, *Jews in the Byzantine Empire*, p. 110, and for the treatment of R. Aaron by Saudan see *Chronicle of Ahimaaz*, pp. 118-119 (pp. 76-77). On the Jews of Bari under Christian rule see Roth, "Italy," pp. 102ff.

92. *Chronicle of Ahimaaz*, p. 119 (p. 77).

93. *Ibid.*, 119ff. (pp. 77ff), and Starr, *Jews in the Byzantine Empire*, p. 124.

94. See above ch. IV, n. 29.

95. Nicholas I, "Responsa ad consulta Bulgarorum," (*MGH, Epist.*, 6, 574, 599). Cf. Blumenkranz, *Auteurs chrétiens*, pp. 204-205. Baron, *SRH*, III, 209, with note 46, p. 330, provides some discussion of the theology involved and includes useful bibliography. Cf. A. Scheiber, "Hungary," *WHJP*, II, 314.

96. *Theophanis contin.*, pp. 341-342. Sharf, *Byzantine Jewry*, pp. 84ff., sees this account as the work of the Macedonian school of historiography that attempted to glorify Michael and his descendants. In fact the author may have been Michael's grandson, Constantine VII (p. 86). For other friendly Greek sources see Sharf, *Byzantine Jewry*, p. 103, n. 5. See also Baron, *SRH*, III, 179-180, and Starr, *Jews in the Byzantine Empire*, pp. 133-134, on the question of authorship with further bibliography.

97. See Starr, *Jews in the Byzantine Empire*, pp. 137-138. The general discussion by Sharf, *Byzantine Jewry*, pp. 84ff., sets this attack in its historiographical as well as its historical perspective.

98. Sharf, *Byzantine Jewry*, p. 86.

99. *Chronicle of Ahimaaz*, pp. 115ff. (pp. 69ff.), and Starr, *Jews in the Byzantine Empire*, pp. 127ff.

100. See, for example, Sharf, *Byzantine Jewry*, pp. 86ff., and Roth, "Italy," pp. 104ff. But cf. Baron, *SRH*, III, 180ff.

101. Sharf,' *Byzantine Jewry*, pp. 87-88. On Amittai's poems see Starr, *Jews in the Byzantine Empire*, p. 127, and the literature cited there. On R. Silano see J. Marcus, "Studies in the Chronicle of Ahim'atz," *PAAJR*, 5 (1933-1934), 88-90, with the literature cited there.

102. It is far from certain that any of the compositions alluded to in note 101, above, are outside the *mouvance* of the *Chronicle of Ahimaaz*. The problems of dating and authorship are considerable; see, for example, Starr, *Jews in the Byzantine Empire*, pp. 131-132, and Roth, "Italy," p. 403, n. 18, where he quotes from a hymn: "The King of Edom forced me / In the Sh^{e}ma' he silenced me . . . / Synagogues in dust he lays, / that My children should not pray." Roth argues that it "describes the persecution [by Basil] in unmistakable terms." This kind of evidence is clearly unreliable, and a close examination of it makes clear why Baron, *SRH*, III, 180-181, rejects the entire line of investigation. For more on R. Silano and Amittai ben Shefatiah see J. Schirmann, "The Beginning of Hebrew Poetry in Italy and Northern Europe," *WHJP*, II, 251.

103. See, for example, Sharf, *Byzantine Jewry*, pp. 87-88. For other contradictions and errors found in the Hebrew sources on Basil's alleged vigorous persecution see Baron, *SRH*, III, 180-181, and Sharf, *Byzantine Jewry*, pp. 87-88, who nevertheless tries to explain them away with observations like "Once more, allow-

ance must be made for rhetoric" (p. 90) and "This contradiction has remained a puzzle" (p. 93).

104. Sharf, *Byzantine Jewry*, pp. 88-90.

105. Auxilius, *De ordinationibus*, pp. 109ff. Auxilius the monk who wrote this letter may well have been echoing Jewish traditions. His phrase "per vim baptizari fecit" is quite vague.

106. *Novel*, 55, ed. Zepos (vol. I, p. 125); and *Les Nouvelles de Leon VI, le Sage* (Paris, 1944), eds. and trans. Noailles and Dain, pp. 208-211; and Starr, *Jews in the Byzantine Empire*, pp. 134, 147, with bibliography on p. 148. Cf. Sharf, *Byzantine Jewry*, p. 92. It is worth noting that the *Chronicle of Ahimaaz*, pp. 117ff. (p. 74), states that Leo VI rescinded the order for forced conversions issued by Basil and permitted the Jews to return to their faith.

107. As Sharf, *Byzantine Jewry*, p. 91, observes, "Basil explicitly intended the *Procheiron* and the *Epanagogē* to be the basis for a re-codification of all Byzantine and Roman enactments." In the *Procheiron* (*Procheires nomos*, XXXIX, 31, 32, ed. Zepos [vol. II, p. 279]) translated by E. H. Freshfield, *A Manual of Eastern Roman Law* (Cambridge, 1928), p. 154, and Starr, *Jews in the Byzantine Empire*, p. 126, two pieces of anti-Jewish legislation were reaffirmed: XXXIX, 31 based on *CJ*, I, 10.1 condemns a Jew to death who buys a slave and circumcises him, and XXXIX, 32 based upon *CJ*, 9.18 (19).3, condemns to death Jews who proselytize by attacking Christianity. The argument put forth by Andreades, "Jews in the Byzantine Empire," p. 12, n. 2, that this legislation was meant to contend with contemporary problems seems reasonable in light of Basil's specific intention to use these laws as the basis for re-codification. Cf. Starr, *Jews in the Byzantine Empire*, p. 127.

108. In the *Epanagogē* (IX, 13, ed. Zepos, vol. II, p. 255, and translated by Starr, *Jews in the Byzantine Empire*, p. 138), which was the introduction to the forthcoming code, Basil repeated the two anti-Jewish acts cited in note 107 and the law that Jews were not to serve in the army or hold any public office as stipulated in *CJ*, I, 5.12. It should be added, parenthetically, that in 883 a book of canon law appeared (*Nomocanon*, XIV, XII.2.3 [pp. 601, 604]) that took no account of Basil's alleged policy but based its position on the Quinisext Council discussed above in ch. II, n. 87. Those canons of 883 can be considered the position of the Patriarch Photius whom Basil had chosen. See Sharf, *Byzantine Jewry*, pp. 91-92, for the secular and canon law, respectively, and cf. Starr, *Jews in the Byzantine Empire*, p. 139, on the latter.

109. The *Basilika* legislation on Jews as shown by Starr, *Jews in the Byzantine Empire*, pp. 146-147, is based on the *Code* of Justinian in all its particulars.

110. *Basilika*, I, 1.16, and Starr, *Jews in the Byzantine Empire*, p. 144, *a*.

111. *Basilika*, 37, and Starr, p. 144, *d*.

112. *Basilika*, 40, and Starr, p. 144, *g*.

113. *Basilika*, 41, and Starr, p. 144, *h*.

114. *Basilika*, 43, and Starr, p. 144, *i*.

115. *Basilika*, 44, and Starr, p. 144, *j*.

116. *Basilika*, 47, and Starr, p. 145, *m*.

117. *Basilika*, XXXVIII, 1.15.6, and Starr, p. 145, r.
118. *Basilika*, XXXIX, 29.7, and Starr, p. 145, s. It should be reiterated that these are only the pro-Jewish enactments of the *Basilika*.
119. I am more inclined to believe that the traditional Jewish lachrymose conception of history exaggerated Basil's nonviolent efforts because of the legal reforms enunciated in the *Procheiron*, *Epanagogē*, and *Basilika*. These compositions revived in detail the rigors of Justinian's *Code* which had been ignored for centuries. Thus new Jewish synagogues were threatened, Jewish proselytism was imperiled, Jewish slave owning and slave trading were endangered, and perhaps most important the religion, itself, was threatened by the mandated use of vernacular scriptures in synagogue. See the *Basilika*, I, 1, 47, 51, 53, 57, and XXXIX, 29.7, 31, 32, 54.23. On the lachrymose conception of history see Preface above. In characterizing Basil's policy Baron, *SRH*, III, 181, writes: "Whatever anti-Jewish measures were taken by Basil and Leo, obviously they were more of an administrative than legislative nature, and probably were but short-lived." Paradoxically, we have official legal evidence but no official administrative evidence.
120. On the general background see Louis de Valdeavellano, *Historia de España*, I, pt. I, 448ff., and E. Lévi-Provençal, *Histoire de l'espagne musulmane* (Paris, 1950), I, 218ff.
121. Manuel Díaz y Díaz, "La historiógrafia Hispaña desde la invasión Arabe hasta el año 1000," *SSCI*, 17 (1969), 314-343, for a general view.
122. Cantera Burgos, "Christian Spain," pp. 357-358.
123. *Ibid.*, p. 358, who quotes an undocumented statement by J. Amador de los Ríos, *Historia social, politica y religiosa de los judíos de España y Portugal* (Madrid, 1875), I, 167, concerning Ramiro I that "it is said that among those put to death were not a few Jews."
124. Cantera Burgos, "Christian Spain," p. 360, admits that Alfonso pursued a pro-Jewish policy in the wake of his successes and argues, "It is therefore hardly surprising that the urgent need for increased population should have led to a modification of the hitherto harsh treatment accorded to the Jews." As noted above there is no evidence that Alfonso III or his predecessors had pursued anti-Jewish policies. It might be worthwhile here to recall the letter written by Pope Hadrian III (see above ch. IV, n. 65) censuring Christians throughout Spain (Christian and Muslim areas) for being too friendly with Jews.
125. Baron, *SRH*, IV, 35 and 250, n. 40, with substantial bibliography. See also Cantera Burgos, "Christian Spain," p. 361. It might be observed that Jewish communities flourished in both Carolingian and Muslim Spain during this period, and Alfonso would have to have made life very attractive for Jewish settlers in the empty spaces he ruled. On flourishing Jewish communities in Carolingian Spain see chapter VI and on nearby Muslim cities see, for example, F. Cantera and J. M. Millas, *Las inscripciones hebraicas de España* (Madrid, 1956), nos. 199, 290, and the observations of Cantera Burgos, "Christian Spain," p. 359.

Chapter VII

1. Parkes, *Church and Synagogue*, pp. 383ff., provides an analytic table of conciliar legislation in the barbarian kingdoms concerning the Jews. Blumenkranz,

Auteurs chrétiens, passim, provides a bibliography and summary of authors who deal with the Jews in virtually any manner.

2. Solomon Grayzel, "Christian-Jewish Relations in the First Millennium," *Essays on Anti-Semitism*, 2nd ed., ed. Koppel Pinson (New York, 1946), 79-92; Baer, *Galut*, p. 116; and Cecil Roth, "European Jewry in the Dark Ages: a Revised Picture," *Hebrew Union College Annual*, 23 (1950), 151-169.

3. Blumenkranz, *Auteurs chrétiens, passim*.

4. See, for example, the treatment of Chilperic and Guntram by Gregory of Tours, *Hist.*, Bk. VI, ch. 17, and Bk. VIII, ch. 23, respectively.

5. This seems to have been the case with Perctarit. Cf. above ch. II, notes 92 and 93.

6. Fredegar's treatment of Dagobert I would seem to fall into this category. This is not to say that Dagobert did not pursue an anti-Jewish policy, but Fredegar seems to have embellished it. See above ch. III, notes 89-90.

7. See, for example, above ch. I, n. 86, and the discussion of Basil's "persecution" in ch. VI above. More generally, in a theological sense, see Baer, *Galut*, *passim*. The survey by H. J. Zimmels, "Aspects of Jewish Culture," *WHJP*, II, 274-281, is of little value on this point.

8. These three sources are Thegan's account of Louis's life, the Astronomer's account, and Hermoldus Nigellus's work on Louis the Pious.

9. Cf., for example, the works cited in note 2 above.

10. This is the thrust of Agobard's argument and of the positions of his successors and advisors, Amulo, Remigius, and Florus.

11. Halphen, *L'empire carolingien*, pp. 65ff., and Ganshof, *Les capitulaires*, pp. 96ff., as a guide to the laws.

12. Although theological considerations may well have influenced learned churchmen such as Gregory the Great or Isidore to advocate the temporary survival of Judaism, it is unlikely indeed that such nuances were of significance to the barbarians who exercised secular power during the period under consideration. See above ch. II, n. 68.

13. Gavin Langmuir, "Anti-Judaism as the Necessary Preparation for Anti-Semitism," *Viator*, 2 (1971), 384, calls attention to the "strongly defensive tone" one finds in the elaboration of doctrinal anti-Judaism. See his note 3 for a guide to further literature in which more theoretical formulations are postulated.

14. Bernhard Blumenkranz, "Anti-Jewish Polemics and Legislation in the Middle Ages: Literary Fiction or Reality?" *Journal of Jewish Studies*, 15 (1964), 125-140, maintains the hypothesis that "every anti-Jewish writing presupposes the existence of an active and energetic Jewish group the fight against which is the purpose of the polemical writings" (p. 140). But cf. H. Liebschutz, "Relations between Jews and Christians in the Middle Ages," *Journal of Jewish Studies*, 16 (1965), p. 46, n. 7.

Bibliography

Primary Materials

Aegidius. *Epitome*: See *LRV*.
Agnellus. *Liber Pontificalis ecclesiae Ravennatis*, *MGH*, *SRL*, ed. O. Holder-Egger. Hannover, 1878.
Agobard. *Epist.*: *MGH*, *Epist.*, V, ed. E. Dümmler. Berlin, 1899.
Alcuin. *Epist.*: *MGH*, *Epist.*, IV, ed. E. Dümmler. Berlin, 1895.
Amulo. *Liber contra Judaeos*, *PL*, 116.
Annales de Saint Bertin, ed. Felix Grat, et al. Paris, 1964.
Ann. Fuld.: *Annales Fuldenses*, ed. F. Kurze, *MGH SS in us. schol.* Hannover, 1891.
Anonymus Valesianus, *MGH*, *AA*, IX, ed. Th. Mommsen. Berlin, 1892.
An. q. d. Einhardi: See *ARF*.
ARF: *Annales Regni Francorum et Annales Q. D. Einhardi*, ed. F. Kurze. Hannover, 1895.
Astronomer. *Vita Hludowici Imperatoris*, *MGH*, *SS*, II, ed. G. Pertz. Hannover, 1827.
Aurasius. *Epist.*: *MGH*, *Epist.*, III, ed. W. Gundlach, Berlin, 1892.
Auxilius. *De ordinationibus a Formoso papa factis*, ed. E. Dümmler, *Auxilius und Vulgarius*. Leipzig, 1866.
Basilika: Basilicorum Libri LX, I. ed. H. Scheltema and N. Van der Wal. Groningen-Gravenhage, 1955.
Bouquet: See *Recueil des historiens*.
Braulio. *Epist.*, *PL*, 80.
Carmen de Synodo Tinicensi, *MGH*, *SRL*, ed. L. Bethmann and G. Waitz. Berlin, 1878.
Cassiodorus. *Varia*, *MGH*, *AA*, 12, ed. Th. Mommsen. Berlin, 1894.
Chrétien de Stavelot. *Expositio in Mathaeum Evangelistam*, *PL*, 106.
Chronici Fontanellensis fragmentum, ed. G. Pertz, *MGH*, *SS*. II. Hannover, 1827.

Bibliography   193

Chronicle of Ahimaaz: Aḥima'atz of Oria, *Sefer Yuḥasin*, ed. A. Neubauer in *Medieval Jewish Chronicles*, Oxford, 1895 and *The Chronicle of Ahimaaz*, trans. Marcus Salzman. New York, 1924.

CIJ: *Corpus inscriptionum judaicarum, Recueil des inscriptions juives qui vont du IIIe siècle avant Jesus-Christ au VIIe siècle de notre ére*, ed. J. Frey. Rome, 1936, vol. I.

CJ: *Codex Justinianus*, ed. P. Krüger, II. Berlin, 1929.

Conc. Narbon.: See *Conc. Tolet.*

Conc. Tolet.: *Concilios Visigóticos e hispano-romanos*, ed. José Vives, Tomas Marín Martinez, and Gonzalo Martinez Díez. Barcelona-Madrid, 1963.

Const. Sirm.: See *CTh*.

CTh.: *Theodosiani libri xvi cum constitutionibus Sirmondianis et leges novellae ad Theodosianum pertinentes*, eds. Th. Mommsen and P. Meyer, 2 vols. Berlin, 1905.

Dhuoda. *Liber manualis: Le Manuel de Dhuoda (843)*, ed. E. Bondurand. Paris, 1887.

Einhard. *Vita Karoli: Eginhard, Vie de Charlemagne*, ed. and trans. L. Halphen. Paris, 1947.

Ekloga (appendix): *Ecloga Leonis et Constantini cum Appendice*, ed. A. G. Monferratus. Athens, 1889.

Eleutherius. *Oratio*, *PL*, 65.

Epaganagogē: See *Ius Graecoromanum*.

Epit. Guelf.: See *LRV*.

Epit. S. Gall.: See *LRV*.

Eugenius. *Carmina*, *MGH*, *AA*, XIV, ed. F. Vollmer. Berlin, 1905.

Exemplar epistole Iohannis patriarche, ed. G. Rauschen, *Die Legende Karls des Grossen*. Leipzig, 1890.

Flodoard. *Historia Remensis Ecclesiae*, *MGH*, *SS*, XIII, ed. G. Waitz. Hannover, 1866.

Fortunatus. *Opera Poetica*, *MGH*, *AA*, IV, pt. 1, ed. F. Leo. Berlin, 1881.

Fredegarius. *Chronica*, *MGH*, *SRM*, II, ed. B. Krusch. Hannover, 1888.

Gelasius. *Epist.*, *PL*, 59.

Gesta Dagoberti, *MGH*, *SRM*, II, ed. B. Krusch. Hannover, 1888.

Gregory. *Epist.*, *MGH*, *Epist.*, I, II, eds. P. Ewald and L. M. Hartmann. Berlin, 1891-1899.

Gregory. *GC.*: *Gregorii episcopi Turonensis, Liber in Gloria Confessorum*, *MGH*, *SRM*, I, ed. B. Krusch. Hannover, 1885.

Gregory. *Hist.*: *Gregorii episcopi Turonensis, Libri Historiarum*, *MGH*, *SRM*, I, pt. 1, eds. B. Krusch and W. Levison. Hannover, 1951.

Gregory. *VP.*: *Gregorii episcopi Turonensis, Liber vitae patrum*, *MGH*, *SRM*, I. ed. B. Krusch. Hannover, 1885.

Hadrian. *Epist.*, *PL*, 98.

Hermoldus Nigellus. *Ermold le Noir, Poème sur Louis le Pieux*, ed. and trans. Edmond Faral. Paris, 1964.

Ibn el-Athir. *Annales du Maghreb et de l'Espagne*, ed. and trans. E. Fagnan. Algiers, 1898.

Ibn Kurradadhbah. *Le Livre des routes et des royaumes*, ed. and trans. M. J. de Goeje. Leiden, 1889.
Ibn Verga, Solomon. *Shebet Yehudah*, ed. and trans. M. Weiner, 2nd ed. Hannover, 1924.
Imp. Form.: *Formulae Merowingici et Karolini aevi*, *MGH, LL*, V, ed. K. Zeumer. Hannover, 1886.
Isid. Contin. Hisp.: *Isidori continuatio Hispana*, *MGH, AA*, XI, ed. Th. Mommsen. Berlin, 1892.
Isidore. *Historia Gothorum*, *MGH, AA*, XI, ed. Th. Mommsen. Berlin, 1892.
Julian. *Historia Wambae regis*, *MGH, SRM*, V, ed. W. Levison. Hannover, 1910.
Julian. *Insultatio in tyrannidem Galliae*, *MGH, SRM*, V, ed. W. Levison. Hannover, 1910.
Julian. *Iudicium in tyrannorum perfidiam promulgatum*, *MGH, SRM*, V, ed. W. Levison. Hannover, 1910.
Ḳebhutsat Ḥakhamin, ed. W. Warnheim, *Wissenschaftliche Aufsätze in hebräischtalmudischer Sprache, enthalten Geschichte, Exegese und Dogmatik*, I. Vienna, 1861 and *Die jüdische litteratur seit Abschluss des Kanons*, eds. and trans. J. Winter and A. Wünsch, II. Trier, 1894.
LB: *Leges Burgundionum* see *LRB*.
Lex Romana Raetica Curiensis, ed. E. Meyer-Marthaler, *Die Rechtsquellen Kantons Graubünden*. Aarau, 1959.
LRB: *Lex Romana Burgundionum*, *MGH, LL*, II, ed. L. De Salis. Hannover, 1892.
LRV: *Lex Romana Visigothorum*, ed. G. Haenel. Leipzig, 1849. Includes also the texts of *Eiptome ab Aegidio Edita*; *Scintilla sive Epitome Codicis Regii Parisiensis* Suppl. Lat. 215; *Epitome Codicis Guelpherbytani*; *Epitome Codicis Lugdunensis*; *Epitome Monachi*; *Epitome S. Galli*; and the *Epitome Codicis Seldeni*.
Lucas of Tuy. *Chron.*: *Lucas Tudensis Chronicon Mundi* in *Hispaniae illustratae*, ed. A. Schott. Frankfurt, a/M, 1608.
LV: *Leges Visigothorum*, *MGH, LL*, I, ed. K. Zeumer. Hannover, 1902.
Lyons' Epit.: See *LRV*.
MGH, Capitularia Regum Francorum, I, II, ed. A. Boretius and V. Krause. Hannover, 1883-1897.
MGH, Concilia, Aevi Merovingici, I, ed. F. Maassen. Hannover, 1893. *Aevi Karolini*, II, pts. 1 and 2, ed. A. Werminghoff. Hannover, 1896-1898.
MGH, Diplomatum Karolinorum, I, eds. E. Mühlbacher, et al. Hannover, 1906.
Monk's Brev.: See *LRV*.
Nicholas I. *Epist.*, *MGH, Epist.*, VI, ed. E. Perels. Berlin, 1925.
Notker. *Gesta Karoli Magni Imperatoris*, *MGH, SSRG*, new series ed. H. Haefele. Berlin, 1959.
Les nouvelles de León VI le Sage, ed. P. Noailles and A. Dain. Paris, 1944.
Paul the Deacon. *Historia Langobardorum*, *MGH, SRL*, eds. L. Bethmann and G. Waitz. Hannover, 1878.
Procheiron: See *Ius Graecoromanum*.
Procopius. *Opera Omnia*, 2nd ed., eds. J. Haury and G. Wirth, 4 vols. Leipzig, 1962-1964.

Recueil des actes de Charles II le Chauve, ed. G. Tessier, 3 vols. Paris, 1942-1955.
Recueil des historiens des Gaules et de la France, ed. M. Bouquet. Paris, 1870, vol. VI.
Scintilla: See *LRV*.
Sedulius Scottus. *Carmina, MGH, Poetae Latini Aevi Carolini*, III, ed. L. Traube. Berlin, 1886.
Sid. Apol.: *Sidonii Apollinaris, Epistulae et Carmina, MGH, AA*, VIII, ed. C. Luetjohann. Berlin, 1887.
Sisebut. *Epist., MGH, Epist.*, III, ed. W. Gundlach. Berlin, 1892.
Stephen. *Epist., PL*, 129.
Teshubhot geoné mizrah u-ma'arabh (Responsa of Eastern and Western Geonim), ed. J. Müller. Berlin, 1888.
Teshubhot haGeonim (Responsa of the Geonim), ed. J. Musafiah. Lyck, 1863-1864.
Thegan. *Vita Hludowici Imperatoris, MGH, SS*, ed. G. Pertz. Hannover, 1827.
Theodoric. *Edictum Theoderici Regis, Fontes Iuris Romani Ante-Iustiniani*, ed. S. Riccobono et al. Florence, 1941, vol. II.
Theophanis continuator, ed. I. Bekker, *CSHB*. Bonn, 1838.
Th. Nov.: See *CTh*.
Vita Anscharii, MGH, SS, II, ed. G. Pertz. Hannover, 1827.
Vita Audoini, MGH, SRM, V, ed. W. Levison. Hannover, 1910.
Vita Columbani, MGH, SRG, ed. B. Krusch. Hannover, 1905.
Vita Ferreoli, Catalogus codicum hagiographicorum latinorum, II. Brussels, 1890.
Vita Sancti Germani: MGH, SRM, VII, ed. W. Levison.
Vita Sancti Zosomi: AA, SS, March, 3, 842.
Vita Sulpicii Biturgi, MGH, SRM, IV, ed. B. Krusch. Hannover, 1902.
Vita vel Passio Sancti Desiderii a Sisebuto Rego composita, MGH, SRM, III, ed. B. Krusch. Hannover, 1896.
Vitae Caesarii episcopi Arelatensis libri duo, MGH, SRM, III, ed. B. Krusch. Hannover, 1896.

Secondary Materials

Abadal i de Vinyals, Ramon d'. *Catalunya carolingia*. 2 vols. Barcelona, 1926-1952.
Adams, Jeremy. "Ideology and the Requirements of 'Citizenship' in Visigothic Spain: The Case of the *Judaei*," *Societas*, 2, 1972, 317-332.
Agus, Irving A. *Urban Civilization in Pre-Crusade Europe*. Leiden, 1965, 2 vols.
———. *The Heroic Age of Franco-German Jewry*. New York, 1969.
Altamira, R. "Spain under the Visigoths," *The Cambridge Mediaeval History*, ed. H. M. Gwatkin, et al. Cambridge, 1926, 159-193.
Altmann, Berthold. "Studies in Medieval Jewish History," *PAAJR*, 10, 1940, 5-98.
Amador de los Rios, José. *Historia social, politica y religiosa de los judios de España y Portugal*. Madrid, 1875, I.
Amencourt, Ponton d'. *Essai sur la numismatique mérovingienne comparée à la géographie de Gregoire de Tours*. Paris, 1864.

———. "Description raisonée des monnaies mérovingiennes de Châlons-sur-Sâone," *Annuaire de la société française de numismatique et d'archéologie*, 4, 1873, 37-152.
Anchel, R. *Les Juifs de France*. Paris, 1946.
Andreades, A. "Les Juifs et le fisc dans l'empire byzantin," *Mélanges Charles Diehl*. Paris, 1930, I, 7-29.
Aronius, Julius. *Resgesten zur Geschichte der Juden in fränkischen und deutschen Reiche bis zum Jahre 1273*. Berlin, 1887-1902.
Assaf, Simchah. "Slaves and the Slave Trade among the Jews in the Middle Ages," *Zion*, 14, 1938-1939, 91-125, in Hebrew.
Bachrach, Bernard S. "Charles Martel, Mounted Shock Combat, the Stirrup, and Feudalism," *Studies in Medieval and Renaissance History*, 7, 1970, 49-75.
———. "Procopius and the Chronology of Clovis's Reign," *Viator*, 1, 1970, 21-31.
———. "Barbarians," "Childebert," "Chlotaire II," "Reccared," and "Sisebut," *Encyclopaedia Judaica*. Jerusalem, 1971, vol. 4, cols. 205-206; vol. 5, cols. 422-423, 616-617; vol. 13, cols. 1608-1609; and vol. 14, col. 621.
———. *Merovingian Military Organization, 481-751*. Minneapolis, 1972.
———. "A Reassessment of Visigothic Jewish Policy, 589-711," *AHR*, 78, 1973, 11-34.
———. "Military Organization in Aquitaine under the Early Carolingians," *Speculum*, 49, 1974, 1-33.
———. "Some Observations on the Role of the Jews in the Establishment of the Spanish March, 768-814," *Hispanica Judaica*, forthcoming.
Baer, Yitzhak, F. *Review*: Salo W. Baron, *SRH*, *Zion*, 3, 1938, 277-299.
———. *Galut*, trans. R. Warshaw. New York, 1947.
Barnett, C. *Britain and Her Army, 1509-1970*. London, 1970.
Baron, Salo W. "Ghetto and Emancipation," *The Menorah Journal*, 14, 1928, 515-526.
———. *SRH*, 1952-1967.
———. "The Jewish Factor in Medieval Civilization," *Ancient and Medieval Jewish History*. New Brunswick, N.J., 1972, 239-267, 502-517.
Bergengruen, A. *Adel und Grundherrschaft im Merowingerreich*. Wiesbaden, 1958.
Björkman, Walther. "Karl und der Islam," *Karl der Grosse*, I, 1965, 672-682.
Bloch, Peter. "Das Apsismosaik von Germigny-des-Pres," *Karl der Grosse*, III, 1965, 234-261.
Blondheim, D. S. *Les parlers judéo-romans et la Vetus Latina*. Paris, 1925.
Blumenkranz, Bernhard. "Deux compilations canoniques de Florus de Lyon et l'action antijuive d'Agobard," *RHD*, ser. 4, 33, 1955, 227-254, 560-582.
———. *Juifs et Chrétiens dans le monde occidental, 430-1096*. Paris, 1960.
———. *Les auteurs chrétiens latins du moyen âge sur les juifs et le judaïsme*. Paris, 1963.
———. "Anti-Jewish Polemics and Legislation in the Middle Ages: Literary Fiction or Reality?" *Journal of Jewish Studies*, 15, 1964, 125-140.
———. "The Roman Church and the Jews," *WHJP*, II, 1966, 69-99.
———. "Les premières implantations de Juifs en France: du Ier au début du Ve siècle," *Comptes Rendus, Académie des Inscriptions et Belles-Lettres*, Paris, 1969, 162-174.

---. "Les origines et le moyen âge," *Histoire des Juifs en France*. Toulouse, 1972, 13-73.
Boshof, Egon. *Erzbischof Agobard von Lyon: Leben und Werk*. Cologne, 1969.
Bosl, K. *Die Reichsministerialität der Salier und Staufer*. Munich, 1950-1951.
Braude, W. G. *Jewish Proselyting*. Providence, R.I., 1940.
Breslau, Harry. "Zur Lehre von den Siegeln der Karolinger und Ottonen," *Archiv für Urkundenforschung*, 1, 1908, 355-370.
Bressolles, Adrien. *Doctrine et action politique d'Agobard*. Paris, 1949.
Browe, P. "Die Judengesetzgebung Justinians," *Analecta Gregoriana*, 8, 1935, 101-146.
Buchner, Rudolf. *Deutschlands Geschichtsquellen im Mittelalter*. Weimar, 1953.
Buckler, F. W. *Harunu'l Rashid and Charles the Great*. Cambridge, Mass., 1931.
Bullough, Donald. "*Europae Pater*: Charlemagne and His Achievement in Light of Recent Scholarship," *EHR*, 65, 1970, 59-105.
---. "Social and Economic Structure and Topography in the Early Medieval City," *SSCI*, 21, 1974, 351-399.
Cabaniss, Allen. *Agobard of Lyons: Churchman and Critic*. Syracuse, 1953.
---. "Bodo-Eleazar: A Famous Jewish Convert," *JQR*, 43, 1953, 313-318.
---. "Paulus Albarus of Muslim Cordova," *Church History*, 22, 1953, 99-112.
---. *Amalarius of Metz*. Amsterdam, 1954.
Cahn, Kenneth. "The Roman and Frankish Roots of the Just Price of Medieval Canon Law," *Studies in Medieval and Renaissance History*, 6, 1969, 3-52.
Calmette, J. "Une lettre close originale de Charles le Chauve," *École française de Rome, mélanges d'archéologie et d'histoire*, 22, 1902, 135-139.
---. "Sur la lettre close de Charles le Chauve aux Barcelonais," *BEC*, 64, 1903, 329-334.
Cantera Burgos, F. "Christian Spain," *WHJP*, II, 1966, 357-381, 450-452.
Cantera, F. and Millas, J. M. *Las inscripciones hebraicas de España*. Madrid, 1956.
Caro, G. *Sozial- und Wirtschaftsgeschichte der Juden im Mittelalter und der Neuzeit*. Leipzig, 1908, vol. I.
Castro, Americo. *España en su Historia: Christianos, Moros, y Judiós*. Buenos Aires, 1948.
Chevrier, Georges and Georges Pieri. "La roi romaine des burgondes," *IRMA*, part I, ab aa b, Milan, 1969.
Classen, Peter. "Karl der Grosse, das Papsttum und Byzanz," *Karl der Grosse*, I, 1965, 537-608.
Claude, Dietrich. *Geschichte der Westgoten*. Stuttgart, 1970.
Clercq, C. de. *La législation réligieuse franque de Clovis à Charlemagne*. Louvain, 1936.
---. "La législation réligieuse franque depuis l'evènement de Louis le Pieux jusqu'aux Fausses Décrétales," *Revue de droit canonique*, 4, 1954, 371-404; 6, 1956, 144-162; 263-289; 340-372; 7, 1957, 15-48.
Coville, Alfred. *Recherches sur l'histoire de Lyon du Vme siècle au IXme siècle (450-800)*. Paris, 1928.
Cowley, A. "Bodleian Genizah Fragments," *JQR*, old series, 18, 1906, 399-405.
Dahn, Felix. *Die Könige der Germanen*. Leipzig, 1861-1909, 11 vols.

198 Bibliography

Deér, Josef. "Karl der Grosse und der Untergang des Awarenreiches," *Karl der Grosse*, I, 1965, 719-791.

Díaz y Díaz, Manuel. "La historiografia Hispaña desde la invasión Árabe hasta el año 1000," *SSCI*, 18, 1969, 314-343.

Diéz, Gonzalo Martinez. *La colección canónica Hispaña*. Madrid and Barcelona, 1966, I.

Doehaerd, Renée. *Le haut moyen âge occidental, économies et sociétés*. Paris, 1971.

Duby, Georges. *Rural Economy and Country Life in the Medieval West*. London, 1968.

Duchesne, L. *L'Eglise au VIe siècle*. Paris, 1925.

Dudden, F. H. *Gregory the Great*. London, 1905, 2 vols.

Dunlop, D. M. "The Khazars," *WHJP*, II, 1966, 325-356.

Ensslin, Wilhelm. *Theoderich der Grosse*. Munich, 1947.

Epperstein, Simon. "Beiträge zur Geschichte und Literatur im Gaonäischen Zeitalter," *MGWJ*, 56, 1912, 80-102.

Ewig, E. "Résidence et capitale pendant le haut Moyen Âge," *Revue historique*, 230, 1963, 25-72.

Fita, Fidel. "Hebreos de Barcelona en el siglo IX," *Boletín de la Real Academia de la Historia*, 4, 1884, 69-70.

Freshfield, E. H. *A Manual of Eastern Roman Law*. Cambridge, 1928.

———. *Roman Law in the Later Roman Empire*. Cambridge, 1932.

Gallia Judaica: dictionnaire géographique de la France d'après les sources rabbiniques, ed. H. Gross. Paris, 1897.

Ganshof, F. L. "Charlemagne et le serment," *Mélanges d'histoire du Moyen Âge dédiés à la mémoire de Louis Halphen*. Paris, 1951, 259-270.

———. "Charlemagne et l'usage de l'ecrit en matiére administrative," *MA*, 57, 1951, 1-25.

———. "Zur Entstehungsgeschichte und Bedeutung des Vertrages von Verdun (843)," *Duetsches Archiv für Erforschung des Mittelalters*, 12, 1956, 313-330.

———. *Recherches sur les capitulaires*. Paris, 1958.

———. "Louis the Pious Reconsidered," *History*, 42, 1957, 171-180.

———. "Note sur le 'Praeceptum Negotiatorum' de Louis le Pieux," *Studi in onore di Armando Sapori*. Milan, 1957, I, 103-112.

———. "L'Eglise et le pouvoir royal dans la monarchie franque sous Pépin III et Charlemagne," *SSCI*, 7, 1959, 95-141.

———. "Les traits généraux du système d'institutions de la monarchie franque, *SSCI*, 9, 1961, 91-127.

———. "Charlemagne et l'administration de la justice dans la monarchie franque," *Karl der Grosse*, I, 1965, 394-419.

———. "Charlemagne et les institutions de la monarchie franque," *Karl der Grosse*, 1965, I, 349-393.

———. "Charlemagne's Programme of Imperial Government," *The Carolingians and the Frankish Monarchy*. London, 1971, 55-85.

Gaudemet, J. "Le Breviaire d'Alaric et les epitomes," *IRMA*, part. I, 2b aa b, Milan, 1965.

Bibliography 199

Germania Judaica: von den ältesten Zeiten bis 1238, 2nd ed., ed. I. Elbogen, et al., vol. I. Tübingen, 1963.

Goffart, Walter. "Byzantine Policy in the West Under Tiberius II and Maurice: The Pretenders Hermenegild and Gundovald (579-585)," *Traditio*, 13, 1957, 73-118.

Görres, Franz. "Konige Rekkard und das Judentum (586-601)," *Zeitschrift für wissenschaftliche Theologie*, 41, 1891, 284-296.

———. "Die Religionspolitik des Westgotenkönigs, Witterich (reg. 603-610)," *Zeitshrift für wissenschaftliche Theologie*, 41, 1898, 102-105.

———. "Charakter und Religionspolitik des vorletzten spanischen Westgotenkönigs Witiza," *Zeitschrift für wissenschaftliche Theologie*, 48, 1905, 96-111.

———. "Das Judentum im westgotischen Spanien von König Sisebut bis Roderich (612-711)," *Zeitschrift für wissenschaftliche Theologie*, 48, 1905, 353-361.

———. "Die Religionspolitik des spanischen Westgotenkönigs Swinthila, des ersten Katoliken 'Leovigild' (621-631)," *Zeitschrift für wissenschaftliche Theologie*, 49, 1906, 253-256.

Goubert, Paul. "Administration de l'Espagne Byzantine," *Revue des études byzantines*, 4, 1946, 70-134.

Graboïs, Aryeh. "Un principaute juive dans la France du Midi a l'époque carolingienne?" *Annales du Midi*, 85, 1973, 192-202.

Graetz, H. "Die westgotische Gesetzgebung in Betreff der Juden," *Jahresbericht des judisch- theologischen Seminars: Fraenckelsche Stiftung*. Breslau, 1858.

———. *Geschichte der Juden von der ältesten Zeiten bis auf die Gegenwart*, 4th ed. Leipzig, 1909, vol. V.

Grayzel, Solomon. "Christian-Jewish Relations in the First Millennium," *Essays on Anti-Semitism*, 2nd ed., ed. Koppel Pinson. New York, 1946, 79-92.

———. "Jews and Roman Law," *JQR*, 59, 1968, 93-117.

Grierson, Philip. "Election and Inheritance in Early Germanic Kingship," *Cambridge Historical Journal*, 7, 1949, 1-22.

———. "Money and Coinage under Charlemagne," *Karl der Grosse*, I, 1965, 501-536.

Griffe, Elie. *Histoire réligieuse des anciens pays de l'Aude*. Paris, 1933.

Guillou, André. *Régionalisme et indépendance dans l'empire byzantine au VIIe siècle, l'example de l'exarchat et de la Pentapole d'Italie*. Rome, 1969.

Halphen, Louis. *Charlemagne et l'empire carolingien*. Paris, 1947.

Heil, Wilhelm. "Der Adoptianismus, Alkuin und Spanien," *Karl der Grosse*, II, 1965, 95-155.

Helfferich, A. *Entstehung und Geschichte des Westgothen-Rechts*. Berlin, 1858.

———. "Zum Capitulare Karoli M. de Judaeis," *Zeitschrift für Rechtsgeschichte*, 2, 1863, 417-420.

Herlihy, David. "Church Property on the European Continent, 701-1200," *Speculum*, 36, 1961, 81-105.

Hertzfeld, L. *Handelsgeschichte der Juden des Alterthums*, 2nd ed. Brunswick, 1894.

Hillgarth, J. N. "Coins and Chronicles: Propaganda in Sixth Century Spain," *Historia*, 15, 1966, 483-508.

Hodgkin, Thomas. *Italy and Her Invaders*. London, 1880-1889, 8 vols.
Hyland, F. E. *Excommunication, Its Nature, Historical Development and Effects*. Washington, 1928.
John, Eric. *Land Tenure in Early England*. Leicester, 1960.
Jones, A. H. M. "The Constitutional Position of Odoacer and Theodoric," *JRS*, 52, 1962, 126-130.
———. *LRE*. Norman, Okla., 1962, 2 vols.
Joranson, Einar. *The Danegeld in France*. Rock Island, Ill., 1923.
Juster, Jean. "La condition légale des juifs sous les rois Visigoths," *Études d'histoire juridique offertes à Paul-Frédéric Girard*. Paris, 1913, 2, 275-335.
———. *Les Juifs dans l'empire romain*. Paris, 1914, 2 vols.
Kaemmerer, Walter. "Die Aachener Pfalz Karls des Grossen in Anlage und Uberlieferung," *Karl der Grosse*, I, 1965, 322-348.
Katz, S. "Pope Gregory the Great and the Jews," *JQR*, new series, 24, 1933, 113-136.
———. *The Jews in the Visigothic and Frankish Kingdoms of Spain and Gaul*. Cambridge, Mass., 1937.
Kestenberg-Gladstein, R. "The Early Jewish Settlement in Central and Eastern Europe: Bohemia," *WHJP*, II, 1966, 309-312.
King, P. D. *Law and Society in the Visigothic Kingdom*. Cambridge, 1972.
Kisch, Guido. *Jews in Medieval Germany*. Chicago, 1949.
Langmuir, Gavin. "Majority History and Post-Biblical Jews," *AHR*, 27, 1966, 343-364.
———. "Anti-Judaism as the Necessary Preparation for Anti-Semitism," *Viator*, 2, 1971, 383-389.
Lauer, Ph. "Lettre close des Charles le Chauve pour les 'Barcelonais,'" *BEC*, 62, 1902, 696-699.
Laurent, H. "Marchands du palais et marchands d'abbayes," *Revue historique*, 180, 1938, 281-297.
Levi, Israel. "Le roi juif de Narbonne et le Philomène," *REJ*, 48, 1904, 197-207.
Lévi-Provençal, E. *Histoire de l'espagne Musulmane*. Paris, 1950, vol. I.
Levy, Ernst. *West Roman Vulgar Law*. Philadelphia, 1951.
Lewis, A. *The Development of Southern French and Catalan Society, 718-1051*. Austin, 1965.
Lewis, Charlton T., and Short, Charles. *Latin Dictionary*. Oxford, 1879.
Liebschutz, H. "Relations between Jews and Christians in the Middle Ages," *Journal of Jewish Studies*, 16, 1965, 35-46.
Llewellyn, Peter. *Rome in the Dark Ages*. New York, 1970.
Loeb. I. "Notes sur l'histoire des Juifs. VIII-Juda, Juif Catalan du IXe siècle," *REJ*, 10, 1885, 248.
Longnon, Auguste. *Géographie de la Gaule au VIe siècle*. Paris, 1878.
Lot, F. and Halphen, L. *Le regné de Charles le Chauve*. Paris, 1909.
Lynch, C. H. *Saint Braulio, Bishop of Saragossa (631-651)*. Washington, 1938.
Lyon, Bryce D. *Henri Pirenne*. New York, 1974.
Mann, Jacob. "The Responsa of the Babylonian Geonim as a Source of Jewish History," *JQR*, 7, new series, 1916-1917, 457-490.

———. *The Responsa of the Babylonian Geonim as a Source of Jewish History.* New York, 1973.

Marcus, J. "Studies in the Chronicle of Ahim'atz," *PAAJR*, 5, 1933-1934, 85-91.

Metz, W. "Die Agrarwirtschaft im karolingischen Reiche," *Karl der Grosse*, I, 1965, 489-500.

Milano, Attilo. *Storia degli ebrei in Italia*. Torino, 1963.

Miles, George C. *The Coinage of the Visigoths of Spain: Leovigild to Achila II.* New York, 1952.

Mitteis, Heinrich. *Der Staat des hohen Mittelalters.* Weimer, 1962.

Morrison, Karl F. *The Two Kingdoms, Ecclesiology in Carolingian Political Thought.* Princeton, 1964.

Murphy, F. X. "Julian of Toledo and the Fall of the Visigothic Kingdom in Spain," *Speculum*, 27, 1952, 1-27.

Newman, L. I. *Jewish Influence on Christian Reform Movements.* New York, 1925.

Niermeyer, J. F. *Mediae Latinitatis Lexicon Minus.* Leiden, 1960- .

Ostrogorsky, George. *History of the Byzantine State.* New Brunswick, N.J., 1957.

Parkes, James. *The Conflict of the Church and the Synagogue.* London, 1934.

———. *The Jew in the Medieval Community.* London, 1938.

Parvan, V. *Die Nationalität der Kaufleute in römischen Kaiserreiche.* Breslau, 1909.

Picotti, G. B. "Osservazioni su alcuni punti della politica religiosa di Teoderico," *SSCI*, 3, 1955, 173-226.

Poupardin, René. *Le royaume de Provence sous les carolingiens.* Paris, 1901.

Rabinowitz, J. J. "Jewish and Lombard Law," *Jewish Social Studies*, 12, 1950, 299-328.

———. *Jewish Law: Its Influences on the Development of Legal Institutions.* New York, 1955.

Rabinowitz, L. *Jewish Merchant Adventurers: A Study of the Radanites.* London, 1948.

Régné, Jean. *Étude sur la conditions des juifs de narbonne du Ve au XIVe siècle.* Narbonne, 1912.

Roth, Cecil. "Jewish History for Our Own Needs," *The Menorah Journal*, 14, 1928, 419-434.

———. *History of the Jews in England.* Oxford, 1941.

———. "European Jewry in the Dark Ages: A Revised Picture," *Hebrew Union College Annual*, 23, 1950, 151-169.

———. "Jewish Antecedents of Christian Art," *Journal of the Warburg and Courtald Institutes*, 16, 1953, 24-44.

———. "Economic Life and Population Movements," *WHJP*, II, 1966, 13-48, 385-390.

———. "Italy," *WHJP*, II, 1966, 100-121, 402-407.

Saaverda, E. de. *Estudio sobre la invasión de los árabes en España.* Madrid, 1892.

Scheiber, A. "Hungary," *WHJP*, II, 1966, 313-318.

Scherer, J. E. *Die Rechtsverhältnisse der Juden in den deutschösterreichischen Ländern.* Leipzig, 1901.

Schieffer, Theodor. "Die Krise des karolingischen Imperium," *Aus Mittelalter und Neuzeit. Festschrift zum 70. Geburtstag von Gerhard Kallen*. Bonn, 1957, 1-16.

Schirmann, F. "The Beginning of Hebrew Poetry in Italy and Northern Europe," *WHJP*, II, 1966, 249-266, 429-432.

Schwab, M. "Sur une lettre d'un empereur byzantin," *Journal asiatique*, 8, 1896, 498-509.

Schwarzfuchs, S. "France and Germany under the Carolingians," *WHJP*, II, 1966, 122-142.

Sharf, Andrew. "Byzantine Jewry in the Seventh Century," *BZ*, 48, 1955, 103-115.

———. "Jews in Byzantium," *WHJP*, II, 1966, 49-68.

———. *Byzantine Jewry from Justinian to the Fourth Crusade*. London, 1971.

Shaw, R. D. "The Fall of Visigothic Power in Spain," *EHR*, 82, 1906, 209-228.

Simonsohn, Shlomo. "The Hebrew Revival among Early Medieval European Jews," *Salo Wittmayer Baron Jubilee Volume*. Jerusalem, 1975, II, 832-858.

Simson, B. *Jahrbücher des fränkischen Reiches unter Ludwig dem Frommen*. Leipzig, 1874.

Starr, J. "Byzantine Jewry on the Eve of the Arab Conquest," *JPOS*, 15, 1935, 280-293.

———. *Jews in the Byzantine Empire, 641-1204*. Athens, 1939.

Stenton, F. M. *Anglo-Saxon England*. 2nd ed. Oxford, 1947.

Stevens, C. E. *Sidonius Apollinaris and His Age*. Oxford, 1933.

Synan, Edward A. *The Popes and the Jews in the Middle Ages*. New York, 1965.

Tailhan, Jules. "La ruine de l'Espagne gothique," *Revue des questions historiques*, 31, 1882, 341-408.

Tangl, M. "Zum Judenschutzrecht unter den Karolingern," *NA*, 33, 1907, 197-200.

Thompson, E. A. "The Barbarian Kingdoms in Gaul and Spain," *Nottingham Medieval Studies*, 7, 1963, 3-33.

———. *The Goths in Spain*. Oxford, 1969.

Valdeavellano, José de. *Historia de España*. Madrid, 1952, vol. I.

Vasiliev, A. A. *History of the Byzantine Empire*. Madison, 1961, 2 vols.

Verlinden, Charles. "A propos de la place des Juifs dans l'economie de l'Europe occidentale aux IXe et Xe siècles," *Storiografia e storia in onore Eugenio Dupré Theseider*. Rome, 1974, I, 21-37.

Vismara, Giulio. "Edictum Theoderici," *IRMA*, part I, 2b aa a, Milan, 1967.

Wacholder, Ben Zion. "The Halakah and the Proselyting of Slaves during the Geonic Era," *Historia Judaica*, 18, 1956, 89-106.

Wallace-Hadrill, J. M. *The Long-Haired Kings and Other Studies in Frankish History*. London, 1962.

———. "Charlemagne and England," *Karl der Grosse*, I, 1965, 683-698.

———. *Early Germanic Kingship in England and on the Continent*. Oxford, 1971.

Weinryb, Bernard. "Reappraisals in Jewish History," *Salo Wittmayer Baron Jubilee Volume*. Jerusalem, 1975, II, 939-974.

Wengen, Paul à. *Julianus, Erzbischof von Toledo*. St. Gall, 1891.

Werner, K. *Alkuin und sein Jahrhundert*. Paderborn, 1876.

White, Lynn T., Jr. *Medieval Technology and Social Change*. Oxford, 1962.

Bibliography 203

Wiegand, Friedrich. "Agobard von Lyon und die Judenfrage," *Festschrift seiner königlichen Hoheit dem Prinzregenten Luitpold von Bayern zum achtzigsten Geburtstage dargebracht von der Universität Erlangen, I, Theologische Fakultät.* Leipzig, 1901, 3-32.

Wilmart, A. "Un lecteur ennemi d'Amalaire," *Revue Bénédictine*, 36, 1924, 317-329.

Ziegler, Aloysius. *Church and State in Visigothic Spain.* Washington, 1930.

Zimmels, H. J. "Scholars and Scholarship in Byzantium and Italy," *WHJP*, II, 1966, 175-188, 415-418.

———. "Aspects of Jewish Culture," *WHJP*, II, 1966, 274-281.

Zuckerman, Arthur. "The Political Uses of Theology: The Conflict of Bishop Agobard and the Jews of Lyons," *Medieval Studies*, 3, 1970, 23-51.

———. *A Jewish Princedom in Feudal France, 768-900.* New York, 1972.

Index

Index

Aachen, 94
Aaron, R., 125
Abbasids, 112
Abd al-Malik ibn Mughith, 70
Abiron, 77, 89
Abraham of Saragossa, 97
Academies, 124
Achila, King, 23-25, 133
Adalard, Abbot, 84, 99
Adaloald, King, 9
Africans, 74
Agobard, Archbishop, 98-102, 104, 109, 110, 121, 122, 126, 131, 137
Ahimaaz, 127-128
Ahwaz, 73
Alaric II, King, 4, 6
Alaric's *Breviary*, 4, 50, 64, 66, 78
Albi, 68
Alfonso III, King, 79, 130, 131, 135
Al-Jabiya, 73
Al-Jar, 73
Al-Mu'tamid, Caliph, 167
Al-Ubullah, 73
Amalarius of Metz, Bishop, 88
Amantius, Jew, 161
Amittai, Jew, 127
Amulo, Archbishop, 109-111, 121, 131
Anastasius, Bishop, 122

Andalusia, 73-74
Anskar, Saint, 123
Antioch, 73
Antonius, Jew, 27-28
Aquitaine, 66-67, 95, 115: dukes of, 134; regional levies of, 70
Arabs, 24-26
Archisynagogus, 8
Argebad, Archbishop, 8
Arians, 3, 9, 32, 42, 44
Aribert, Archbishop, 67
Aripert I, King, 42
Arles, 4, 44-45, 47, 121, 122
Arno, Archbishop, 71, 72, 123, 124
Asclepiodatus, priest, 155
Asturias, 79, 103, 129, 130
Auch, 63
Augsberg, 123
Aurasius, Archbishop, 10
Ausona, 68-71, 113-118. *See* Vich
Austrasia, 52, 53, 58
Avitus, Bishop, 55-57

Baghdad, 73, 125
Balkh, 73
Barcelona, 16, 68, 70, 79, 113-119
Barcelonians, 117-119
Bari, 104, 124, 125
Basil I, Emperor, 126-131, 134

207

Index

Basilika, 128
Basques, 18, 24
Basra, 73
Bavarians, 76-77
Beneficia, 107
Benevento, 40, 125
Berbers, 38
Bernard, Bishop, 101
Bernard of Septimania, 115
Bernesga River, 130
Bodo, convert, 88, 114-116
Bordeaux, 57, 60, 68, 114, 115
Bourges, 49, 68
Braulio, Bishop, 17
Britain, 74, 79
Brunhild, Queen, 9, 38, 58-64, 135
Bulgars, 126
Burgundian Roman Law, 51, 70
Burgundians, 50, 51
Burrellus, Count, 68-70
Byzantine Empire, 8, 24, 27, 33, 38, 42, 56-58, 61, 73, 80-83, 103-105, 125-129, 131

Caesarius, Bishop of Arles, 4
Cagliari, 35
Capitulum, Capitula, Capitularies, 87-94
Cardona, 68-69
Carolingian Spain, 18, 113, 116, 119
Carolingians, 43, 46, 65-67, 136
Caspian Sea, 73
Casseres, 68, 69
Cassiodorus, 30
Catechumenate, 4
Cato, priest, 53
Cautinus, Bishop, 53-55
Cenaticum, 96
Cespitaticum, 96
Châlons-sur-Sâone, 56, 101, 121
Charibert, King, 54
Charlemagne, 27, 66, 67, 71-84, 91, 92, 112, 135, 137, 138
Charles, king of Provence, 122
Charles the Bald, King, 106, 107, 110-122, 131

Chichek, Khazar Princess and Byzantine Empress, 168
Childebert I, King, 47, 51, 53, 54
Childebert II, King, 58
Childeric, Count, 18
Childeric I, King, 44
Chilperic, King, 54-57, 62
China, 73
Chindasuinth, King, 13-17
Chintila, King, 13-17
Chlodomir, King, 47
Chlotar I, King, 47, 53-56
Chlotar II, King, 59-64
Chorespiscopus, 102
Chramn, 53-54
Civitas, civitates, 27, 47-49, 70, 71, 76, 85, 97
Civray-sur-Cher, 161
Claudius of Turin, 172
Clermont, 3, 49-57, 161
Clovis, King, 44-53, 58
Coimbra, 130
Coloni, 34, 37
Constantine V, Emperor, 168
Constantinople, 32, 38-40, 80, 126, 127
Constantius, Bishop, 28
Conversion: of Arians, 9, 86; of Christians, 4, 7, 15, 33, 40-41, 52, 64, 86, 99, 109, 110; of Jews, 5, 11, 15, 39, 41, 56-57, 60, 99, 107, 109, 110, 121-122, 126-127, 134; of pagans, 4, 52, 86, 88. *See* Bodo
Cordova, 25
Councils: Agde, 3; Châlons-sur-Sâone, 63; Clichy, 60, 61; Epaone, 51; Mâcon, 54-58; Meaux-Paris, 107; Nicaea, 80; Orange, 5; Orleans I, 45, 46; Orleans II, 48, 49; Orleans III, 54; Orleans IV, 53-54; Paris, 59; Pavia, 120, 123, 131; Quinisext, 41; Rheims, 60, 61; Rome, 40; Toledo III, 18; Toledo IV, 13, 15, 17, 20; Toledo V, 12; Toledo VI, 13, Toledo VIII, 15; Toledo IX, 18; Toledo X, 16, 18; Toledo XII, 19, 20;

Index 209

Toledo XVI, 21; Toledo XVII, 22; Toledo XVIII, 24

Dagobert I, King, 60-64
Damascus, 73
Dathan, 77, 89
Defensor civitatis, 46
Desiderius, Bishop, 8-9
Dignitas, dignitates, 87, 107
Domatus, R., 92
Domitian, Emperor, 63
Dhū Nuwās, 156
Duero, 130

Easter, 51, 55, 56, 108
Ecloga, 81, 82
Edict of Paris, 59
Egica, King, 20, 22
Egypt, 73
Einhard, 79
Eirene. *See* Chichek
Eleutherius, Bishop, 44, 48
Epanagogē, 128
Épernay, 110, 116, 120
Epitomes: Aegidius, 64; *Codex Guelpherbyteni*, 78; Lyons, 78; *Monk's Breviary*, 78; Saint Gall, 78; *Scintilla*, 78
Erwig, King, 19, 20, 21
Esther, Book of, 186
Eugenius II, Bishop, 17
Eunuchs, 73
Euphrasius, priest, 55
Euric I, King, 133

Faof, Bishop, 101
Farama, 73
Fars, 73
Fasting, 3
Felix, Bishop, 21
Felix, senator, 3
Ferreolus, Bishop, 53, 54
Fidelis, fideles, 13, 111, 117, 118
Fontenoy, battle of, 106
Formulary, 90-96
Francia Occidentalis, 106, 107, 111, 113, 115, 120

Francia Orientalis, 106, 123, 124, 131
Fredegar, 60-63
Fredric, *missus*, 100
Frodo, Bishop, 117
Froga, Count, 10

Gaeta, 125
Galasuintha, Queen, 62
Galicia, 130
Gallia Narbonnensis, 12
Gallus, Bishop, 53
Garic, *missus*, 100
Garrisons, 4, 25, 30, 69, 113
Gascony, 70
Gaul, 112, 133
Geila, 11
Gelasius, Pope, 27, 28, 31, 135
Genoa, 29, 30
Germanus, Bishop, 161
Gerona, 68
Gibraltar, 73
Godepert, King, 42
Gregory I, Pope, 6, 35, 36, 38, 39, 43, 58, 60, 80, 93, 133, 135, 138
Gregory III, Pope, 40, 41
Gregory of Tours, Bishop, 56, 58
Grimoald, King, 40, 42
Gundemar, King, 7
Gundobad, King, 50
Gundovald, usurper, 55-58
Guntram, King, 54-58
Guntram Boso, Duke, 57

Hadrian I, Pope, 80
Hagia Sophia, 39
Harun al Rashid, Caliph, 73-74
Heliodorus, Jew, 171
Helisacher, Abbot, 89, 99
Heraclius, Emperor, 8, 39, 43, 60, 62, 81
Himyarites, 156
Hincmar, Archbishop, 107, 114, 119
Hispania, 67
Holocaust, 144
Honoratus, Bishop, 49
Honores, 87, 97, 107
Honorius I, Pope, 13

Huesca, 68, 69

Ibn Kurradadhbah, 72
Idalcarius, Bishop, 69
India, 73
Irene, Empress, 81-82
Isaac, legate, 74, 168
Isaac, R., 8
Isidore of Seville, Bishop, 9-11, 16, 133
Italy, 27, 58, 80-82, 103, 106, 125
Iudex, iudices, 49, 54, 87, 97, 107, 120, 124
Iudila, King, 12

Jerusalem, 104
Jewish law. *See Lex Judaeorum*
Jewish Life of Jesus. *See Toledoth Jeshu*
Jidda, 73
John, Bishop of Barcelona, 118, 119
John of Ephesus, 32
Joseph, R. of Ausona, 113
Judah, Judas, Judacot, 117, 118
Judices reipublicae, 34
Julian of Toledo, 20, 63, 134
Julius, Jew, 42
Justinian, Emperor, 27, 33, 35, 81, 155
Justinian's *Code*, 36, 37, 81, 128
Judex, see iudex

Kairouan, 112
Kalonymus, 71, 86
Khamlij, 73
Khazars, 73, 103
Kirman, 73
Kufa, 73

Lachrymose interpretation, 144
La Janda, battle of, 24
Latifundium, latifundia, 34, 37
Laurentius, Bishop, 28
Lent, 3, 98
Leo III (the Isaurian), Emperor, 41, 43, 80-81
Leo IV, Pope, 122
Leo VI, Emperor, 128, 129
Lérida, 68
Levi Samuel, 8
Lex Judaeorum, 76, 85, 86, 87, 120
Lex Langobardorum, 120
Lex Romana Curiensis, 40, 41, 78
Lex Romanorum, 76
Lex Salica, 45
Liber Contra Judaeos, 109
Limoges, 68
Liuva, 7
Lombards, 35, 38, 40, 41, 67, 71, 76, 77, 133
Lothair, Emperor, 106, 119-122
Louis II, King, 119-122
Louis the German, King, 106, 119, 123, 124
Louis the Pious, King, 68, 84-92, 103-108, 111, 130, 135, 137, 138
Lucas of Tuy, 22, 23
Lucca, 71
Luna, 35
Lyonnais, 70, 94, 99
Lyons, 102, 137

Macedonian dynasty, 126
Mâcon, 121
Magister Judaeorum, 84, 85, 99-101
Magister ostiariorum, 84
Magistri, 84
Mainz, 71, 86
Marseilles, 56-57
Masona, Bishop, 4
Mayors of the palace, 66
Mecca, 73
Medina, 73
Meir ben Joseph, R., 113
Merchants, 3, 55, 72. *See* Radanites
Mercia, 73, 79
Michael II, Emperor, 103-105, 124
Michael Bogar, King, 126
Middle Kingdom, 106, 119, 120
Milan, 31
Militia, 87, 111
Ministeriales, 117

Index   211

Mintmaster, 56, 63, 75
Mints, 56, 111
Missaticum, 84
Missi dominici, 84, 85, 100, 101
Mixed marriage, 5, 6, 40-42, 48, 51, 63
Moneylenders, 58
Monk's Breviary (*Monk's Brevarium*). *See* Epitomes
Moses, 77, 89
Mount Sinai, 77, 89
Mummolus, 56
Muslims, 24, 25, 39, 67-68, 80, 83, 96, 97, 103-105, 110, 112-115, 124, 125, 129

Naamen, 77, 89
Najrān, 156
Nantes, 44
Naples, 33-34
Na'ran, 157
Narbonnaise, 3, 66, 67, 70, 102
Narbonne, 6, 7, 18, 68, 69
Nasas, Jew, 155
Nathan ben Ephraim, 104, 125
Natronai, R., 69, 112
Nibridius, Bishop, 101, 120
Nicholas I, Pope, 126
Nile, 73
North Sea, 106
Nordmen, 74
Notkar, 123

Oaths, 89
Odoacer, King, 27
Offa, King, 73, 79
Oise, 59
Oman, 73
Oppas, Bishop, 24
Ordoño I, King, 130
Oria, 82, 104, 124-128
Orleans, 47, 56, 58. *See* Councils
Ostrogoths, 4, 5, 27, 30-33

Pagans, *pagani*, 61, 62, 69, 70
Pamplona, 69

Paravereda, 95
Paris Program, 107-109, 114, 120, 123
Paul, Duke, 18
Paul the Deacon, 40, 42
Peppin I, 66-68, 135
Peppin, king of Aquitaine, 82, 115, 116
Perctarit, King, 41-43
Persians, 39, 148
Peter, Archbishop of Ravenna, 31
Peter of Pisa, 42
Phatir, convert, 56
Pilgrimages, 104
Placitum, 13
Poitiers, 44, 68
Polygamy, 42
Praecepta, 66-68
Praeceptum negotiatorum, 90
Priscus, Jew, 56
Privilegium, privilegia, 4, 29-36, 43, 45, 78
Procheiron, 128
Procopius, 33
Proselytism, 45, 46, 48, 116, 121. *See* Conversion
Provence, 70
Prudence, Bishop, 114
Pumbeditha, 112

Quinigesius, Bishop, 27
Quiricius, Bishop, 16
Qulzum, 73

Rabanus Maurus, 88
Radanites, 72, 97, 112, 126, 131. *See* Merchants
Ramiro I, King, 130
Ranosind, Count, 18
Ravenna, 31
Reccared I, King, 5-7, 11, 18, 38, 62
Reccared II, King, 11
Reccesuinth, King, 15-17
Reconquest, 130
Red Sea, 73
Refugae, 13, 22
Regensburg, 123

212 Index

Regnum Francorum, 53, 54, 59-67, 78, 111, 112
Remigius, Archbishop, 121, 122, 131
Rhine, 58, 61, 62
Rhône, 72
Ripuarian Franks, 76
Roderic, King, 24, 25, 133
Rois Fainéants, 63, 133
Roman law, 55
Romani, 76, 87
Rome, 27, 30, 39
Rothadus, Bishop, 119

Sages of Barcelona, 113
Saint Gall, monastery, 123
Salian Franks, 45, 76
Salomon II, Bishop, 123
Salzburg, 71, 123
Samaritans, 32
Samuel, Jew, 92
Saracen, 74, 161
Saragossa, 17, 97, 103
Saudan, governor, 125
Saxons, 76, 77, 136
Scandinavia, 123
Sedechias, physician, 114
Seine, 59
Septimania, 5, 7, 18, 67, 68, 70, 89, 95, 102
Serfs, 37
Servi, 118
Seville, 21, 24, 25
Shefatiah, Jew, 125-128
Sicily, 39, 80, 104, 124
Sidonius Apollinaris, 3
Sigibert, King, 54-56
Silano, R., 127, 128
Siracusius, Bishop, 28
Sisebert, Bishop, 21, 24
Sisebut, King, 7-8, 14, 15, 20, 59, 62
Sisenand, King, 11, 12, 14, 15, 62
Slavery, slaves: conversion of, 11, 28-29, 55, 60, 64, 76, 78, 81, 87, 88, 92; Jewish-owned, 4, 7-12, 19, 28-30, 34, 37, 46, 58, 64, 75, 76, 81, 87, 88, 92; slave trade, 34, 36, 58, 61, 62, 72, 73, 79, 88, 92, 96, 97, 108
Stephen III, Pope, 67, 80
Suez, 73
Suinthila, King, 11, 12, 14, 62
Sulpicius, Archbishop, 60
Sunie Fred, 20
Sura, 112
Symmachus, Jew, 29
Syrians, 72

Taio, Bishop, 17
Tangier, 73
Taranto, 104, 124
Tarik ibn Ziyad, 24
Tarraconensis, 16, 18
Taxes, 103, 109, 111, 120
Telesinus, Jew, 27-30
Tellonarius, tellonarii, 54, 87, 96, 97, 107
Theodore, Bishop, 56, 57
Theodoric, King, 4, 27-33, 135, 138
Theodoric's *Edict*, 29-30
Theodosian Code, 28-33, 36, 37, 40
Theophanes, 126
Theophilus, 124
Theudebald, King, 53, 54
Theudebert I, King, 48, 49-50, 53
Theudebert II, King, 38, 58
Theuderic I, King, 47-49, 52, 53
Theuderic II, King, 9, 38, 58
Theudimer, Byzantine general, 24
Tiberius II, Emperor, 57
Tigris, 73
Toledo, 17, 25
Toledoth Jeshu, 87, 109
Torah, 77
Torío, 130
Tortosa, 68, 70
Toulouse, 44, 68
Tournai, 44, 48
Tours, 44, 58
Transoxiana, 73
Tsemah, R., 112
Tughuzghur, 73
Tulga, King, 13-17

Tuy, 22, 23
Urban, Count, 24
Uzés, 53

Vandals, 33
Velay, the, 68
Venice, 82
Venosa, 82, 104, 113, 125, 127
Verdun, Treaty of, 106, 120
Vich, 68-71. *See* Ausona
Vienne, 101, 121
Vikings, 74, 114, 115
Vir clarissimus, 28

Visigoths, 3-27, 42, 54, 59, 62, 65, 67, 70, 130, 133

Wala, Count, 99
Wamba, King, 18-20, 22, 63, 139
Wilfrid the Hairy, 69, 118, 119
William, Duke, 114-116
Witgarius, Bishop, 123
Witiza, King, 22, 23
Witteric, King, 7

Yotabē, 156

Zacharias, Pope, 41
Zaddo, governor, 68
Zeno, Emperor, 134

ABOUT THE BOOK AND AUTHOR

This history of Jewish policy in Western Europe during the early medieval period challenges what the author terms the myth that the Church dominated the early medieval world. In his comprehensive account Professor Bachrach analyzes the political realities underlying the formulation and implementation of Jewish policies. Bernard S. Bachrach is a professor of medieval history and associate director of the Program in Jewish Studies at the University of Minnesota. He is the author of two other books published by the University of Minnesota Press, *Merovingian Military Organization, 481-751* and *A History of the Alans in the West*.